MENS-REA — GUILTY MIND AND INTENT

NO " " — GUILTY ACT

MISFEASANCE = To do something wrong
NON-FEASANCE = not to do something but
              has duty to

"CAVEAT EMPTOR" LET THE BUYER BEWARE
VOLENTI NON FIT INIURIA
        INFANT ? TORTS
        MINOR ? CONTRACTS
        VOLENS = ONE ACCEPTS THE RISK

FUNDAMENTALS OF
CANADIAN LAW

FUNDAMENTALS OF

CANADIAN LAW

F. A. R. CHAPMAN, M.A. (Laws) Cantab.

Ryerson Polytechnical Institute, Toronto

McGRAW-HILL COMPANY OF CANADA LIMITED

TORONTO, *New York, London, Sydney*

Printed and bound in Canada by

John Deyell Limited, Lindsay, Ontario

PREFACE

A book of this nature is necessarily a compromise. In view of the vast material covered, which it takes law students many years of intensive study to assimilate, it is not possible to delve into too great detail. On the other hand, the danger of oversimplification must be avoided: this can easily lead to an actual misstatement of the law. The problem, then, is to a much lesser extent what to put in than what to leave out.

Next, regard must be had for the class of person reading this book. He will certainly not be a lawyer but either an established businessman or a person preparing himself to become one: namely a student—either at the senior high school or the college level. Both can be assumed to have a sound knowledge of the English language, but it would be pointless to bombard them with legal jargon. On the other hand, while homey examples and illustrations are always useful in driving home a point, the pitfalls of becoming childish and repetitive in doing so must be avoided equally assiduously.

If, with the above in mind, this book turns out to be of some value to the businessman for reference; of some assistance to the student in mastering a notoriously dull subject; and, perhaps, even of some interest to the casual reader, it will have served its purpose.

Grateful acknowledgment is made to Gerald J. Morris, B.A., LL.B., for unstintingly devoting his time to checking the manuscript for legal inaccuracies; and to my wife for unselfishly serving as guinea pig and of her untiring assistance.

F. A. R. Chapman

CONTENTS

vii

Introduction to
Our Legal System

CHAPTER ONE

Definitions, History, and Jurisdiction

DEFINITION OF LAW

Definitions, like dates in history, are something from which the student instinctively recoils. They are a chore to memorize and do not appear to serve a useful purpose. Often, however, they constitute a convenient device for determining whether something really is what it appears to be—as a yardstick will show whether an article is truly three feet long.

The topic of this book being law, let us work out a definition for it. First, we shall take a number of laws everyone has heard of and analyze them: for example, the laws of nature (many of them gathered in the science of physics); the laws of health (the science of medicine); the laws of etiquette (see Emily Post and others); and the laws of morality (the basis of sociology), among many others. One thing common to all these laws is the consequence of their being disobeyed: in all cases the offender is punished!

Thus, the pre-Wright Brothers birdmen, attempting to defy the law of gravity, had their limbs broken; defying the laws of health by burning the candle at both ends for too long results in a breakdown; poor social behaviour, contrary to Mrs. Post's tenets, means lost invitations; and immoral conduct leads to rejection by society. We can therefore say that: *Law consists of rules, laid down by various authorities, which cannot be broken without penalty.*

We, of course, shall not concern ourselves with any of the above, but only with *governmental law: a body of rules and regulations which our law courts will enforce.* As we shall see, it is this law, made by our government, that lays down our rights and obligations and, most important of all, provides us with the means of enforcing our rights.

NEED FOR LAWS

Another point it might be well to clear up before embarking on the study of law is the reason for having man-made laws at all. One might easily think that in a decent community, consisting of honest, God-fearing folk, the Ten Commandments, the golden rule, and the law of God should suffice. But these—call them morality, ethics, or conscience, if you like—are often not enough. While our law has these for its foundation, they may often offer us two (or more) choices, both equally correct and moral. What, for instance, is morally wrong with driving a car on the left-hand side of the road? Many good people in Britain and Sweden do just that and will not, necessarily, wind up "down below." Also, moral standards vary according to geographical regions and religions.

It is, however, extremely important that one of the alternatives be chosen as the accepted one and that this choice be then made public, so that everyone should either know of it and/or be able to refer to it easily. If this is omitted, one needs no great imagination to picture the resulting confusion! Why, even games must be played according to certain rules with a referee to supervise their administration and to mete out fair and predetermined penalties.

REASONS FOR STUDYING LAW

Having determined the reason for having laws, one might now ask why we, non-lawyers, should study them? After all, isn't that what we pay lawyers for? The answer is that an elementary knowledge of law might save us from getting into trouble from which even a lawyer might not be able to extricate us. In an analogy with medicine, while the majority of us are not doctors or nurses, we all realize the value of knowing something about first aid.

There is nothing so easy as breaking a law which you never knew existed! And don't forget that, except in most criminal cases, "Ignorance of the law is no excuse." (This, by the way, is the first of numerous legal "maxims," or proverbs, appearing in this book.) Most people

4

know that they are violating a law if they fail to pay certain taxes to the authorities: for example, income tax; withholding tax on employees' wages; property tax on their houses; and sales tax on buying certain articles. They also know that it is unlawful to drive an automobile, to hunt, to ride a bicycle, to own a dog older than six months, or to get married—without an appropriate licence, that is. But, do they know of the dozens, if not hundreds, of occupations they may not engage in without first obtaining a licence from the city, the county, the province, or the federal government? (The author sometimes wonders if the Toronto requirement for a petty chapman to take out a licence at ten cents a year, applies to him.)

In addition, the businessman needs to know even more law to keep out of trouble and to avoid losses. For example, when trading with youngsters and the feeble-minded, he should know that the legal dice are loaded against him (see Chapter 8). He should realize the legal danger of extending credit, or letting claims slide, beyond certain time limits (see Chapter 13); the necessity for putting certain contracts in writing, or even under seal (see Chapter 6); the consequence of doing certain work, or entering into certain contracts on Sundays (see Chapter 9); and he should be aware of his rights against and his duties toward his neighbours and fellow-citizens generally. This knowledge will also aid him when drawing up contracts and when examining contracts presented to him for his signature.

A word of warning before you embark on a study of the law: If you think that a full knowledge of the law will protect you against all acts that are dishonest, immoral, or unethical, you are mistaken. You will, for example, have no legal remedy if the other party:
- Fails to keep some of his promises to you;
- Fails to pay bets he has lost to you;
- Fails to accept cancellation of orders you might only just have placed with him;
- Fails to take back certain defective goods you bought from him.

Why the law does not protect you against the above, and other, unethical conduct should be obvious—it would be a physical (and financial) impossibility to furnish courts and judges to deal with every promise that is broken.

It is similarly obvious why the normally well-balanced person will

5

not habitually "make a fast buck" by taking advantage of these legal loopholes or other technicalities. Even if he could continue sleeping easily at night by "keeping just within the law," he would be ostracized in the community and blacklisted by his business associates.

What, then, are you entitled to expect when you have assimilated the contents of the following pages? Not, certainly, to become a "do-it-yourself" lawyer. But you will have learned enough: (1) To prevent you from becoming enmeshed in certain legal difficulties; (2) To recognize situations on which you should consult your lawyer; and (3) To confer intelligently with your lawyer, and to speak his language, once you do get into a legal scrape.

It may be that you will never find yourself in an emergency where you will have to apply your knowledge of law, and you might, therefore, consider your studies wasted. If that is the case, please think of the insurance you carry, or of the fire extinguisher in your home: you may not need it often, if at all; but if you ever should, you will need it very badly indeed!

HISTORY OF LAW

From the dawn of civilization, people needed laws when they began living together. The community chores had to be divided among its members equitably, and its weaker members were entitled to protection against their more aggressive and dishonest neighbours. While Adam, alone in his Garden, and Robinson Crusoe, alone on his island, needed no law (who was to complain at whatever they chose to do?), the need for it became immediate with the advent of Eve and Man Friday, respectively.

Who was it that made the laws and enforced them in pre-historic times? Then, as today, it was the head of the community or tribe. How he became head—whether by physical strength, mental superiority, influence, inheritance, or democratic process—is immaterial. It is even likely that the laws were very one-sided, outrageously in favour of the law-giver; for instance, the penalty for stealing an apple from the chief's orchard may have been death. However, the interesting thing to note is that the severity of the penalty was not considered nearly so important a matter as that the prospective apple thief should be fully aware of the penalty lying in store for him—in

6

other words, that the law be publicly known.

Precedent. Since every creature in nature (including man) is conservative by instinct, the doctrine of following an established *precedent* is as old as law itself. After all, if something has worked well once in any field, it is natural to apply the same procedure automatically when a similar situation arises again later. So it is, and always was, also in law: if the chief, in his capacity as judge and law maker, rendered his decision once in a certain case, he himself would probably render a similar decision in some similar future case. After his death, his successor in office would certainly render an identical decision, if only out of piety or superstition. The logical development of this early practice was the binding rule that decisions in all similar cases had to be the same— in other words, "Precedent must be followed."

Codification. That the above conjectures are not empty theorizing is borne out by examining the legal systems of some ancient civilizations. While the details of the undoubtedly intricate Egyptian legal system have become lost to us because they were inscribed on perishable papyrus, those of the Babylonian Empire are available to us because they were, fortunately, inscribed on baked clay tablets preserved to this day and decipherable by our archaeologists. In fact, in 1902 archaeologists discovered a green basalt rock about seven feet high and six feet around (now standing in the Louvre Museum in Paris) on which King Hammurabi had engraved in about 2100 B.C. a summary, or *codification,* of all Babylonian law as it had developed to that date. It had obviously occupied a prominent position in central Babylon. It is amazingly comprehensive and often rings a familiar note as, for instance, it sets out the punishments for dishonest contractors, bribed witnesses, or incompetent doctors. Incidentally, in their carefully indexed libraries are preserved various Babylonian contracts: bills of sale, mortgages, marriage contracts, and wills; as well as examples of an elaborate accounting system.

It was about 1500 B.C. when Moses made public the Ten Commandments, as recorded in Exodus 20. These, again, were obviously not new laws. They merely put on permanent record a summary of the already existing laws of God, in a manner designed to make them as widely known as possible. While no penalty was specifically mentioned for the breach of any of these ten laws, the fear of the wrath of God obviously sufficed. However, in Exodus 21 and 22 further laws are given to Moses together with fairly explicit penalties—based on the principle of "an eye for an eye and a tooth for a tooth" (Ex. 21, 23-25).

ROMAN LAW

Finally, we shall take a quick look at the most famous of ancient legal systems, the Roman Law. Of this system we know every last detail since it has never been allowed to perish; it survives in many modern cultures—the closest being no farther away than the Province of Quebec.

This system had its legendary beginning with the erection of the Twelve Tables (stone tablets, similar to the two of Moses) in the public meeting place of Rome, the Forum, about 300 B.C. The Tables have been destroyed long ago, and their contents are not exactly known. It is believed that they contained what we would call *constitutional law*: how Rome was to be governed, who the office holders were to be and their qualifications, who had the right to vote, how voting was to take place, and similar matters. This, again, was not new law; but it has always been recognized that, for laws to be good, they must be generally known and easily accessible.

The territories that were occupied by the ever-victorious Roman forces also received the benefits of Rome's highly advanced civilization: its roads, aqueducts, and coinage—to mention just a few—and also its masterly legal system. Thus, when Julius Caesar conquered Britain in 55 B.C. (and began an occupation that was to last until 412 A.D., when the occupation forces had to return to the defense of Rome), he naturally also brought to it Roman law.

It will be remembered that 412 A.D. marks the beginning of the Dark Ages—when Europe was overrun by the Goths, the Vandals, and other savage hordes, when might was right and chaos reigned everywhere. Light did not emerge from this darkness for centuries; in England we might put a date for this emergence at 1066, when the Duke of Normandy invaded England to become William I, "the Conqueror." Now, it is by no means claimed that Roman law had survived in Britain (later England) for all those years in its pure

8

form. But its principles were so sound that substantial portions of it did survive in the form of traditions. Being a good colonial administrator, William tried to apply the local law as much as possible; when local law was inadequate, he supplemented it with his own law, called *Norman and Paris custom*—again based substantially on the laws used by the Romans during their occupation of Gaul.

And that is how English law comes to have so many elements of Roman law in it—and consequently also the law of most of Canada and the United States, which is similar to English law in many respects.

COMMON LAW

The law governing in England at the time of William's arrival was called the *common law of England*. It was the law handed down through the generations by tradition, and it was administered by the local nobles and important land owners. Whenever they could, they rendered decisions themselves. In more complicated cases they had recourse to various forms of *trials* in which they virtually asked the Almighty to help indicate who had right on his side.

There was, for instance, Trial by Combat: The contestants fought it out with arms, under certain ceremonials, and the winner of the combat was declared the winner of the dispute. Women and priests who were involved in disputes could have "champions" fight for them on their behalf. This form of trial was not finally declared obsolete in England until 1818, when a man charged with murder claimed it as his right against his accuser.

There were, also, numerous forms of Trial by Ordeal: for example, the Trial by Hot Iron, where both parties to the dispute had to grasp a red-hot iron rod—the party who let go of it first was the loser. Trial by Cold Water was based on the idea that a body of water, the symbol of purity, would receive the innocent, but reject the guilty. Thus, a person charged with a crime would be immersed in the water; if he did not sink, he would be regarded as guilty; if he sank, he was innocent. Incidentally, there were safeguards against letting an innocent person drown—after being submerged for a specified time, he was fished out again.

In Trial by Hot Water the accused had to place his arm in boiling

9

water; his guilt or innocence were determined by the length of time it took for his wounds to heal. The credibility of parties to legal proceedings was tested by the Trial of Bread and Cheese. The parties were given dry bread and stale cheese to eat and then were observed for signs of choking when answering questions: a sure sign of a guilty conscience! (Might this have been the forerunner of our present-day lie detectors?)

The most important form of early trial (because it is the foundation of our jury system) was Compurgation. If the accused, or a party to a private dispute, could get twelve "compurgators," or "oath helpers," to swear that they believed his statements to be true, he would win. In other words, the compurgators were character witnesses, rather than the present-day impartial jurymen.

The reason for calling this ancient law of England the *common law* was that everybody believed it to be the law common to all of England. Such, however, was far from being the case. Because of the distances involved and the poor means of communication from one end of the country to the other, the law on many points might have been completely different in the various regions without anyone being aware of it.

This situation changed under the Norman kings of England. From the beginning William, who had a strong sense of justice, made it a practice to listen to appeals from his subjects against unjust decisions by the local judges. This practice was followed by the two sons who succeeded him—William II (Rufus "the Red") and, particularly, Henry I (Beauclerc, "the fine Scholar") who gave the English back many of their suppressed laws and constitutional freedoms.

RULE OF LAW

It was Henry II, the first of the Plantagenet kings, who delegated his judicial functions to full-time judges, called *the King's Justices*. Henceforth, they were the only people with the authority to judge the more important cases in the country; this power being taken away from the local judges. The change did away with many malpractices, such as tyranny and bribery; and, approximately one hundred years after the Conquest, the "rule of law" was firmly established in England, as contrasted to a rule by force and corruption.

To make justice available to all, the Justices held sittings not only at the royal courts at Westminster, but they went on regular *circuits* of the country, holding sittings (or *assizes*) at all important centres of population. What was more natural than for them to meet together on their return to London from their journeyings and to compare notes on the cases they had heard and the decisions they had given? (They soon began meeting in what developed into the Inns of Court: places where they lived and dined when in London. The Inns of Court are, virtually, the lawyers' guilds and law schools. It was the strong Inns of Court that successfully resisted the invasion of England in the sixteenth century renaissance by the newly rediscovered Roman law, which swept the rest of Europe.)

Directly due to the regular meetings of the Justices, the same law soon came to be applied all over England. Precedent was followed rigidly in identical cases; in non-identical but similar cases, the principle established in the earlier case was followed as closely as possible. Notes of the more interesting cases were taken by the judges themselves, their secretaries, law students, or interested spectators and circulated in the form of *reports*. The law all over the country thus became universally available and did in fact, and not only in name, become the common law of England.

EQUITY

The original Justices were, as a whole, a fine body of conscientious, intelligent men. Later generations of judges, unfortunately, degenerated into hidebound bureaucrats. They were content to follow precedent slavishly where it existed; but if some new situation or conflict arose, they refused to display any initiative and declared themselves powerless to deal with it. Consequently, many cases of unrighted wrongs arose, and the only person to turn to for relief was the king, who stood above the law (even today "the king can do no wrong"). Theoretically at least, the king saw to it that true justice was done, whether in accord with the law or not—in other words, he applied the principles of *equity*.

For example, it became common practice for a knight, before departing on a crusade, to will his property to a trusted relative or friend, under a sacred "trust" for it to be administered for the benefit of the knight's defenseless widow and children. If the trust was betrayed, there was no legal remedy against the betrayer who, after all, was the legal owner of the property. It was only the king who could uphold the equitable rights of the trust beneficiaries, and he was frequently called upon to do so.

The administration of equity was eventually delegated by the king to his secretary, who had charge of the royal office or chancery—in other words, to his *chancellor* (today the Lord Chancellor, or the Minister of Justice). At first the chancellor was bound by no precedent and acted strictly according to the dictates of his conscience (which could vary "according to the length of the chancellor's foot"). In time, precedent came to be followed even in equity cases where possible. Today, equity is not even administered in separate courts by separate judges, but is dispensed right alongside the common law.

LAW MERCHANT

Before finishing the discussion of the body of law that we inherited from England, we should mention our laws of banking, bills of exchange, charging of interest, sale of goods, marine insurance, and similar mercantile matters called the *Law Merchant* (in this old-fashioned term the noun comes before the adjective, as in "Little Boy Blue" or the "Lord Almighty"). The Law Merchant had its birth at the time of the crusades, when commerce and communications started in Europe. The ships that transported the crusaders to the Holy Land returned to their ports of Venice and Genoa, in what is now northern Italy, with rare goods from the East. If northerners, for example, wanted to buy these goods, they had to pay for them with gold resulting from the sale of their furs, lumber, or whatever else they produced. Thus markets, or fairs, sprang up all over Europe, which were visited regularly by the merchants of many lands who wanted to trade there. The fairs were the birthplace of credit, of paper money, and of the other conveniences covered by the Law Merchant.

When disputes arose among the merchants, as was (and is) unavoidable, they were decided on the spot by a tribunal of the senior merchants present, whose decisions were scrupulously obeyed. These tribunals were curiously called the *Pie Powder Courts*, a garbling of the French term for the Court of Dusty Feet—which the travelling merchants, both litigants and judges, had no chance to clean before coming into court. The decisions of the Pie Powder Courts developed into the Law Merchant, which was adopted into its own law by England and by many other civilized countries.

DIVISIONS AND MAKING OF LAW

Practically all our law is based on English law which, as we have seen, is composed principally of the common law. Much of this law has been put into statute form by Parliament, as we shall presently see; but vast portions of it can only be established by referring to the reports of previous cases dealing with similar circumstances. For this reason, the common law is also often called *case law.*

Then, since in our system of justice a judge *must* follow the principles established by a judge of equal or higher standing in earlier cases dealing with similar circumstances, this law is also called the *law of precedent.*

Further, because these laws are not codified anywhere formally, they are also called the *unwritten law.* This does not mean that you cannot read about them in great detail in any of the law libraries—actually, they are published in the various law reports issued by the courts themselves, by the law societies, or by commercial publishers. They are also quoted, analyzed, and discussed by lawyers in text books and magazines.

The advantage of case law is that it is elastic; its principles can be adapted to changing circumstances without having to create new law. For example, the common law principles of negligence apply equally to the driver of a horse and buggy and to the pilot of a jet airplane. However, it is sometimes cumbersome to establish what exactly the law is; in complicated cases, you may find the lawyer for one party citing dozens of cases which will help his side; while the lawyer for the other party will have an equal number of cases to help prove his point. It is then for the judge to decide which of these many cases, with their fine distinctions, applies most closely to the case before him.

STATUTES

It is for this reason that British Parliament, and subsequently our own law-making bodies, have systematically embodied specified portions at a time of the common law into acts of Parliament, or *statutes*. This process is called *codification* of the law. We have already encountered examples of it in Hammurabi's Babylonian code, in the Ten Commandments of Moses, and in the Twelve Tables of Rome. Other important examples in history are the complete codification of the vast body of Roman law (in the incredibly short space of two years) under the Roman Emperor Justinian in 533 A.D.; and the Napoleonic Code—a similar undertaking in 1804 involving the laws of France.

Examples of codification of Canadian federal law are the Bills of Exchange Act and the Criminal Code; of provincial law, the various Partnership Acts and the Sale of Goods Acts. These statutes seldom attempt to create new law; they merely set out to record formally the existing common law. As a matter of fact, one section of the Canadian Criminal Code specifically states that, in the case of any omissions from the Code, the English common law is to be followed. This codified common law is called *statute law* or the *written law*. (In the rare case of any conflict between statute law and cases, the statute will overrule the inconsistent case law.)

The British North America Act. Who makes the laws for Canada? Until 1867 it was Great Britain; in that year of Confederation, British Parliament passed the British North America Act, by which Canada was, henceforth, to make its own laws beginning July 1, Dominion Day. According to the B.N.A. Act, our federal Parliament has the power to make laws in all matters not expressly assigned to the provinces; twenty-nine topics are specified. (As you probably know, Parliament consists of three sections, each one of which must approve a *bill* before it passes into an *act of Parliament*: namely, the House of Commons, the Senate, and the "Queen in Parliament"—acting through her representative, the Governor-General.)

The B.N.A. Act gives the provinces the exclusive right to make laws on sixteen specified topics. In these matters the provinces make their own statutes in their provincial legislatures. Each province has also made a number of laws empowering its counties and municipalities to make certain ordinances and by-laws for themselves—in matters of local application, such as traffic, zoning, local elections, etc.

14

It should be noted that our laws apply to everyone in the country or province, respectively, whether he is a native or a visitor. There are two seeming exceptions to this rule. First, there exists a doctrine that "a king can do no wrong." "King" in this context includes the head of any government, or his representative. If our own monarch broke the law, she could be tried in the courts only with her consent; if she withheld consent, our only remedy—an extreme one, but used in the past—would be for Parliament to depose her. This it has the power to do, since "Parliament can do anything, except change a man into a woman, or a woman into a man." Nor can our courts try visiting royalty, foreign ambassadors, or registered members of embassy or legation staffs. In such cases a remedy must be sought through diplomatic channels.

Second, by the doctrine of *extraterritoriality*, foreign embassies and legations (but not consulates) are regarded as foreign soil, and not as Canadian. That is why no one, not even the Police or Fire Department, may set foot there without invitation. Our representatives in foreign countries naturally enjoy reciprocal privileges. Such privileges used to be enjoyed also by foreign business communities in Shanghai, under a treaty with pre-war China.

On the other hand, our courts cannot try a person (Canadian or foreign) for a crime committed elsewhere (except treason). However, *extradition treaties* exist between most civilized countries whereby one country will hand over to another country, at its request, people genuinely suspected of specified serious, non-political crimes.

PUBLIC AND PRIVATE LAW

The vast field of law can also be classified according to the topics with which it deals; the two main categories are *public law* and *private law* (or *civil law*)—both of which are composed partly of common law and partly of statute law. This division is quite arbitrary. There is nothing official or particularly scientific about it; we make it purely for the sake of convenience.

We shall reserve the term *private law* for those topics in which only the contending parties are involved; all other matters we shall consider as belonging to *public law*.

PUBLIC LAW

The following are examples of public law—they form by no means a complete list:

Criminal law covers violations of the law that are so grave as to cause society to initiate proceedings against the wrong-doer—in most cases even if the directly injured party might be inclined to forgive the miscreant. (See Chapter 2, Crimes.)

Constitutional law consists of the laws which determine our system of government.

Administrative law is the name for the innumerable regulations which the various ministers of the Crown are authorized to make on their own responsibility by almost every statute and for the operation of many boards and tribunals.

Private international law governs situations where more than one set of laws might apply. According to determined rules, the courts can decide which territory's laws are to apply to a certain set of circumstances; and also which territory's courts have the jurisdiction to hear the dispute. More descriptively, this field of law has the alternative name of *conflict of laws*.

Public international "law," popularly referred to as "international law," deals with relations between nations involving rules of peace, war, and neutrality; territorial waters, and (recently) air space and the like. These rules have developed through the centuries and have been accepted by the nations of the world by usage. Much international law is also created by countries entering into contracts (or treaties) regarding such matters as fishing rights, extradition, the use of radio frequencies and air lanes.

In case of disputes, the nations involved often turn to the Hague International Arbitration Court in Holland, by whose decision they agree to abide. However, since as yet there is no efficient international law enforcement agency with the power to inflict penalties, this topic cannot properly be classified as *law* according to our definition of the term at the beginning of this chapter; and that is the reason for placing it between quotation marks in the heading above. The more serious disputes can only be handled by diplomacy and may result in the breaking of diplomatic relations, or in war.

Admiralty law deals with marine matters, such as collisions at sea.

16

Military law imposes regulations on the conduct of the members of the armed services, over and above their obligations as citizens.

Martial law refers to the emergency measures which can be imposed in times of crisis such as riot and disaster. It is administered by the military authorities that are called to the assistance of the insufficient regular law enforcement agencies.

Ecclesiastical, canon or church law. In addition to being the source of our marriage, incest, and succession laws, ecclesiastical law also regulates the conduct of the members of the clergy.

PRIVATE LAW

Private (or civil) law can be conveniently sub-divided into (1) the law of obligations and (2) the law of property.

The law of obligations. It has been said that every one of us is a bundle of rights and duties: we have certain rights against other people, and we have, correspondingly, certain duties (or obligations) toward them.

TORTS. Many of these obligations have been imposed on us by the law of the land. Apart from not being permitted to commit crimes, we have obligations not to trespass on the land, goods, person, or reputation of our fellow-men. If we violate any of these obligations we commit a *tort* (from the French word for a "wrong" and the Latin word for "crooked" or "winding"), and the injured party has the right to sue us. The law of torts is discussed in Chapter 3.

CONTRACTS. Besides the above duties, we might also be under obligations to pay our fellow-men sums of money, to supply them with certain goods, or to render certain services for them. These obligations will have been undertaken by us voluntarily, for reasons of our own—generally because we think we are getting fair value in exchange. It is these obligations that will comprise the bulk of this book—for they have been incurred by entering into a *contract*.

The law of property somewhat overlaps the law of contracts. Please note that when a lawyer speaks of *property*, he means not only land and houses (which he calls *real property* or *immoveables*) but also goods (which he calls *personal property, moveables,* or *chattels*). The topic can be divided into:

OUTRIGHT OWNERSHIP: (1) How it is acquired; for example, by grant from the Crown, by purchase, gift, or inheritance, or by long-term occupation. (Students regularly suggest "by stealing" which is, of course, wrong; a thief can obtain only physical possession but not the rights which go with ownership.) (2) The rights and duties of the owner or co-owners.

INTERESTS IN PROPERTY— amounting to less than full ownership. Thus, if you lease an apartment and rent a typewriter, you certainly have the right to the use of these premises and goods, even though you have no right to sell them.

Similarly, when lending money on the security of a mortgage, you have certain contingent rights over the mortgaged property in case the loan or the interest on it are not properly paid. Also, a repairman has a *lien* on, or the right to hold back, an article he has repaired until he is paid the repair charges; as has the pawnbroker the right to retain the pledge until he is repaid the loan for which it was given as security. One can also have interests in another's property in the form of an *easement*, such as a right of way over his land, or the right to take water, hay, or wood from it. (See Chapter 26.)

SUCCESSION TO PROPERTY. The ownership of property can change, not because of someone's voluntary action, but on account of:

1. Death. The deceased person's property passes according to the terms expressed in his will; or if no will is left, according to the laws of intestate succession. (See Chapter 30.)

2. Bankruptcy. A person also loses ownership of his property in this case of "financial death"; it passes into the hands of a trustee for equitable distribution among the creditors. (See Chapter 25.)

3. Insanity. Similarly, in this case of "mental death" ownership vests in a trustee, curator, or committee. (A convict remains owner of his property.)

Please note that foreclosures of mortgaged property or repossessions by finance companies do not come under this heading. In both cases the creditors were previously given these rights by the debtor in the form of contracts.

Besides the classification of all laws as public or private, other groupings of the law are, of course, also possible. For example, a distinction between common law and equity used to be made because it was once important. But it is no longer of practical consequence; neither are the other divisions, and we shall therefore not be concerned with them.

LAW COURTS

We have now analyzed, chronicled, and catalogued the law. But you will remember from the definition at the beginning of this chapter that the only reason why governmental law is effective is because it can be enforced in the courts of law. We shall now take a closer look at these law courts, of which there are several different kinds. First we shall list the courts dealing with criminal cases and briefly discuss proceedings in them.

CRIMINAL COURTS

Police Court or Magistrate's Court. Whenever a person is charged with an offense, he is first brought into this court—whether it be for a parking violation, a theft, or even murder. The Police Court magistrate has several courses of action open to him:

1. The magistrate himself will summarily try the relatively unimportant *summary conviction offenses* (in England and the United States called *misdemeanours*), such as traffic offenses, rowdyism, "petty thefts" below $50, and others for which the maximum punishments are fixed at a $500 fine and/or six months' imprisonment.

2. If the accused is charged with a more serious offense (either a grave misdemeanour, punishable with up to two years' imprisonment or an indictable offense, popularly called a "felony" and punishable with at least two years in a federal penitentiary), he has the right to be tried before a higher court, with a *petty jury* (the traditional "twelve good men and true"). It is then the magistrate's function to hold a *preliminary hearing* to decide whether there is a *prima facie* case against the accused—in other words, whether the prosecution has gathered sufficient evidence to warrant the accused being made to go through the ordeal of having to defend himself in court.

If the magistrate decides that the evidence warrants it, he will "commit the accused for trial" before a higher court; this means that the Crown Attorney's department will prepare an *indictment* (pronounced inditement) against him. Even then the accused will not come up for trial forthwith, for his case will be re-assessed by a *grand jury* —seven to twenty-three people whose function it is to double-check the magistrate's findings, to make sure that no obviously innocent person is submitted to the ordeal of a court trial. Many provinces and American states have abolished the grand jury, feeling that its function is a needless duplication of effort; however, where it has been retained, it also inspects public institutions such as prisons, asylums, old-age homes, etc.

3. Instead of committing an accused for trial the magistrate may, with the consent of the accused, himself try the accused and punish him if he finds him guilty. For example, recently an escaping bank robber in Toronto was tackled and caught by a passer-by. He was brought up before a magistrate the next day; he elected this method of summary trial before the magistrate, and was immediately tried by the magistrate and given fourteen years!

The magistrate is appointed by the Lieutenant-Governor of the province and paid by the municipality in which he officiates. In communities where there is no need for a full-time magistrate, warrants and summonses are issued by Justices of the Peace—who can also try offenses against municipal laws. Two J.P.'s sitting together possess the powers of a magistrate under (1) and (2) above, but not under (3).

If the accused—or the prosecutor, for that matter—is dissatisfied with the decision of the magistrate or the justices, he can ask to have a summary conviction offense retried in the County Court, to be discussed next.

County Court (the criminal section of which is called the Court of General Sessions). Staffed by a professional judge, appointed by the Governor-General of Canada—as are also the Supreme Court judges referred to below—there is one of these courts in each county town. Where there are *districts* instead of counties, this court is called the District Court. Here are tried the more serious cases for which the accused has been committed for trial by the magistrate earlier; but not the most serious ones, such as murder, manslaughter, treason, piracy, and rape.

20

Provincial Supreme Court.

1. HIGH COURT DIVISION.   This is the highest trial court of Ontario; the other provinces have other names for it (e.g., Common Pleas, or Queen's Bench). It has its headquarters in the provincial capital (in Toronto it is at Osgoode Hall), but it periodically holds *assizes* throughout the province. This court has the power to try even the gravest crimes. (If an assize town, on occasion, has no criminal case for the circuit judge to try, it traditionally presents him with a pair of white gloves!)

2. APPEAL DIVISION.   Staffed by different judges from those in the High Court Division, the Appeal Division is the court that listens to appeals from the County Court, from the High Court, and from the magistrate with regard to the serious cases he was specifically authorized to try (see 3. under Police Court or Magistrate's Court above). It also hears appeals from the Juvenile Court, Surrogate Court, and Family Court, to be mentioned later.

The Supreme Court of Canada, located in Ottawa, is not a provincial but a federal court. No proceedings can be commenced in this court, but it is the "court of highest instance" in Canada since it can hear appeals from the supreme provincial Appeal Courts. Since 1949 appeals from it to the British Judicial Committee of the Privy Council (judges of the House of Lords) are no longer possible. However, convicted criminals can still beg the Queen to exercise her "prerogative of mercy," exercised on her behalf in Canada by the Minister of Justice along policies determined by the Canadian Cabinet.

Juvenile Court is a special court for dealing with youngsters, not over sixteen years of age, who have committed an offense. Where the youngster is over fourteen and has been charged with an indictable offense, the Juvenile Court can, at its discretion, order him to stand trial in the ordinary courts. The general public is not admitted to Juvenile Court trials, and the names of the accused must not be published in the newspapers. If convicted, they are sent to reform institutions; here they will not be exposed to contact with "old lags," and a good percentage leaves these institutions to become valued members of society.

The coroner. Once the personal representative of the monarch (the "Crown-er") whose duty it was to investigate all cases of unnatural death, Treasure Trove (unearthing valuables of unknown source), Wreck, and Flotsam and Jetsam (broken-up ships, floating goods, and pieces of cargo deliberately jettisoned to lighten a ship in distress, respectively) washed up on the sea-shore, the coroner is today generally a medical practitioner concerned with the first function only, viz., unnatural death. In simple cases, such as obvious heart attacks, etc., he conducts the inquiry, or *inquest*, by himself at the scene of death.

In more involved cases he is assisted by a jury in a court room, with the power to call witnesses. The coroner's jury will decide whether the death resulted from natural causes; accident; suicide (while of sound, or unsound mind—this distinction being sometimes of importance for life insurance purposes); from causes unknown; or, in cases of killings, "from wounds inflicted by a person or persons unknown." An interesting point to note is that there are no legal consequences to the Coroner's findings. The coroner's verdict is only an opinion as to the cause of death, and there is no charge laid against anyone; thus no one has cause to lodge an appeal against the verdict. But if the verdict alleges some person to have committed murder or manslaughter, and that person has not yet been charged with the offense, the Coroner has the power to issue a warrant for his arrest.

CIVIL COURTS

Of more concern to the student of business law are the courts which try civil, rather than criminal, cases.

Division Court is the name in Ontario of the lowest of the civil courts. It deals with small claims only, involving a maximum amount of $400. The court is staffed by a professional judge. Usually there is more than one such court in a county; in York County, containing Metropolitan Toronto, there are twelve. An appeal from the Division Court lies to the provincial Court of Appeal (2. under Provincial Supreme Court above), provided the dispute involves at least $100; for lesser amounts special permission to appeal is required from the Court of Appeal.

County Court (see above under Criminal Courts) tries cases involving intermediate amounts: for example, in Ontario, cases up to $3,000. However, in undefended cases, the County Court may give judgment

22

by default (see below) for unlimited amounts. Appeals again lie to the provincial Court of Appeal.

High Court Division of the provincial Supreme Court. (Its criminal functions have already been discussed above.) This court also has civil jurisdiction over cases involving unlimited amounts. Some cases are tried with a petty jury (of six in Ontario), and appeals lie as above. However, appeals from the provincial Court of Appeal to the Supreme Court of Canada can be lodged only if the amount involved is at least $2,000 (unless special leave to appeal is obtained from the Supreme Court of Canada).

Surrogate Court deals with the estates of deceased persons; for example, the *probate* (proving the authenticity) of wills; the appointment of an administrator, where the deceased failed to appoint one; and the partitioning of estates in case of an *intestacy* (see Chapter 30). Appeals go as above.

Family Courts deal with domestic disputes, and appeals go as above.

The above civil courts are all provincial. But some matters, beyond provincial jurisdiction, must be begun in the following federal civil court:

Court of Exchequer. This federal court has two imposing court rooms in the Supreme Court of Canada building in Ottawa, but it has sittings in all the provincial capitals also. In it are tried cases involving patents and copyrights; taxation disputes; Crown corporations, such as the CBC or the CNR; disputes between provinces; and claims against the Crown—for example, if someone is negligently injured in a federal building or by a federal employee. As a matter of interest, in this latter case we still have evidence of the fact that "the Queen can do no wrong" in that the writ she grants expresses her permission (fiat) to be sued. Appeals from the Court of Exchequer lie directly to the Supreme Court of Canada, provided the amount involved is at least $500 (except with special leave).

There are other Tribunals and Boards dealing with specialized matters; one which should be of particular interest to the business man is described below.

Court of Arbitration. Frequently, business contracts contain a clause whereby the parties, beforehand, agree that any dispute between them should not be brought before a court of law but tried by a named person, or group of persons, in whose judgment they both place complete confidence. He, the arbitrator, is less generally a lawyer than an intelligent, disinterested person who is completely familiar with the subject under contract. The terms of the contract usually permit no appeal from the arbitrator's decision; which is one reason why arbitration is, generally, much cheaper and faster than litigation (going to law).

PROCEDURE IN CIVIL CASES

Except perhaps for small cases in Division Court, the layman seldom sets the machinery of the law in motion without the assistance of a lawyer. Therefore he need not be concerned with too much detail about the progress of a law suit; but he should have a general knowledge of the various stages of a civil law suit.

• In all the courts, the *plaintiff* seeks a remedy for the injury he has suffered through the *defendant's* wrongful act or breach of contract by having the court issue a *writ of summons* (in Division Court, it is known as a *claim*).

• This document is then *served on* (handed to) the defendant. In it the Queen commands him:

• *To enter an appearance* (defend himself) within ten to fifteen days from date of service; otherwise judgment will be entered against him "by default." (In Division Court, the defendant must *enter a dispute*.) On the eleventh (or sixteenth) day, the plaintiff goes to the court offices and finds out if the defendant has "appeared"; that is, let the court office know that he disputes the claim (by entering his name in a book kept for that purpose in some courts). If the defendant fails to enter an appearance:

• The plaintiff (or other person acting on his behalf) makes out *affidavits* (sworn statements) that the writ was properly served on the defendant and that the latter failed to enter an appearance in time. The plaintiff is then awarded a judgment against the defendant by default.

• If the defendant enters an appearance in good time, further *pleadings* take place:

1. The plaintiff supplies the defendant with a detailed *statement of claim*.

24

Plaintiff = π
Defendant = Δ

2. The defendant replies to the statement of claim with a detailed *defense*. (A not-too-far-fetched defense might read as follows: (i) The defendant denies the existence of any contract as claimed in #1 of the plaintiff's statement of claim. (ii) However, if such a contract is held to exist, the defendant denies that he ever received the goods as claimed in #2 of the plaintiff's statement of claim. (iii) However, if the defendant is held to have received such goods, he claims that they were not according to specifications. (iv) Even if the goods are held to have been according to specifications, the defendant claims he need not pay for them because of—the Statute of Frauds, the Statute of Limitations, duress, infancy, or "what have you.")

3. The defendant might also have a *counterclaim* or *set-off* against the plaintiff, for which the plaintiff will then furnish:

4. A *defense*, together with:

5. A *reply* to the defendant's defense.

• If, after all this, the litigants (parties to the law suit) have not yet reached a settlement out of court (and even a poor settlement is, generally, preferable to a promising law suit), further preliminaries must be settled before the case comes up for trial in court. These matters are attended to by various officials; such as, a County Court judge; a High Court master; or a special examiner. For example, after the questioning of the parties in the *examination for discovery*, the examiner may decide, among other things, whether the documents (letters, books of account) of one party should be open for inspection by (or "discovered to") the other party. In case of a dispute on the topic, he will decide whether the case should be tried with or without a jury; and the place and time of trial. The master or judge might also disallow a claim or strike out a defense altogether if these pleadings are obviously frivolous.

• If the parties still have not settled their claim out of court, the case comes up for *trial* in due course. (At present this might take months in the County Court, and even a year or two in the High Court.) Both parties, usually through their lawyers, present their case before the court according to recognized procedure. The judge (with the aid of a jury, if any) decides which side to believe. And then:

• The judge renders his *judgment*. The judge, in his discretion, may additionally (and usually does) order the loser to make good to

25

the winner his legal expenses or *costs* which are awarded according to the rules of court.

• If the loser (the *judgment debtor*) does not make payment to the winner according to the terms of the judgment, the winner (the *judgment creditor*) may apply to the court for a *writ of execution*— the carrying out of the judgment terms by a court official (bailiff or sheriff's officer[1]). The judgment debtor's property may be seized and sold; his bank account, safety deposit box, and business interests may be "attached" (frozen) and his wages "garnisheed" (i.e., his employer is ordered to withhold a portion of them). The execution is also registered against his land. Incidentally, in an examination under oath, the judgment debtor is forced to reveal all his assets and income; if he makes false answers, he is guilty of perjury, a serious offense.

What if the judgment debtor owns and earns nothing and carries no insurance? In that case, the judgment creditor is out of luck. Imprisonment for debt went out with Charles Dickens, and the judgment creditor could have saved himself a lot of time, worry, and the costs of the action by finding out about the defendant's finances before starting legal action. A just resentment and eagerness to obtain one's legal rights often result in a won law suit which, however, turns out to be an extravagant luxury.

The only exception which comes to mind is the Motor Vehicles Accident Claims Fund which some provinces maintain to compensate, to a limited extent, victims of uninsured, penniless, or hit-and-run motorists. Getting payments from its predecessor, the Unsatisfied Judgment Fund was often slow and involved—so that one student was less wrong than at first apparent when he misnamed it the Unsatisfactory Judgment Fund.

QUESTIONS

The answers to many of the following questions will have to be sought outside the pages of this book.

1. (a) What is the distinctive feature of a valid law?
   (b) Is *international law* properly so termed? Explain.

---

[1] The sheriff is the Crown's representative in the county.

2. Name two activities that may not be engaged in without a licence or a permit from:
   (a) Your province;
   (b) The federal government.
3. What features common to Hammurabi's Code, the Ten Commandments, and the Twelve Tables have made these laws strong?
4. Distinguish between the English common law in 1065 A.D. and in 1166 A.D.
5. (a) What are three other names for the "unwritten law"?
   (b) In what works can one study it?
6. (a) What is equity?
   (b) How did the need for it arise?
7. Give the historical explanation why commercial law is just about the same in all European countries.
8. List 15 major topics which are the subject not of provincial, but of federal legislation.
9. (a) What is meant by diplomatic immunity?
   (b) Give reasons for according diplomatic immunity.
10. What distinguishes public law from private law?
11. What courses are open to a magistrate when dealing with a person charged with an indictable offense?
12. What cases are tried in County Court?
13. What cases are heard in the Supreme Court of Canada?
14. (a) Why is arbitration preferable over litigation?
    (b) Draft an arbitration clause for insertion into a contract.
15. Make a list of the various steps that might be taken in the course of a lengthy *civil* law suit.

CHAPTER TWO

Crimes

CRIMINAL INTENT

Common law crime may be defined as *the intentional breach of a law which is designed to protect society*; the breaker is prosecuted and punished by society (the state). This definition holds true even of criminal negligence which has been defined as "intentionally doing without care," and of manslaughter which is often the lack of restraint over one's passions. Obviously, climbing into a neighbour's house on a foggy night, mistaking it for your own to which you have mislaid the key, is not a crime since there was no intention to commit a wrong. Nor do you commit a crime if a pedestrian walks into the car you are driving or you otherwise injure, or even kill, someone by pure accident; that is, without a trace of negligence.

Children under seven years of age are held incapable of committing a crime because they are not sufficiently mature to tell between right and wrong, and thus they cannot possess a guilty mind (whatever you or I might think about some precocious brat!). However, any Fagan training and employing them as thieves would be guilty of committing a crime "through an innocent agent." If the young malefactor is between the ages of seven and fourteen, the prosecution must be able to prove his "guilty knowledge"; above that age, the perpetrator of a criminal act will generally be assumed to have been aware of its consequences, and it will be up to him to disprove his guilty intent. While a person is asssumed innocent until proved guilty in our system of law, the burden (or *onus*) of proof on the prosecution generally, is only to show the commission of the act beyond a reasonable doubt; the onus is then on the accused to prove lack of intent.

Insanity. An insane person, or one drunk to the extent of insanity, is deemed to have had no criminal intent. To be successful in a plea of insanity, however, the accused must satisfy the court that he complied with the McNaghten Rules of Insanity: that is, that he either did not appreciate the nature of his act (an example being the poor soul who slit a boy's throat under the delusion that he was slicing bread—there is nothing wrong in slicing bread!); or that he did not know his act to be wrong. Thus, the deranged person who killed certain people under imagined divine instructions was found guilty of murder because he knew that such killings, while quite justified in his own eyes, were unlawful under the law of the land. It was shown that he would not have committed them "had a policeman been standing at his elbow." (That is also why religious sects must obey laws—Mormons must be monogamous, and Doukhobors must send their children to school—even if doing so is contrary to their sincere beliefs.)

A person found to be insane is declared *not guilty*. If the insanity is not temporary, he is placed in a mental institution "at the pleasure of the Lieutenant Governor" (usually for life).

Provocation. Irresistible impulse (e.g., stealing by a kleptomaniac), therefore, will not serve as a defense; it does not comply with the McNaghten Rules. Nor does our law condone "crimes of passion"; however, if violence is done immediately upon receiving severe provocation, this will serve to reduce the punishment. But there must exist no time or opportunity for the aggrieved person to form an intention to hurt the other. It is similarly excusable, though not justifiable, for a person to commit a crime against another's belongings (though not to his person) while he is in the presence of someone who is threatening to do him some violence unless he commits this crime. This is called *coercion*.

In concluding our comments on criminal intent, it is important to remember that criminal law in Canada has been codified into a statute, the Canadian Criminal Code, and that this law, together with many other laws (e.g., the Official Secrets Act, the Narcotics Act, the provincial liquor and traffic laws), makes a number of actions punishable even though there was no intention to commit a crime. It is well known that ignorance of the law is no excuse (although the court may be more lenient in such cases). Examples of such punishable acts are

29

the serving of liquor to people not known to be on the Interdicted List and intimacy with mature-looking young women below specified ages ("jail bait").

CLASSIFICATION OF CRIMES

Common law crimes are divided into the following three groups:

Treason: a Canadian conspiring with the Queen's enemies, at home or abroad. (The traitor's property was, once upon a time, confiscated to the king.)

Felonies: grave, indictable crimes, punishable by death or incarceration in a penitentiary for at least two years. (The felon's property used to be forfeited to his feudal lord.)

Misdemeanours: transgressions of the law punishable by fine or imprisonment up to two years.

The innumerable crimes in the above three groups can also be arranged according to their nature, whether they are:

1. Offenses against public order in general;
2. Offenses against someone's person; or
3. Offenses against someone's property or belongings.

It might be well to define some of them so as to remove popular misconceptions—even though most of them have little to do with business law.

OFFENSES AGAINST PUBLIC ORDER

Treason, already defined, belongs at the top of this list. Treason is still punishable by death, although this penalty is seldom inflicted in peace time (but note the Rosenberg case in the U.S.A. after the war ending in 1945). Related to treason is the offense of

Sedition: advocating the overthrow of the government by force.

Riot is an *unlawful assembly* that has "gotten out of hand." After the Riot Act has been read to the rioters (by a magistrate or mayor who gets as close to them as he prudently can), the rioters must disperse within thirty minutes or they may be liable to an offense punishable by life imprisonment.

Blasphemy is referring to religious subjects in other than decent and

30

respectful terms. (*Heresy* is no longer a punishable offense.)

Conspiracy was "invented" by British Parliament after Sir Guy Fawkes' unsuccessful attempt to blow up the Parliament on November 5, 1605. It consists of "two or more persons planning an unlawful act," even though no attempt has yet been made to commit it. Curiously, husband and wife cannot commit this offense with one another since, in this case, they are regarded as one, and "you cannot conspire with yourself."

Perjury is deliberate lying by a witness in a judicial proceeding when sworn to tell the truth. This extends to a person who, on religious grounds, has made a *solemn declaration* instead of taking the oath and to a person signing an affidavit or *statutory declaration* (a document sworn to before a notary public or a Commissioner for Oaths).

Subornation is the influencing of a witness to give false evidence or to withhold it altogether; or influencing a juror in his decision. Witness and juror are equally guilty with the influencer. This is also called *embracery*.

Bribery, or the giving of a "secret commission" to an agent or a public official to act against the best interests of his superiors, is also a crime by both giver and taker of the bribe. A licencing official can be guilty of this offense by refusing to grant a licence until "given a present."

Disturbing the peace, vagrancy, and other forms of disorderly conduct are all punishable on summary conviction. In this connection, a person finding himself in the unfortunate and embarrassing position of being the victim of foul-mouthed abuse might find it valuable to know that he can lay a charge against the bully for "inciting to a disturbance of the peace"; in other words, inciting the victim to punch the bully in the nose! A *public mischief* is committed by falsely reporting fires and crimes.

OFFENSES AGAINST THE PERSON

The most serious offenses in this category are the various *culpable homicides* (unlawful man-killings): The gravest is

Murder: deliberately and unlawfully taking a human life; or, deliberately doing an unlawful act intrinsically dangerous to life (e.g., brandishing a gun during a robbery; accompanying an armed robber;

performing an illegal operation; kidnapping; rape), from which death results within a year and a day. Until recently, all persons convicted of murder were sentenced to death (although there were many reprieves). In 1961 a distinction was made between *capital* and *noncapital* forms of murder (literally between those which do and those which do not "cost you your head"); the latter, fractionally less serious type, is punished with imprisonment for life.

Manslaughter is killing a person without premeditation; for example, in a sudden rage; or while merely intending to harm; or while criminally negligent. The maximum punishment for manslaughter is life imprisonment.

Infanticide is the killing by a mentally deranged mother of her young child (not older than one year).

Abortion, while a serious offense, does not properly belong under this heading, since the life that is being taken does not yet enjoy a separate existence. The maximum penalty is life imprisonment.

Suicide. While it cannot be classed as a crime since there is obviously no legal punishment for it (but consider the probable loss of insurance benefits; the possibility of not being buried in consecrated ground; the possible stigma on the surviving family members), an attempt to commit suicide while of sound mind is still a summary conviction offense in Canada (abolished in England in 1961), and the instigation or abetting of a suicide by another is an indictable offense. Note that "mercy killing" (euthanasia) *is* an offense.

JUSTIFICATION.   On the other hand, there are several forms of *justifiable homicide;* for example, the soldier or the hangman taking life in the line of duty; or the police while attempting the arrest or preventing the escape of a felon, as an absolutely last resort; or while defending your own life or that of persons entrusted to your care (e.g., immediate family) with absolutely no more force than is necessary. Note that when a person is being resisted while exercising his "citizen's right" of arresting someone who has actually committed an indictable offense, he is being technically attacked and can use the same *self defense.* If you come upon a burglar in your house, your only justification for shooting him is your reasonable belief that otherwise you yourself would be harmed by him; there is no requirement, however, for you to wait until he has taken a shot at you first!

After the culpable homicides, in point of seriousness, come
Kidnapping and rape (in some of the United States these are even
punishable by death) and other less serious sexual offenses. Note that
adultery, while immoral, in itself is not a crime unless accompanied
by aggravating circumstances. It might also form the basis of a civil
action for damages.
Woundings range in seriousness from "causing bodily harm with
intent to maim, wound, or disfigure" (such as knifing and acid throw-
ing) to a simple *assault* which might be just a slap in the face. (The
Criminal Code no longer uses the antiquated term "assault and battery": where the battery was the actual infliction of the injury, and the
assault was, literally the "jump toward" or the preliminary to it.)

Note that no assault is committed when properly ejecting a trespasser: that is, after he has refused your request to leave, you are
entitled to escort him peaceably off your premises (e.g., home, store,
restaurant, hotel, theatre, etc.); if he resists this, he is technically
assaulting you, and you are entitled to use as much force as necessary
—to the extent, perhaps, of giving him the "bum's rush."
Bigamy and polygamy. Bigamy is the offense of going through a
marriage ceremony while married; and polygamy is the doing of this
even oftener. (The classic answer to the question of "What is the
punishment for bigamy?" is, of course, "Two mothers-in-law.")

OFFENSES AGAINST PROPERTY

Arson, the most serious of the offenses against property, is setting fire
to anything with intent to harm or defraud someone (often an insurance company).
Mischief, a much more serious offense than it might sound, is wilful
destruction or damage to property other than arson.

Next come the many offenses wherein one person helps himself to
the goods of another, usually without the owner's permission or knowledge. The basic offense is
Theft (popularly called *stealing* or *larceny*—petty or grand, depending
if under or over $50). Theft is defined in common law as taking
something from its owner without his consent with the intention of
depriving him of it permanently. The element of gain to the taker

33

does not enter the picture (as it does under systems that adopted the Roman law); thus, the cook on a Thames pleasure steamer who in a fit of rage tossed all the galley's pots and pans, crockery and silver overboard into the soft, muddy river bottom was successfully charged with theft. On the other hand, special statutes had to be passed (now incorporated into our Criminal Code) to cover adequately the following:

Joy riding. Since there is no intent to deprive the owner of his automobile permanently, the most the young scamps could be charged with under the old definition of theft was the theft of the gasoline. The Code now reads "to deprive temporarily or absolutely" and makes joy riding a summary conviction offense.

Embezzlement. The cashier, teller, or other trusted employee who absconded with the cash box was not "taking" it, since he already had physical possession of it. To cover this case, the Code definition of theft now reads "takes, or converts to his own use." To cover the case of the optimistic embezzler who merely "borrows" the funds to put them "on a sure thing" at the local track and then intends to return the "loan" before it is discovered, the Code deems it theft to deal with the funds in a way which may make it impossible to restore them to their owner.

Theft by finding is keeping a found article if its owner is known or could be readily established (e.g., by reporting it to the Police, a Lost and Found department, or by advertising). If the true owner cannot be traced within three months, the article is returned to the finder.

Being in possession of goods while knowing them to have been unlawfully obtained is the crime that, until recently, used to be called *receiving stolen property*. "Knowledge" includes deliberately closing your eyes to circumstances that are, or should be, suspicious to the normal person.

Breaking and entering into a "place" (building or vehicle) with intent to commit an offense therein used to be called *housebreaking* if done by day and *burglary* if by night (9 p.m. to 6 a.m.). Technically, "breaking" can consist of nothing more than unlocking a door with a key that was already in the lock. Opening the latch on an unlocked door is not "breaking"; however, an unlawful "entrance" takes place—and is punishable by itself also—as soon as any part of the body is inserted in the place (e.g., a finger through a broken screen to unfasten a bolt) or any part of an instrument (e.g., a bent wire through the hole in a shop window).

Obtaining (money, goods, or credit) by false pretenses or fraud is the specialty of confidence tricksters and other swindlers. The offense includes the ordering and eating of a restaurant meal without paying for it; or the issuing of a cheque to obtain something knowing there to be no, or not sufficient, funds.

Robbery is theft with actual or threatened violence, for example, by a purse-snatcher or a "stick-up artist." To speak of "robbery with violence" is therefore as redundant as referring to "yellow jaundice" or to a "widow woman."

Forgery is the crime of "making a false document"—a document that tells a lie about itself—with intent to harm someone. It can consist of changing just a part of an otherwise genuine document; for example, its signature, date, or an amount—this is what happens when a cheque is "raised." It is an offense to falsify books of account; to make false statements in a company prospectus, in income tax returns, and other documents; and to imitate trade marks, etc.

The forgery of paper and metal money, of postage and excise stamps, and of government seals is called *counterfeiting*. *Uttering* is the placing of forgeries into circulation. Incidentally, defacing a current coin, even if not done with fraudulent intent, is technically a summary conviction offense.

Extortion, popularly called *blackmail,* is "inducing someone to do anything by threats, criminal accusations—on a genuine or concocted basis—menaces, or violence."

Defamatory libel, which is malicious defamation of character in a permanent form, such as writing, is also a criminal offense. The defamed party will far more frequently start civil proceedings for damages, than criminal proceedings. He will do the latter only if he cannot do the former: for example, if the statements are true, but were made only for spite and not in the public interest; and if there has been no publication to anyone but the maligned person himself. (As will be explained in the next chapter, to succeed in a civil tort action for libel, the statements must be false and published to someone other than the libelled person.)

Anyone repeating a libel is equally guilty with its originator; there-

35

fore publishers of newspapers, books, etc., must be most careful to verify anything they print—they are equally liable with the author. Even the bookseller can be liable if he sells a publication that he knows to contain a libel.

Other offenses. There are many other offenses specifically mentioned in the Criminal Code and other statutes, such as:

Using false weights and measures;

Smuggling;

Running lotteries and gambling places;

Narcotics and liquor law violations;

Cruelty to animals;

Salting mines;

Spying and other violations of the Official Secrets Act.

Special mention should be made of the many crimes the businessman can be guilty of: for example, the mishandling of other people's money and goods placed in one's charge; the failure, either by an individual or by the company of which he is an officer, to keep proper books or make proper returns to the respective authorities; in the case of an insolvent person about to go bankrupt, the commission of any one of innumerable irregularities, such as hiding assets or listing them under the name of friends or relatives (this is called *fraudulent conveyance*) for the purpose of defeating the claims of his creditors; and fraudulent stock exchange manipulations. Also, there are always prosecutions going on under the Combines Investigations Act (usually against large companies) for engaging in conspiracies to restrain trade by monopolies, price-fixing rings, etc.

• It must be noted that merely to *attempt* most crimes is a punishable offense. This would apply to one who shoots at another person but misses him, and to the pickpocket who inserts his hand into an empty pocket.

ACCOMPLICES

An accomplice can be punished for being:

1. *An accessory before the fact*; for example, by instigating someone else to commit the crime.

2. *An accessory during the fact*, by assisting him, such as keeping a look-out.

3. *An accessory after the fact*, by hiding or otherwise aiding the criminal, or by helping him to escape (no married person can be an accessory after the fact to his or her spouse). Concealing a serious crime for reward is called *compounding an indictable offense*; an offense of this nature can be committed, perhaps surprisingly, by advertising a reward for the return of anything lost or stolen and using words indicating that "no questions will be asked" if it is returned.

PENALTIES FOR CRIME

Death (by hanging) is, of course, the most serious form of punishment. As previously mentioned, this is the maximum sentence for treason, and it is mandatory for capital murder. It can also be meted out for piracy in circumstances endangering life, and under military law for desertion or cowardice in the face of the enemy. While the Criminal Code allows the death sentence on a pregnant woman to be postponed, it is never carried out in practice. Murderers under the age of eighteen years are sentenced to life imprisonment.

Whipping can still be ordered by the judge. It is administered, to men only, with a "cat o' nine tails" (leather strips, but no longer with metal tips) under careful medical supervision for crimes of violence. It can also be used as a disciplinary measure against prison inmates.

Imprisonment can take place in a federal penitentiary from two years to life—which is usually twenty years, unless it is the commutation of a death sentence or the punishment for non-capital murder. A convict can also obtain remission of a maximum of ten days out of every thirty for good behaviour. A penitentiary sentence is usually accompanied by useful employment, still called *hard labour*. Deprivation of liberty can also take place in jails, reformatories, prison camps, reform schools, and other specialized institutions likely to be best for the convict. A prisoner may be released before the expiration of his sentence under *parole* under certain conditions, such as periodically reporting to the police.

Fines can be levied from trifling amounts (e.g., for over-parking) to six-figure amounts (e.g., for violations of the Combines Investigation Act).

Confiscation of property. Many years ago all of a traitor's or felon's belongings were subject to forfeiture. Until the 1830's inanimate objects that killed or injured someone or caused damage were impounded: for example, a runaway wagon: the entire wagon if there was some degree of negligence; if it was a case of pure accident, then only that part of the wagon which actually struck the victim was impounded. This "Deodand" ("to be given to God") was abolished when railroads were built—too many trains became subject to seizure every time they killed a sheep. Today smuggled goods can still be seized; also hunting and fishing equipment (including tents, cars, and boats) while flagrantly violating the game laws; also cars and boats that are caught illegally transporting liquor; and equipment in a gambling establishment.

Suspension of privileges. An example of this penalty is having one's hunting or driver's licence suspended or revoked.

Deportation. A non-Canadian is subject to deportation to his country of origin for crimes or for transgression of the immigration laws. Our system of punishments no longer provides for exile (e.g., to Russia's Siberian salt-mines; or to France's Devil's Island, which was discontinued after the last war; or to Britain's American Colonies until these gained their independence—after which Australia's Botany Bay was used for that purpose until 1840).

Other penalties. The judge may give the accused a suspended sentence, or he may place him on probation if he is a first offender and if there are extenuating circumstances. He may order the accused "to give a recognizance to keep the peace"; he may place an alcoholic on the *interdicted list*; he may declare "public property" the premises of persons convicted of gambling, bootlegging, etc.,—that is, the police may enter them at will, without a search warrant. He may also order restitution of unlawfully obtained goods or money to their owner and even payment by the accused to the complainant of an amount in the way of damages. While a convicted person usually has to pay the court costs only when fined, he may be made to pay the successful complainant's costs in a case of criminal libel.

Excommunication by the church and the stigma and disgrace imposed by society would not properly be discussed here.

DEFENSES

A person who is proved to have committed an act that is usually regarded as a crime can sometimes plead certain defenses. We have already discussed lack of intention (e.g., insanity) and justification (eg., self-defense) as valid defenses.

There remains the defense of *pardon*. If the accused can produce the Queen's Pardon, he cannot be punished. Nor can a person be tried a second time for a crime for which he has stood trial once before; he cannot be placed "in peril" or "in jeopardy" twice. This defense goes by the old Norman French name of *autrefois acquit* or *autrefois convict*. Once such a person is convicted or acquitted (and the time for an appeal by the Crown has elapsed), he is immune from further accusations even if irrefutable new evidence against him is uncovered. On the other hand, if a person is unjustly convicted and later released from prison when the regrettable mistake is brought to light, the Crown cannot be made to compensate him—but it will generally do so as "an act of grace." In 1962 a Toronto man was given $125 for one day's wrongful imprisonment.

AIMS OF PUNISHMENT

It might be well to round off the topic of crimes with a digression into penology. Why do we punish our criminals? The atavistic reason is, undoubtedly, atonement—the wrong-doer should be made to suffer for the good of his soul and to give the rest of society satisfaction. An eye for an eye, a tooth for a tooth, a life for a life.

Ideally, we should punish criminals for no other purpose than that of reforming them into useful members of society—to give treatment to them, the same as to other sick people. Our aims are probably a mixture of these two extreme attitudes plus a desire to protect life, limb, and property. We want the fear of punishment to help a tempted person resist temptation; for example, the threat of imprisonment may check the impulse to steal in a person entrusted with funds or a shopper in a self-service store surrounded by small, unguarded articles. The first punishment of a criminal should create a distaste in him for a second dose of this unpleasant medicine, and seeing the punishment carried out on one person should act as a deterrent to others.

The dangerous criminal can also be prevented from harming society again either by hanging him[1] or by placing him in safe-keeping—even for life; this is what can happen to a "three-time loser" (an incorrigible *habitual criminal*, convicted of three indictable offenses punishable by five years or more).

The cynic might also justify fines as a convenient source of revenue.

QUESTIONS

1. Strictly speaking, only a person under fourteen is assumed completely innocent until proved guilty. Explain.
2. Why does a plea of insanity seem to be used only in murder trials and almost never for other crimes?
3. Are you justified in killing a bandit who threatens you with a realistic toy gun? Explain.
4. Is it criminal to speak in favour of atheism and the abolition of the monarchy? Explain.
5. Under what circumstances is it a crime to plan an unlawful act?
6. What crime, if any, does an agnostic commit who lies in court while sworn to tell the truth?
7. May a doctor ever take a human life? Explain.
8. What offense, if any, does a Moslem commit who marries a second wife in Canada?
9. Differentiate between mischief and public mischief.
10. Is there anything wrong with making a bracelet of dimes?
11. To make sure that his wife can continue living in comfort, a man gives to her all the money he still has, just before declaring bankruptcy. Is there anything wrong with this? Explain.
12. With what offense can a doctor be charged who nurses back to health a man suffering from unexplained bullet wounds?
13. A man has been summarily sentenced to six months in prison for wounding another. While he is in prison, his victim dies as a

---

1 The author refuses to be involved in a discussion regarding the merits, or otherwise, of capital punishment.

result of the wounds. Can the prisoner now be charged with homicide? Explain.

14. Draw up a list of arguments for and against capital punishment.

CHAPTER THREE

Torts

NATURE OF A TORT

In Chapter 1 we have defined a tort as the breach of an obligation that is imposed on us by society and for which we can be sued by the harmed party, even if the wrongful act is not sufficiently grave to be classified as a crime; the perpetrator of a crime, as we have heard in Chapter 2, being subject to punishment by the state. We can, therefore, call a tort a civil (or private) wrong as contrasted to a public wrong (or crime). Many wrongful acts can create both criminal liability and a liability in tort; for example, a motorist might be tried criminally and receive punishment by the state for criminal negligence and then be sued for damages by the injured party for the tort of negligence; or a swindler might be tried and punished for the crime of obtaining by false pretenses and also be sued for damages by the victim for the tort of fraud. Other examples are assault and malicious damage to property. In a few cases the aggrieved party must make a choice between instituting criminal or civil proceedings; an example would be a case involving a victim of a defamatory libel.

It should also be noted that there is no duty on the victim of a tort to institute civil proceedings; whereas the state may institute a prosecution for crimes regardless of the injured party's wishes.

Another distinction between crime and tort is that a crime is generally not committed unless there exists a "guilty mind"; while in tort the question of intention is, generally, immaterial. The basic rule is that a person must compensate another whom he has harmed, whether intentionally or not. It is for this reason that children, while often immune from criminal prosecution, enjoy no immunity from tort actions being brought against them, provided, of course, that they have attained the age of reason. Thus, in theory at least, there is nothing to prevent a mischievous or clumsy youngster from being sued in tort for any damages he causes. In practice, however, there is little point in suing a child (or any other person, for that matter) who is without means, since any judgment obtained against him under such circumstances could not be enforced.

Responsibility of parents for children's torts. Note, that there is no *legal* obligation on the parent of a youngster to make good the damage the latter caused; although it is customary for him to pay for windows broken by his offspring's poorly aimed baseballs, etc., as a moral obligation. However, the parent is equally responsible with his child if he instigates the commission of the tort; or authorizes it previously; or if the child's tort is due to the parent's negligence—for example, where damage was caused because the parent let the child have matches, fireworks, or arms without proper instructions or supervision. It has been held to be "constructive negligence" by the parent when the child caused damage in his presence—the parent should have kept his child under control. "Presence" in one case consisted of the parent being on the same floor as the child in a large department store—even though at the extreme other end of it.

CLASSIFICATION OF TORTS

It is a perennial subject of argument among lawyers whether there is as clearly defined a list of torts as there is of crimes, or whether there are just a few basic principles for being sued in tort. An example of such a basic principle would be that a person must not carry his right to freedom of action to such an extent as to harm another (e.g., while a person certainly has a right to swing his arms to his heart's desire, the right ends "where the other fellow's nose begins"). Another example of a person over-stepping his rights is causing harm to another by "taking, but not giving"; or by "living, but not letting live."

Whichever lawyers are right in this argument, there is no question about all tort cases being subject to precedents established in earlier cases. However, our judges have little hesitation in adapting old cases to modern developments and changing philosophy. Nor is it seriously disputed that the law is sometimes, while not changed, at least slightly twisted the one way or the other to accord with popular sentiment (to take an example from criminal law, accused persons who were clearly guilty of theft used to be acquitted by juries wholesale until the punishments that were considered too severe—death or exile— were relaxed). As has been humorously observed, "Public policy is a well-known unruly horse which the courts frequently mount and ride off in all directions." On this latter basis, an action for flagrant invasion of privacy might yet, one day, succeed in Britain or Canada, as it already has in a few cases in the U.S.A. (e.g., taking and publishing unauthorized photographs or wire-tapping telephones).

Be that as it may, there follows a partial list of the more important torts.

Assault and battery, or trespass to the person. As mentioned under Crimes, a tort action can lie even for an intentional push or for spitting. This may seem trivial, but it is considered sounder in the public interest for affronted persons to seek a legal remedy than to resort to physical counter-measures of self-help. The courts will naturally not penalize insignificant physical contacts which are unavoidable in urban living.

Trespass to goods is injuring or just using another's property without his express or implied consent.

Trespass, without qualifying words, usually refers to going on another's land without his express or implied consent and during no emergency. While in the open spaces of Canada it is not considered wrong to go on another's land for camping, hunting, or fishing unless such implied consent is expressly negatived by fences, posted notices, or verbally, you are certainly not welcome to cross people's front yards in a built-up area without the owner's permission.

It is similarly improper, without permission, to burrow under someone's land (unless the digger has the mineral rights), to string wires over it, or fly over it. While military and commercial aircraft have statutory protection from trespass actions when flying on their prescribed routes, a trespass action could well be brought against a pilot for "buzzing" your land. (An English farmer who, in the early days of radio, sued the British Broadcasting Company to make good the damages that their radio waves allegedly caused as they trespassed over

44

his tomato plants, did not succeed in his action.)

Defamation of character (which could also be called "trespass to the reputation") is the "publication of false statements that will bring a person, even unintentionally, into hatred, ridicule, or contempt"—in other words, that will lower him in the esteem of right-thinking persons. Defamation of character is either *libel* or *slander*.

Libel. The statement constitutes libel if it is in some permanent form, such as writing—though it could also be a movie, a faked photo, a drawing, or a sculpture. For example, in the frieze over the entrance to the Toronto Stock Exchange there is shown a top-hatted financier with his hand in a cloth-capped worker's pocket; if the financier's face were identifiable as that of a living person, he could sue the sculptor for libel.

Slander. Slander usually consists of spoken words, but it might also consist of gestures; for example, tapping one's forehead to indicate mental weakness, or a circular motion of the hand and fingers indicating a propensity in someone for helping himself to the goods of others.

PUBLICATION. To constitute defamation, there must have been publication of the slander or of the libel by the defamer to someone beside the defamed person; even though this be to no one but the defamer's secretary, to whom he had dictated the libellous letter.

INTENTION. Nor need the defamation be intentional. If an author makes up a fictitious name for his story's villain, and the plaintiff can show that certain normally intelligent persons came to a reasonable conclusion that this story was supposed to be a true account of the plaintiff's misdeeds, the plaintiff will win against the author and publisher, even if there was a notation on the flyleaf of the book to the effect that "no reference was intended to any person living or dead."

Newspapers run even greater risks when reporting criminal cases. When printing the criminal's name, they should be sure to spell it correctly, and they will be wise also to give his age, description, and address so that innocent people with similar names should not be able to claim that their friends had taken them for the criminal in question. Advertisers must be equally careful when making up names—for example, a policeman resented, with success, being pictured soaking

45

his malodorous feet in certain bath salts. An amateur golf champion collected damages from a chocolate manufacturer who published his picture in an advertisement without permission—the "innuendo" (or logical conclusion) being that, since people usually get paid for their endorsement of products, the golfer had violated his amateur status. But a named stockbroker who was shown, in an advertisement, to have lost his reason through an over-indulgence in the Yo-Yo craze did not win his case; it was held that no normal acquaintance of his would really think the less of him as a consequence, and that he was obviously just trying to "cash in" on the advertisers' accidental use of his name.

TRUTH. A defamation action will fail if the statements are true in every particular, even though they were published purely out of spite and malice. In this case, however, the maligned party might succeed in a criminal prosecution, as set out in Chapter 2.

PRIVILEGE. Some persons enjoy complete protection, or *absolute privilege* from defamation actions: these are judges, lawyers, and witnesses in court; and members of the legislature (e.g., members of Parliament) in the Legislative Chambers (e.g., Parliament). Their privilege ends outside, as Mayor Lamport of Toronto found out to his cost when he made some statements, later held slanderous by the courts, to newspaper reporters on the City Hall steps. The damages that he was ordered to pay were ultimately paid by the City of Toronto.

Qualified privilege is enjoyed by persons who make false statements about others not out of malice but for good motives, and where they are under an express or implied duty to "stick their necks out" for the protection of others. Thus, a parent is protected when warning his child against consorting with someone whom he suspects; as is a person who, in good faith, gives a bad reference on an ex-employee to a prospective employer who requested the reference in confidence. Similar to this is "fair comment": a reporter, giving his views on a public performance by an actor, athlete, politician, etc., is permitted to be quite uncomplimentary, provided he is voicing his honest opinion and is not venting some personal spite. Similarly, people in the public eye must submit to having fun poked at them in cartoons, etc.

Negligence is the most common type of tort case before the courts—

46

not surprising when you consider that it includes all the many claims arising out of motoring accidents. The basic rule is that anyone doing anything at all has the duty to do it with proper care, and that he is responsible for any injury caused by his lack of care. To take an extreme example, a person walking along the sidewalk in daylight should watch his step; if he does not, and he stumbles on a pebble or some refuse lying there openly, he is liable for the cost of a store window he may break in his fall. Motorists can be held negligent for not keeping a proper look-out, or for failing to have their vehicles under complete control; and property owners for not maintaining their premises in a safe condition—for example, for failure to sand slippery walks (the famous story about Alexander Woolcott, "The Man who Came to Dinner," is based on this theme), or to fix loose floor boards or dangerously faulty wiring, plumbing, etc.

In this last connection, the property owner's degree of responsibility varies, depending on the type of person injured. He owes the highest amount of care to the invitee.

INVITEE. An invitee is a person whom the property owner asks onto his property, expressly or by implication, for his own advantage; for example, a shopper into his store, a guest into his theatre, hotel, or restaurant, or the deliveryman and serviceman into his home. The invitee is entitled to protection from hidden dangers which the owner knows of, or which a prudent owner ought to know of. The owner should eliminate these dangers by having the trouble repaired, railed off, or guarded.

LICENCEE. A licencee is a person entering on property with express or implied permission; for example, a social guest, or a door-to-door salesman or charity collector (unless there is a "No Canvassers" sign posted). These persons are entitled to a *warning* of unusual hidden dangers actually known to exist. Thus, steep stairs would not be an "unusual" or hidden danger—a prudent person would naturally use the handrail; but atttention should be drawn to a slippery rug, a loose floor board, a "live" light switch, or to a tap emitting boiling water. A lettered sign would not be considered sufficient warning to an illiterate or sightless person who could reasonably be expected on the premises.

TRESPASSER. A trespasser who knows that he is not wel-

47

come "trespasses at his own risk" and has hardly any rights if injured. The only proviso is that he is not "fair game" (e.g., if you see one sleeping on your driveway, obviously you are not entitled to drive your car over him), and you must not set "hidden traps" for him. Thus, you may have your grounds patrolled by fierce dogs, but the public should be made aware of them by their barking or by "beware of the dog" signs; fences must not be secretly electrified; mantraps and spring guns must not be set; and spikes and broken glass on walls must be visible from the outside (if not prohibited by local ordinances altogether). Note that the courts give recognition to the innate nature of children by regarding them not as trespassers, but as licencees, when they are attracted onto land by "attractive nuisances"; that is, things or situations which they do not recognize as dangerous, such as building materials, machinery, pits, pools, etc. (allurements). It is thus the land owner's responsibility to make these hazards inaccessible to children.

AGONY OF THE MOMENT.   Sometimes a defendant will deny liability, claiming that the plaintiff brought the injury entirely on himself. Even if this contention is correct, the plaintiff will succeed if he can prove that in the "agony of the moment" he had to make a quick decision which turned out to be the wrong one, but which was forced on him by the defendant's negligence, in the first place. So it was in the following case: The sole passenger on the open upper deck of a bus was injured when he jumped from it after the bus went into a violent skid and he feared that it might topple over and into the river running alongside the road; however, the bus maintained its balance. Although the plaintiff was the only passenger to be injured, he won his action on the above grounds. In another case, a voluntary rescuer collected the cost of having his drenched suit and watch cleaned from the almost-drowned skinflint who refused payment on the grounds that he had not asked to be saved; the plaintiff was held to have his instinctive heroic action forced on him by the defendant's act of falling in the water.

CONTRIBUTORY NEGLIGENCE.Where the person who is injured as the result of another's negligence is partially himself to blame for the accident (i.e., if he is guilty of contributory negligence), he used not to be able to collect anything; but nowadays, the courts will award to him that fraction of the damages which it considers attributable to the other party's fault. Thus, a negligent jay-walking Hamilton teacher collected $1,875 in damages from an also negligent motorist for the loss of her ability to smile; this being 25% of the $7,500 at which the court valued her smile.

'VOLENTI NON FIT INIURIA.' This Latin maxim means that a person willingly exposing himself to danger has no legal cause of action if he gets injured. This includes athletes and spectators at sports, such as auto racing, golf, baseball, and hockey who get hurt by out-of-control cars, balls, and pucks; and workers in dangerous occupations who get hurt in the normal course of their jobs.

A person who sells a potentially dangerous article, or even lends it without reward, is responsible for warning the other party of the dangers and for instructing him in its use. That is one of the reasons for labelling a bottle of iodine, for example, with the skull and cross-bones, indicating poison.

ANIMALS. The owner of a dangerous article or of an animal that he knows to be dangerous is also guilty of negligence if it gets out of hand and causes injury. Since pets are sometimes not known to be vicious until they try to bite someone the—by no means infallible—saying has arisen that "a dog is entitled to his first bite." (This has, possibly, been taken over from the Bible. Exodus, Chapter 21 says that the owner of an ox who gores someone to death for the first time is to be under no liability; but if the ox does it a second time, its owner shall also be put to death.) While the dog's master might escape tort liability under these circumstances, municipal legislation frequently provides the death penalty for a canine first-offender.

VICARIOUS LIABILITY. Note that, by statute, the blameless owner of a car can be held responsible for the negligent acts of a person who drives his car with his consent. (He is even "criminally" liable to punishment for minor traffic violations committed by such a driver.) Also, at common law, the blameless employer of an employee (or the principal of an agent) can be held responsible for the negligence (or other torts) committed by the employee (or agent) in the course of his employment. (For greater detail, see Chapter 14.)

Nuisance is the tort of using your land or abusing your freedom of personal conduct in a manner that will injure or molest others: for

49

example, emitting a stench from your factory; polluting a stream with chemicals or waste; causing water to overflow onto a neighbour's land; creating offensive noises at unreasonable hours; in a few isolated cases, still, obstructing "ancient lights"—that is, cutting off, with new buildings, the daylight from windows (lights) which have long enjoyed it; obstructing roadways, etc.; allowing branches of your tree, or eaves on your house to overhang your neighbour's land. Strangely enough, a person obtains the legal right "by prescription" to commit certain nuisances if he has continuously committed them openly and without permission or objection for twenty years.

False imprisonment consists, as the name implies, of depriving someone of his freedom without good cause. This tort is also committed when preventing someone from going his accustomed way; or detaining him in, or forcing him into, a place where he does not wish to be.

Malicious prosecution is the laying of criminal charges knowing them to be unfounded or even starting civil proceedings for no good cause, but merely with the purpose of discomfiting the defendant.

Inducing a breach of contract is committed when a person, *A*, persuades another, *B*, (for other than health or moral reasons, or other pure motives) to commit a breach of a contract which he knows to exist between *B* and a third party, *C*. *C* can then sue *B* for breach of contract (see Chapter 11) and/or *A* for the tort of inducing a breach of contract. On similar grounds, a man can be sued by a husband for alienation of his spouse's affections; or a husband-snatching woman by a wife.

Passing off is the common law tort of imitating the appearance of a competitor's goods. The infringements of others' patents, copyrights, trade names, trade marks, etc., are torts by statute; thus stealing another's brainchild is also called plagiarism (see Chapter 31). If done deliberately, it is also punishable as a crime.

Slander of title is falsely alleging that a competitor does not own the goods he is selling.

Slander of goods, another business tort, is falsely alleging that a competitor's goods are defective in some respect.

Deceit or fraud embraces a variety of wrongs, such as *fraudulent conversion* of property and *fraudulent misrepresentation*. These torts are

50

seldom sued upon as such: the former is usually associated with a criminal action, such as embezzlement or obtaining by false pretenses, in the course of which the complainant will request restitution of property and damages; and the latter is usually connected with a breach of contract, which will be discussed in detail in Chapter 11.

REMEDIES FOR TORT

The traditional remedy available to a wronged party in tort cases is damages.

Damages is money to compensate for the loss caused by the wrongdoer. Damages cannot be collected if no loss can be proved, with the following few exceptions: Some loss is taken for granted and need not be proved by the plaintiff in cases of trespass, assault, libel, and in some cases of slander; namely, where a person is wrongfully alleged (1) to have committed a crime; or (2) to be suffering from some anti-social disease; or (3) to be dishonest in his business, or (4) to be incompetent in his profession; or (5) to be an unchaste wife; or (6) to be an immoral beneficed clergyman.

DEFINITE LOSS. To collect damages, the plaintiff must be able to prove that the loss he suffered was definite, and not imaginary. Proving the value of damaged or destroyed articles, hospital and medical bills, lost wages, and reduced earning capacity will not be difficult. The courts also have no hesitation in awarding, sometimes liberal, compensation called *general damages* for indeterminate items such as pain, suffering, mental anguish, and shortened life expectancy. However, one cannot sue for "the loss of a kingdom" merely because the defendant was the cause of a "lost nail." More specifically, suppose that a lad on his way to apply for a job as office-boy is knocked down by a car and is slightly injured, and thus prevented from keeping the appointment. He cannot sue for the loss of a general manager's salary, on his claim that the defendant's act prevented him from attaining that position.

DIRECT CONSEQUENCE. Nor will a person have to pay damages if the consequences are too remote from his wrongful act; for example, a person who, after being publicly slandered, is blinded with mortification and runs into the path of a car, getting severely injured, will surely not get compensation from the slanderer for these injuries.

However, the manufacturer of a defective article or of noisome food will be liable to any person (not only the buyer) who ultimately uses or eats it and suffers injury: for it is to be expected that such things will often pass through many hands—from manuafcturer to jobber, to wholesaler, to retailer, to purchaser, who in turn may make a gift of it to the consumer.

UNBROKEN CHAIN.   An old English case established the "unbroken chain" doctrine: A prankster at a county fair tossed a lighted fire-cracker onto one of the many stalls, constructed of wood and canvas, that were crowded together. The owner of the stall grabbed the fire-cracker and tossed it away; it landed on a second stall, whose owner threw it onto a third stall, where the fire-cracker exploded and set fire to the stall. It was held that the injured stall owner had no remedy against the owners of stalls one and two because these had acted in the "agony of the moment." The prankster claimed that he did not toss the fire-cracker onto the third stall and that therefore he should not be liable for its destruction, this being too remote. However, it was held that he initiated the "unbroken chain of events" which directly resulted in the damage, and that he was thus liable. The maker of the fire-cracker was absolved from liability, as being too remotely connected with the happenings.

DAMAGES TO BE MINIMIZED. The injured party is under a duty not to aggravate the damages negligently, or purposely; in fact, he must try "to minimize the damages"—to hold them to as low a level as possible. Thus, if a person wounded by someone else's wrongdoing fails to apply or to seek prompt first aid, he will be disentitled to compensation for the resulting graver consequences. In other words, if he does not apply the proverbial "stitch in time," he cannot collect for the resulting "nine."

PUNITIVE DAMAGES.   While the general rule is that the courts award damages purely to compensate, they will sometimes order a defendant to pay the plaintiff *punitive*, or *exemplary* damages. This can happen in fraud actions where the feeling of the court is that the defendant should be penalized in addition to compensating the plaintiff. It can also happen in defamation cases, where the defendant has unsuccessfully pleaded the truth of his statements as a defense; here the court feels that the original wrong has been aggravated by being aggressively repeated in open court.

NOMINAL DAMAGES. On the other hand, the court might award only *nominal* damages to a plaintiff who does not want to enrich himself but who might merely want to have his legal rights established; or it might award *contemptuous* damages (often of 1¢) to a plaintiff who is technically in the right but who commenced proceedings "frivolously" or "for trivialities." A person who is thus considered to have wasted the court's time needlessly is labelled a *litigious plaintiff*, and he will often be penalized by not being granted his court costs.

FATAL ACCIDENTS ACT. Until late in the last century "a personal action died with the person"—so that someone injuring another so severely as to cause his death was free of liability. This has been changed by the Fatal Accidents Act under which the surviving dependent relatives of the killed person inherit any claims (such as for negligence) he might have had against the person causing his death. The deceased's estate may sue for any tort injuries (except libel and slander) suffered by the deceased in his lifetime. The estate may similarly be sued by anyone who was so injured by the deceased.

Replevy is the other common law remedy available to a plaintiff in addition to, or in place of, damages. The court will issue a *replevin order* against the defendant, commanding him to return to the plaintiff any wrongfully detained goods, valuables, or documents of the plaintiff's.

Injunction is a remedy that was first made available to a plaintiff by equity in cases where it was felt that money damages could not afford sufficient compensation. It is a court order either commanding a person to do something (e.g., to *abate* a nuisance by cutting off overhanging branches; to remove obstructions from roadways; to repair dangerous premises; or forbidding him to do certain acts (e.g., ordering him to desist from trespassing, committing a nuisance, repeating slanders, or producing articles in violation of patents, copyrights, or trade marks).

While it usually takes many months for ordinary cases to come up for trial before the courts, *interim* (or provisional) *injunctions* can be obtained very speedily if they are required urgently. For example, if you see your neighbour about to build a structure upon your land, you can apply for such an injunction from a judge—even at his

53

private home, should it be needed on a court holiday. Provided you can present to him a *prima facie* need for the injunction, he will grant it, temporarily, without even hearing the other party's objections.[2] However, to protect the other party in case your application is unfounded, you will have to lodge a substantial amount as security with the court so that the amount will be available, as indemnity, to the other party in case it is decided at the *final hearing* that the interim injunction should be lifted, rather than made permanent.

Self-help in abating a nuisance, such as lopping off the neighbour's tree branches overhanging your land, should be avoided since it can result in serious legal difficulties; for example, it might lay you open to a charge of *malicious damage to property*. However, you are within your rights in plucking the fruit off such a branch, provided you do not harm the tree.

QUESTIONS

1. What are the two basic distinctions between a crime and a tort?
2. To what extent can a parent be held legally responsible for torts committed by his children?
3. What rights have you to prevent someone from taking a photograph of you and displaying it publicly?
4. List four different types of trespass.
5. Your neighbour owns two hills, one on either side of your low land. He habitually engages in target practice, firing from one hill to the other. Have you any legal means to prevent him from doing this? Explain.
6. *A* writes a defamatory letter to *B*, who indignantly shows it to his friend *C*. Has *B* grounds for bringing a libel action against *A*? Explain.
7. Is the following newspaper paragraph grounds for a libel action? "The trustees of the local art gallery are worried about the absence of a valuable painting from its usual position. The gallery's curator departed on a long vacation yesterday for parts unknown."
8. *A* suddenly arisen tornado hurls a pedestrian against a store

---

[2] The urgency in this situation lies in the fact that, once the building is erected, you can only get damages; the courts will not order it to be torn down.

window. Can the window's owner compel the pedestrian to pay for its breakage?

9. A hotel guest, returning to his room at 3 a.m., slipped and injured himself while crossing the hotel lobby, whose floor was being washed with liberal soap suds. Explain the hotel's liability.

10. Motorist *A*, while driving on his proper side of the road, suddenly sees approaching him a car on its wrong side of the road. To avert disaster, *A* steers into a ditch on his right, severely damaging his car. When sued, the other motorist *B* correctly claimed that had *A* swerved into the open left lane, no damage would have resulted. Who will win, and why?

11. While crossing an intersection on the green light at 90 m.p.h., motorist *A* is hit by a car going against the red light. What damages, if any, will *A* be able to collect from the other motorist?

12. A construction worker was injured when a falling piece of masonry penetrated his protective helmet. A good helmet would have saved him, but the one furnished by his employer was cheap and defective, though sturdy in appearance. When sued, what defense might the employer plead and with what success?

13. Under what circumstances would a dog not be "entitled to a first bite"?

14. What torts does *A* commit by going on *B*'s land in the night and fixing a solid barricade across the front door of *B*'s house?

15. A motorist negligently upsets a street vendor's pushcart full of fruit. Within the next few hours all the fruit lying in the roadway is squashed by passing traffic. How much can the motorist be made to pay to the owner of the fruit? Explain.

16. *A* sues *B* and *C* for trespass. *B* has cut across *A*'s lawn once, while in a hurry to catch a bus. *C* persistently walks across *A*'s lawn in spite of repeated warnings. What remedies will *A* get against *B* and *C*, respectively?

Basic Principles
of Contract

CHAPTER FOUR

Legal Agreement

DEFINITION

We now come to that portion of private law which is the backbone of the subject loosely called business law: namely, the law governing those obligations which are incurred by a person voluntarily and which are called *contracts*. As explained on page 17, a person usually has a reason which he considers sound for entering into an obligation of this nature. We shall spend considerable time discussing the basic principles of contract in this chapter; in Chapters 14 to 29 we shall explain the additional rules governing certain special contracts.

As has just been said, a person cannot come under a contractual obligation unless he has voluntarily agreed to be placed under one; we can therefore say that all contracts are based on agreement, of one kind or another. But, just as all men are people but all people are not men, all agreements do not amount to contracts: only those agreements are contracts which conform to certain rigorous requirements, as summarized in the following definition;

A legally enforceable contract is a *deliberate agreement* between two or more *competent* parties (not necessarily in *writing*) which is supported by mutual *consideration* to do some *legal* act *voluntarily*.

Whenever it has to be decided whether a transaction or a set of circumstances amounts to a valid contract, it must be checked to see whether it conforms with each of the seven items in this definition; if it does not comply with every one of them, the so-called contract will be void or, at best, voidable. Each of the italicized words in the

59

definition has a technical meaning which we shall now set forth, one by one.

THE MEANING OF A "DELIBERATE" AGREEMENT

When an agreement is "deliberate," it is understood that the parties have the intention that a breach of their agreement is to be followed by legal consequences; in other words, they intend "to go to law" or "to be taken to law" if the agreement is broken. Since a person making a "date" or receiving or extending a dinner invitation cannot have contemplated being sued for cancelling it, such social engagements are obviously not contracts that are enforceable in a court of law. Even if one of the parties had incurred substantial expense, such as travelling quite a distance to keep the date; or preparing an elaborate meal; or buying tickets to a performance, the courts will not penalize the other party for having broken an agreement of this nature.

THE MEANING OF "AGREEMENT"

Often it is at once apparent whether two parties have arrived at a mutually satisfactory way of handling a transaction involving them both—in other words, if they have "reached an agreement": but, sometimes, it is not easy to determine whether an agreement has been reached. Agreement has been defined as "a meeting of the minds": both parties having a clear understanding of their rights and duties under the contemplated dealings between them.

Preparatory negotiations to a business deal are often lengthy and involved. There might have been an exchange of letters, telegrams, and telephone conversations back and forth, containing requests for information; price and delivery quotations or estimates (sometimes called pro-forma orders or invoices); options to buy, offers, suggestions, counter-suggestions, and acceptances, etc. To determine whether these negotiations have culminated in an agreement, the courts have evolved a formula over the years; namely that:

• Agreement equals *offer* plus *acceptance.*

In other words, if the courts find that one party (the *offeror*) has said, written, or done something which amounts to a clear-cut offer to do some definite thing (such as to buy, sell, or rent some goods; or to render or to engage some services); and that the other party (the *offeree*) has done something that can be interpreted as an unconditional acceptance of that offer, the courts will consider an agreement to have been reached. It now becomes necessary to examine the exact meaning of these two terms, offer and acceptance.

OFFER

The offer may be made in express words or writing, or it may be implied from the offeror's conduct.

Serious intention. To be capable of acceptance the other party (the offeree) must have reasonable grounds for believing that the offer was seriously intended by the offeror. If the "offer" was made in an *obvious* spirit of fun or burst of temper, an unscrupulous person cannot, by his acceptance, convert this into a binding agreement. What golfer has not heard another say, after a bad round, "For two pins, I'll give my clubs away!"? Obviously, a person, accepting such an "offer" would not have much success in court if he tried to enforce it. However, if an offeror, with a straight face, makes an offer to sell something at a price which he thinks is too ludicrously low to be taken seriously, he is bound by his offer if it is accepted by someone who is genuinely unaware of the offeror's thoughts; for the courts can only interpret a person's thoughts by his words or actions and not by psycho-analysis.

Clear offer. While it is not necessary for an offeror to use any set expression (such as "I offer to sell you this book for $5 cash"), the words or conduct of the offeror must be made in a manner that clearly indicate his willingness to carry out the promise contained in his offer if it is properly accepted by the other party.

Thus, the following statements would clearly be legal offers to *sell*:

"You can have it for $5."

"Will you give me $5 for it?"

"It is $5. (In response to a request: "How much do you want for it?")

The following would be examples of offers to *buy* a book marked $5 in a book store: "I will take it."; or merely taking it to the cashier with your money, with no words spoken by either party. Ordering a meal in a restaurant is as much an offer as a customer sending an order to a firm on the basis of its current price list. On the other hand, the words "I might sell it for $5" would not constitute an offer.

Invitations. The reader may have noticed that the price tags and price lists referred to above were not treated as offers. They are merely quotations which serve to invite the public to make offers to the seller. Nor are the following considered as offers, but merely as "invitations to the public to make offers": catalogues; advertisements in newspapers, over the radio, etc.; handbills and circular letters distributed indiscriminately; invitations to tender; or an auctioneer putting up articles for bids by the public (the public's bids—offers—are accepted when the auctioneer "knocks down" the goods to them or says "sold" or "gone").

It is for this reason that a seller cannot be legally held by a prospective buyer to an erroneously low price marked on a price tag or printed in an advertisement: they are not offers, but merely invitations. (Commonly, of course, a reputable store will waive its legal rights and will voluntarily sell one of the wrongly priced items at the low price, for the sake of good public relations and to avoid the charge of deliberate misleading advertising.) To avoid arousing ill-feeling in frustrated customers, circulars, catalogues, etc., should bear the clear notation: "Subject to existing stocks and to changes in price without notice." Conversely, requests for price information should be stamped, "This is not a firm order."

Definite terms. Another requirement for a valid offer is that it be definite in every important particular. If the offer concerns a sale, then the articles or the goods should be clearly designated so that there can be no misunderstanding about them. The quantities should also be clearly stated (e.g., U.S. or Imperial gallons; long or short tons); so should the price be stated and the terms of payment (e.g., immediate cash; or 2/10, net 30; or payment in stated instalments); as well as date, place, and method of delivery. In many instances some of these details need not be expressly stated if they are implied from the circumstances or from customary usage. For example, if you buy a small, inexpensive item that carries a standard price, it is obviously implied that you will pay this price, without expecting credit; that you will get the goods at once; and that they will not be delivered to your home—in other words, the sale is on a "cash and carry" basis.

Similarly, you seldom ask your dentist how much he will charge for filling your tooth. You know that at the end of the month he will send you a statement for his customary charges. If the price (or other particular of the offer) has not been expressly stated, and this is not a transaction in which a price has been set by custom, it is implied that a reasonable price will be charged for the delivered article or the rendered service.

Omitted terms. In deciding on the validity of agreements from which a vital term has been omitted, the courts will draw a distinction between *executory* agreements, where everything to be done still lies in the future, and *executed* or partly *executed* contracts, where both or one of the parties have performed all or some of their obligations respectively. In wholly executory agreements, the courts will not "make your bargain for you" by making up the omission of the vital term; in other words, they will consider no agreement to have been reached. However, if there has been some execution of the agreement (e.g., if goods have been delivered and consumed with no price yet agreed upon), the courts will decide on a price and terms they consider fair.

Agreements to agree

• Problem: "I can let you have 100 pounds of this new product "X" next week at a price you and I will agree upon tomorrow." If this offer is accepted, will it constitute an agreement?

Solution: No; because no price has yet been quoted in this executory-agreement, and there is no assurance that an agreement will be reached on it "tomorrow"; therefore the offer is not sufficiently definite.

There would have been agreement if the offer had stated ". . . at a price Mr. Y will decide upon," and if Mr. Y then had decided upon a price.

And, if *A* and *B* draw up a rough agreement which they plan to have put into formal language later, such a rough draft becomes binding on them—provided it contains all the important elements of the agreement—even though the formal document never does come into existence (unless the draft had stated "*subject to* formal contract").

63

Communication. The offer must be communicated to the offeree, and it must reach him. Let us suppose that I leave a note in my son's room promising him $1 if he will wash my car for me; and let us suppose that, without having seen the note, my son decides to do me a favour and washes the car. When he discovers the note, will he have a legal claim against me for $1? The answer is "No" because he had not received my offer, and therefore his washing of the car did not constitute an acceptance of my offer.[1]

• Problem: Hill writes the following letter to McGraw: "Toronto, February 1, 19—. Dear Mac: I offer you, for immediate delivery, 100 boxes of fresh Grade "A" Widgets at $12 a box. Yours truly, (signed) Greg Hill."

On the back of this letter there is a post script stating that the price has been increased to $13 a box. Not knowing what is on the back of the letter, McGraw accepts the offer. Will he have to pay $1,200 or $1,300?

Decision: The court will probably decide that there has been no communication of the P.S. to McGraw. Where a business letter appears to be complete on the face of it, it is surely not necessary to examine its back; unless, of course, it said on the front "See back," "Over," or "P.T.O." (Please turn over), etc. Therefore, McGraw probably will have to pay only $1,200.

Similarly, if on your parking lot receipt it stated in microscopic print that the parking lot operator is to be allowed the unrestricted use of your car while parked in his lot, this part of the offer (which the receipt, technically, is) will not be deemed to have reached you. While normally a person is supposed to read and is bound by conditions printed on receipts, etc., which are handed to him, he is not expected to search beneath the surface for anything hidden or unusual. (Incidentally, a person such as this parking lot operator cannot contract himself out of liability for the consequences of his own wanton recklessness or criminality, or that of his employees, merely by printing words to that effect on the receipt or by painting them on a sign.)

---

[1] Please note the use of the expression "a legal claim." Few fathers would "welsh" on their sons like this, and neither will businessmen always make full use of their legal rights. This distinction between the letter of the law and actual practice should be borne in mind when some legal technicalities in this book may appear to be unduly stressed.

• Problem: If Temple drafts an offer to Urban, and if Urban finds out the contents of this offer before it is sent to him, can he accept it?

Decision: No; Urban cannot, by his acceptance, convert Temple's offer into an agreement because there was no communication of the offer to him.

• Problem: If Lewis makes an offer to Brook which Brook refuses, can Jackson accept it instead?

Decision: No; because, again, no communication of Lewis' offer was made to Jackson.

Note, that an offer need not necessarily be addressed to a person whose identity you know. For example, a $10 reward may be offered to the finder of a lost article or to the first person to furnish a required piece of information. This is a definite offer—not to the public at large, but to one individual. His identity is, as yet, unknown, and the offer can only be communicated to him by publicizing it in a newspaper advertisement or over the radio, etc. The "double your money back if not satisfied" guarantees similarly constitute offers to purchasers of products which carry such promises.

Offer lapses. How long does an offer stay open? Certainly not forever, and there are some fairly definite rules, to establish when an offer "lapses" (i.e., comes to an end) automatically:

1. The offer lapses after the expiry of a specific time limit that may have been mentioned by the offeror.

2. If no such time limit has been specified, the offer will no longer be effective if acceptance of it is attempted beyond a reasonable time after the offer was made. For example, in the case of perishables, or of goods subject to rapid turnover, or to fast price fluctuations, an offer will have to be accepted much more promptly than transactions where more time is customarily taken to form a decision.

3. The offer lapses if either the offeror or the offeree dies, becomes bankrupt, or is declared insane before acceptance of the offer. Thus, the offeree cannot compel a deceased offeror's executor to sell him an article which the deceased, while still alive, had offered to him but had died before acceptance; nor can a bankrupt offeree's trustee in bankruptcy force the offeror to sell him an article which he had offered to the offeree before he went bankrupt. However, if an agreement had been reached before any of these calamities had befallen

65

either party, the dead person's executor or the bankrupt's trustee, respectively, would succeed to their claims or obligations (of a commercial nature only, of course; and nothing involving personal services). For other examples of impossibility of performance see Chapter 11.

4. The offer, naturally, comes to an end when it is properly accepted; it then merges into the resulting agreement.

5. An offer also lapses automatically once it is refused by the offeree. If the offeree then changes his mind and decides to accept the offer after all, it is too late for him to do so.

• Example: If *A* says to *B*: "You can have this book for $5"; to which *B* replies: "No, that is too much"; but a minute later *B* continues: "I guess you have me over a barrel—here is your $5"; to which *A* says: "Sorry, it'll cost you $6 now," *A* cannot be made to sell for $5. When *B* said "No," the offer lapsed. When *B* subsequently tendered the $5 to *A*, he was making a new offer (called a *counter offer*) to *A*, which it was open to *A* to accept or to refuse. In this example *A* refused *B*'s counter offer (and caused it to lapse, thereby) and made yet another counter offer to *B*, this time at $6.

6. In (5) above we had an illustration of an offer lapsing by an express refusal. An offer can also lapse if it is refused by implication; for instance, by making a counter offer:

• Example: *A* to *B*: "I offer you this book for $5." *B*: "I shall be delighted to buy it for $4." Although *B*'s statement sounds like an acceptance by *B*, it is not an unconditional acceptance, but a qualified acceptance. In effect, it is really a refusal of *A*'s $5 offer and a counter offer by *B* to buy for $4. The effects on the offer of an implied refusal, such as this, are identical to those of an express refusal; namely, the refusal causes the offer to lapse. Other examples of counter offers will be given under the heading "Acceptance."

7. In addition to the above automatic offer lapses, it is also open to an offeror to *revoke* (withdraw) his offer, or to change its terms, before it has been accepted; once it has been properly accepted (see "Acceptance"), it is too late for the offeror to change his mind. Complementary to this is the rule that it is too late for an offeree to accept an offer once he *learns of its revocation*—even from sources other than the offeror himself. For example, it is too late for *A* to accept

66

B's offer to sell him an article after he learns that *B* has, meanwhile, sold it to *C*.

Options. Note that one party's promise to hold an offer open to the other party for a certain length of time is not legally binding upon him; unless he received some payment or some other form of "consideration" (see Chapter 5) for this "option."

ACCEPTANCE

Let us assume *A* to have communicated a clear and otherwise valid offer to *B* which appeals to *B* so much that he decides, in his mind, to go along with *A*'s proposition. Does this decision by *B* create an agreement between him and *A*? No, because there has not yet taken place the second step required for an agreement; namely, the *acceptance* of the offer by the offeree.

Just as the offer had to meet with certain requirements, so must the acceptance, to wit:

Unconditional acceptance. As mentioned above under Offer Lapses (item 6.), an acceptance must be absolutely unconditional and without qualification. If the offer is not accepted exactly as made, the so-called "acceptance" serves merely as a bargaining counter offer. This applies not only to the price, but also to the other terms of the offer. If the offer specifies stated goods at a stated price, payment terms, interest rate, and delivery conditions; and if the offeree wants to clinch the bargain by his acceptance, he must not amend any of these specifications in his acceptance.

Inquiries. A counter offer should not be confused with a preliminary inquiry which an offeree may make before deciding to accept or to refuse. The following questions are examples of "inquiries" that the offeree could make in response to an offer to sell him an item for $5:

"Is that your lowest price?"
"Are you sure you wouldn't take $4?"
"May I see something else first?"

In borderline cases the court will have to decide whether a statement by the offeree constitutes a counter offer or a non-committal preliminary inquiry, which would still leave it open to the offeree to make a binding acceptance.

Manner of acceptance. We know (see page 61) that an offeror can make his offer in any reasonable way he pleases: by word of mouth, writing, or conduct. While there are also several ways of making acceptance, the governing factor is that, to be binding on the offeror, the acceptance must be made in a manner that the offeror wanted or in which he expected it to be made, in accordance with the following rules:

PERFORMANCE. The offeree can accept the offer by making immediate performance in accordance with the offeror's proposition. Thus, if *A* wires to *B*: "Send me by air express 12 "number fifteens" from your current price list," *B* will have accepted *A*'s offer by despatching these items to *A* according to instructions. If *B* should send *A* a wire informing him of the despatch, it will only be out of courtesy; the agreement will already have been formed previously by the despatch of the goods.

Similarly, if a customer in a store points to an article with a price tag on it (it will be remembered that price tags constitute "invitations") and asks the cashier, "O.K. if I take this now and pay for it by the end of the month?"; the cashier will have accepted this offer by the act of wrapping the article and handing it to the customer. Or, if a man tells a boy with a shoe-shine kit that he will pay him a quarter for a shine, it is obviously sufficient for the boy to do the job to earn his money, without any formal acceptance speech.

COMMUNICATION. Where the offeree cannot immediately supply the goods or perform the services asked by the offeror, it will be necessary for the offeree to communicate his acceptance to the offeror. Where the parties are negotiating a deal orally, it is obvious that acceptance of an oral offer can be communicated orally or by clear gestures, such as a nod of the head, a handshake, or the fall of an auctioneer's hammer. Incidentally, it is taken for granted that an oral offer that has not been accepted while the parties were conversing, lapses after they part company (unless the offeree was given extra time in which to accept).

Most business transactions take place between people at a distance from one another so that they must communicate by mail, telegram, etc. To decide whether acceptance has been made in the proper manner, we must first establish whether the offeror has or has not clearly instructed the offeree how to communicate his acceptance.

Communication By　　　If such instructions have been given, and the
Indicated Methods.　　　offeree did not observe them punctiliously,
there is no binding agreement. Any such improperly made acceptance
serves only as a counter offer, which the original offeror may, in his
turn, accept or ignore. The following are examples of instructions for
communicating acceptance that might be given by the offeror:

> "If you like my offer, send your acceptance by attaching it to, and
> releasing, the enclosed carrier pigeon."
>
> "If you like my offer, accept it by flashing a light three times from
> your attic window at 9 to-night."
>
> "If you like my offer, indicate your acceptance by firing your shot-
> gun twice at noon to-morrow in your front yard."
>
> "If you like my offer, sign the attached copy of it and give it to the
> messenger who delivered this offer to you."

In all these illustrations, if the offeree wants his acceptance to be
binding upon the offeror, he has no choice but to accept by the indicated methods, even if he considers them foolish. On the other hand,
by selecting these methods of acceptance and forcing them on the
offeree, the offeror assumes the risk of the acceptance not getting back
to him. Once the offeree has released the pigeon, flashed his light, fired
his gun, or handed the message to the messenger respectively, the
agreement has been completed—even if the pigeon is killed by a
hawk, the light cannot be seen on account of fog, the sound of the
shots is drowned out by the noise of machinery, or the messenger for-
gets to return the message. The offeror could then be sued for breach
of contract if, wrongly assuming that the offeree had not made acceptance, he sold the offered article to someone else.

More commonly used today than carrier pigeons are the mails and
telegrams, for which the same rules hold good. If the offeror had stipulated that the acceptance be made by wire, no other method will do—
the offeree must accept by wire. If he accepts by any other method,
such as the mail, it is not a proper acceptance but merely a counter
offer. This rule even extends to the situation where an offeror requires
acceptance to be made by mail only, but the offeree accepts by wire;
this method of acceptance is faster than the other, but it is made contrary to instructions and therefore is not binding on the offeror. (It is,
of course, open to the offeree to let the offeror know by wire that an

69

acceptance has been mailed.) Again, the offeror assumes the risk of the acceptance not getting into his hands; if the offer is accepted by the stipulated manner (e.g., if the letter is dropped in the mail-box, or if the wire is handed to the telegraph boy) within the specified time limits (or, failing which, within a reasonable time), then an agreement has been completed, even if the properly addressed letter of acceptance is destroyed, lost or delayed after mailing it, or if the properly worded telegram of acceptance is garbled in transmission.

To protect himself against these eventualities, it is good business practice for an offeror to stipulate that an acceptance must actually *reach* him within certain time limits, beyond which the offer is to become ineffective.

Communication By Reasonable Methods. While it is common practice for business men to indicate the time within which acceptance is to be made, it is relatively rare for them to stipulate expressly (as in the foregoing examples) the manner of acceptance. If no such manner is expressly indicated, it is implied that he authorizes the offeree to accept in any *reasonable* manner. The rule-of-thumb test for "a reasonable manner" is an acceptance by a means that is at least as fast, efficient, and safe as the manner of making the offer (unless there is some other customary manner in a particular trade of making acceptance). For example, reasonable manners of accepting a mailed offer would be by mail or by wire. However, accepting a wired offer from the other end of the earth by ordinary surface mail would not be considered reasonable and would not be regarded as a binding acceptance.

Time of agreement. The only other matter to be decided is the precise moment at which such a "reasonably" made acceptance converts an offer into an agreement. We have learned that acceptance of an offer that required acceptance by mail, takes place at the moment that the properly addressed acceptance is dropped into the mail-box by the offeree; this is so because the offeror had expressly appointed the mails as his duly constituted representative or agent. The same reasoning accounts for the handing of a telegram of acceptance to the telegraph boy being considered the moment of acceptance (where the offer required acceptance to be made by wire); since the boy is the offeror's implied agent. But where the offeror leaves it open to the offeree to accept in any reasonable manner, the moment of acceptance will vary, according to whether the offeree used the offeror's implied agency or *his own*.

If the offeree accepts in exactly the same way in which the offer was sent, he is held to be communicating through the offeror's agent. For example, a mailed offer is accepted at the moment that the acceptance is dropped into the letter box, and a wired offer is accepted at the moment that a wire of acceptance is telephoned to the telegraph office.

However, if the offeree chooses some other reasonable manner of communicating acceptance, he is employing his own agency and assumes responsibility for its proper functioning. Thus, if the mailed offer did not specify the manner in which acceptance should be made, we have learned that it is reasonable for this offer to be accepted by wire. But, since the telegraph company is now the offeree's agent, he is assuming responsibility for the wire reaching the offeror; in other words, no agreement is reached until the wire of acceptance is actually delivered to the offeror's own hands, or office.

Incidentally, if two people verbally discuss a deal and one says to the other: "Go back to your home town and let me know your decision in a few days," it has been held that acceptance by mail is acceptance through the offeror's implied agent.

Apart from the possibility of the acceptance being lost or garbled en route, there are other reasons why the moment of acceptance is important. For example, the offeror might die or become bankrupt; in which case, the existence of an agreement will depend on whether this event occurred before or after the moment of acceptance. Similarly, if the offeree learns of the revocation of an offer, the validity of the agreement might depend on the exact moment at which acceptance was effected.

Silence and inaction. We have seen that positive action can take the place of an oral or written acceptance (e.g., firing a gun, flashing a light); but maintaining silence or remaining inactive will not be construed as making an acceptance. For example, if a stamp dealer sends some postage stamps to your house, *unasked*, and states that you will have to pay him $5 for them if you do not return them within ten days, you are under no obligation to return them. Of course, if you accept his "offer" (e.g., by pasting the stamps in your album or by giving them to your nephew), you do become liable for the price.

Your only duty toward those stamps is to be reasonably careful of them and to hand them to the dealer should he call for them at your house. If, instead of stamps, these unasked-for goods were perishables, you would be held to have accepted them by consuming them; on the other hand, you would be entitled to put them in the garbage eventually. If the items were bulky, you might, conceivably, charge for the storage of them! In one case it was even held that an offeree who liked the goods offered on these terms could not convert the offer into an agreement by deliberately maintaining silence—with the consequence that, when these goods were accidentally destroyed, it was the original owner who had to suffer their loss, and the "buyer" did not have to pay the "seller" for them.

Naturally, if you had ordered the goods (perhaps by sending in a coupon), you would have to comply with the other party's terms.

Cancellation. It follows that, once acceptance has been properly communicated to the offeror, an agreement has been formed; and, if the offeree (now the *acceptor*) subsequently changes his mind, it is too late for him to withdraw his acceptance. This holds true even in the following example: If a person accepts an offer by mail (which we shall assume to have been the proper method of acceptance in this case), and if he then changes his mind and in a wire to the offeror instructs him to disregard the letter of acceptance, the offeror still has the legal right to treat the letter as a firm acceptance. What happens if the offeree sends his acceptance by an agent of his own? It would then be open to him to cancel his acceptance by getting word of its cancellation to the offeror before the acceptance reached him; the reason being that, in this latter case, there was no complete communication yet of the acceptance and thus no agreement.

And, for the benefit of any reader who wants to delve into this topic still more deeply, it is open to an offeree to cancel any refusal of an offer he may have sent to the offeror, if he can get this cancellation to actually reach the offeror before the offer refusal actually reaches him. If the offeree is successful in this, he may still accept the original offer provided that any specified time limits for accepting have not yet expired.

Communication "by the offeree to the offeror." As already stated, communication of the acceptance must be made by the offeree to the offeror. While these two persons can be replaced by their properly constituted representatives, the latitude extends no further. Therefore, assuming *A* to be the offeror and *B* the offeree, there is no proper acceptance if *B* tells *C*, a friend of his, that he has decided to accept *A*'s offer—the communication not having been made to the offeror. Nor is there an acceptance if this friend, *C*, tells *A* of *B*'s decision to accept *A*'s offer—the communication not having been made by the offeree. Of course, if *C* was instructed by *B* to deliver this message to *A*, *C* would be *B*'s properly appointed agent, and proper communication would have taken place. Nor is there proper communication to the offeror if the offeree places an incorrect address on the envelope, or otherwise does not give the acceptance a proper chance to reach the offeror.

Finally, it should not be necessary to mention that an acceptance needs no further confirmation or acceptance by the offeror. The agreement is completed once there have been a valid offer and acceptance.

Note 1. Referring back to the statement that an acceptance which is to be made by mail is properly made at the moment it is dropped in the mail box even if it never reaches the offeror, the question is often asked how the offeree can prove that he ever mailed such a lost acceptance. Now, to deal with the question of proof and evidence in full, would require a large volume all to itself. Therefore, we beg the reader's indulgence henceforth and ask him to assume all the facts in the examples of this book to be capable of proof; and suffice it to explain that the courts will accept as evidence of a lost letter (even if it was not sent by registered post) a properly filed and dated carbon copy and oral evidence by the writer and mailer. The presumption is that the offeree has not fabricated a false copy and thus committed the serious crime of forgery; and that the original of this copy was mailed on the date it bears, along with all the other outgoing letters of that day. In other words, it is presumed that all routine matters were carried out in a routine manner, unless the contrary can be proved.

Note 2. An important practical lesson to be learned by the businessman from the above legal theory is not to offer an item for sale to Prospect #2 until an offer of the same item to Prospect #1 has expired

73

or been refused. Otherwise, if both accept the offer, without knowledge of the item's previous sale, the seller may find himself saddled with a claim for breach of contract by the disappointed party. A practical way of avoiding such legal complications is to follow the system adopted by the sellers of houses and cars; namely, to invite offers from prospective buyers. It then remains possible for the seller to compare offers and to select for acceptance the offer which appeals to him most.

QUESTIONS

1. Abel and Brown sign a document which contains the following clause: "If either party breaks the contract, the other party agrees not to take court action." If Abel breaks a term of the agreement, what legal action may Brown take? Explain.
2. Man to car dealer: "I want a good used car." Dealer: "I have several at $1,000 each." Man: "That suits me fine." Give six reasons why this conversation does not constitute a contract.
3. Cox places a sign on his car: "For Sale, $100." If Digby tenders $100 to Cox, will Cox have to take the money and let Digby have the car?
4. Earl mailed an offer to Finch without specifying a manner or time for acceptance. Sixty days later Finch mailed an unconditional acceptance to Earl. On what legal grounds might Earl refuse to regard Finch's acceptance as binding?
5. Gordon writes to Higgins: "I accept your offer on condition that you make punctual delivery, and that you supply the full quantity of goods as promised by you." Does this constitute a valid acceptance? Explain.
6. Merchant: "I will give you $39 for these goods, to be delivered to my store one month from today." Wholesaler: "Let me think about it. But, how about your taking them from my overloaded warehouse tomorrow for just $32?" Merchant: "No." Wholesaler: "O.K. then; I will supply the goods on your terms." Explain whether this conversation has resulted in a contract.
7. Irving sent an offer to Jones by air mail, instructing Jones to accept by a wire which was to reach Irving not later than November 27. Jones accepted by an air mail letter which reached Irving on November 26. Was there a legal agreement? Explain.

74

8. On May 16 King airmailed an offer to Lennox which reached Lennox on the morning of May 18. That afternoon Lennox accepted the offer by a wire which reached King on May 19. On the evening of May 18, King had telephoned a revocation of his offer to Lennox. Would there be a legal agreement:
   (a) If King had stipulated that acceptance be made by wire? Explain.
   (b) If King had not stated how acceptance was to be made? Explain.

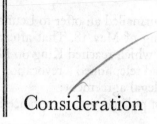

CHAPTER FIVE

Consideration

THE MEANING OF CONSIDERATION

Assuming a deliberate agreement to have been consummated between two parties, we know from our definition of contract that this does not, necessarily, amount to a legally enforceable contract—it does so only if all other requisites have also been complied with. The next one we shall discuss is the need for *consideration*.

The rule is that the courts will not enforce a promise to do or to give something unless the person benefiting from this promise *does or gives something in exchange* or, at least, promises to do so. The courts simply refuse to believe that a promise to do something for nothing could have been seriously intended, this being contrary to human nature! They will only be convinced of the serious intention of the promisor if the contract consists of a formally sealed document (see Chapter 6) or if it is "supported (or, upheld) by valuable consideration"; namely, "giving, or doing something, or giving up some privilege, in return for having something given or done for one." Or, oversimplified perhaps: on the one hand, a man must earn what he gets; and, on the other hand, a man cannot be legally compelled to keep a promise to make a gift. In normal business transactions, the consideration for a sale or hire of goods consists of the price or rental to be paid for them; and in a contract for work or other services, the consideration is the salary or other fee.

ADEQUACY OF CONSIDERATION

It is interesting to note that the court is not concerned whether the consideration is adequate; that is, whether a fair price or fee is being paid. As long as the court is satisfied that the parties have troubled to agree on some consideration, it will uphold the contract; for the court will not "make a person's bargain for him" (unless it can be proved that the consent to accept insufficient value was procured by fraud). If this were not so, anyone could escape the unfortunate consequences of a poor bargain he had made by claiming that he was not receiving sufficient consideration. It is for this reason that public-spirited public servants, by accepting a dollar a year for their services, render themselves liable to the discipline of the service and become entitled to the benefit of any compensation plans, etc.

While the consideration can have a very low value, it must not be obviously entirely valueless commercially, e.g., a drink of water from a near-by tap under normal conditions. And, moral values are held not to be commercial values: thus a relative's promise to love and respect, or an employee's promise to be loyal (while dignified by the term "good consideration") do not have the effect of "valuable consideration" in upholding a contract.

It is to be noted that the person promising to do or to give something is held to his promise even if he gets nothing in exchange for himself personally—since, according to our rules, there is sufficient consideration present if the other party does something to earn his money, or other reward. Thus, a promise to pay someone if he gives up a favourite pastime, or achieves some feat, or renders some service to charity, is enforceable if the other party actually fulfils these requirements.

As mentioned once before, while it is best for a contract clearly to specify all details of the transaction, including the consideration, omission of its mention from the contract will not invalidate it if there exists a customary price for the goods involved or where a reasonable charge is expected to be paid for services.

PRESENT AND FUTURE CONSIDERATION

To be effective, consideration must take place in the *present* or in the *future*; it must *not* have happened in the *past*. Thus, paying $5 for a book in a store is exchanging performance (giving the money) for performance (delivering the goods) and constitutes valid, present consideration. Also, paying $5 in advance for later delivery of the book is exchanging performance (giving the money) for a promise (to deliver the goods). This amounts to present consideration on one side and future consideration on the other, which is equally valid—as is the promise to pay $5 at a later date for immediate delivery of the book. A promise in exchange for a promise is equally valid consideration. In fact, it represents the most common type of credit transaction; namely, an order that is placed for the future delivery of goods, coupled with a promise to pay for them on delivery, or even later. In this example there is future consideration on both sides.

PAST CONSIDERATION

On the other hand, a promise by *A* to pay *B* for some free service or gift that *B* had already given to *A* previously, is held to be made in exchange for "past consideration" which cannot be used to enforce a promise. For *A*'s promise to be enforceable by *B*, *B* must do something for *A* simultaneously or subsequently to *A*'s promise. *B*'s "past consideration" is not valuable consideration but, at best, a motive for *A* promising to make a gift to *B*. And, as already mentioned, a promise to make a gift will not be enforced by law because, obviously, a gift is made for no consideration of value.

EXISTING OBLIGATION

Another requirement for a valid consideration is that it be given for a new obligation, and not for an already existing one. Supposing a builder to have contracted with a buyer to erect a certain house for a stated price by a specified time; and supposing that, some time later, the buyer had promised the builder a bonus for completing the house on time; would the builder be legally entitled to the bonus if he did complete the house on time? The answer would be "No" because the builder was already obligated to do this, and he was not giving any new consideration to earn the bonus. If, in return for the bonus, the builder had promised completion of the house earlier than the original contract date (or to furnish some extra items not originally contracted for), he would have earned the bonus on fulfilling his new obligations and would thus be giving fresh consideration.

But, contrast the following situations: In front of a burning house, Woman No. 1 says to Fireman No. 1: "Save my baby, just inside the front door, and I will pay you $1,000!" And Woman No. 2 says to Fireman No. 2: "Save my cat from the fiercely flaming fifth floor, and I will pay you $100!" Both firemen effect the respective rescues. But while Fireman No. 1 will have no legal claim (since it is assumed that he was merely carrying out his routine duties), Fireman No. 2 is probably entitled to his reward since he seems to have acted "above and beyond the strict call of duty."

UNLAWFUL CONSIDERATION

The consideration must not be unlawful or impossible. If I promise $10 to a man if he will give a beating to an enemy of mine, and he does so, he obviously has no legal claim against me. Also, if I promise a man $100 for a magical tonic that will make me live to be a 1,000 years old, I need not keep my promise for such an impossible consideration.

PARTIAL PAYMENTS

What happens in cases where a creditor, exasperated at not being able to collect a long overdue debt, asks his procrastinating debtor to let him have a portion only of his claim, and that he would then "forget about" the rest of the claim? Let us suppose that, on the basis of such a suggestion by a creditor, a debtor pays $75 out of an overdue $100 debt. Is the creditor then entitled to enforce payment of the $25 balance? The answer is "Yes" because he received no consideration for giving up his claim to $25. What he did, in effect, was to promise his debtor a gift of $25; and we know that such unsupported promises are not upheld in court. The only circumstances under which the creditor would lose his claim to the $25 would be the following:
• Where he received something in the way of consideration from the debtor, however little: for example payment of $75 before the due date of the $100 debt; a promissory note or a draft drawn on the debtor for $75 to replace the $100 book debt; or some slight service or trifling article.
• Where the debtor could prove that the creditor forgave him the

79

payment of $25 because he genuinely intended to make the debtor a gift of this amount. (While unsealed promises to make gifts will not be enforced, the courts will not rescind an executed gift—one that has already taken place; they will not allow a person to be an "Indian giver.")

• Where the debtor could prove that he and the creditor had come to a genuine agreement to make a change in the original terms of the contract; for example, where a landlord voluntarily reduced a tenant's rent during a period of depression.

• Where there has been a *voluntary composition with creditors.* This takes place where a debtor owes money to several creditors but does not have enough to pay them all in full. If, in a meeting with all his creditors, during which he lays all his cards frankly on the table, they unanimously agree to take a proportionate share of their debts in full satisfaction of their claims, the debtor is freed from further obligations toward them when he makes all the agreed-upon payments. (This arrangement is the common law forerunner of our federal laws of bankruptcy, which operate on the same principle.) The consideration received by each creditor for giving up a part of his claim is the fact that he is now receiving no less than each of the other creditors, by reason of each of these having given up a part of their claims also.

• Where the debtor and the creditor had effected a *compromise;* namely, where the debtor had sincere grounds for contesting all or part of the creditor's claim and offered to pay part of it (e.g., by "meeting him half-way") for the sake of avoiding litigation. The consideration for the creditor's giving up part of the claim, in this case, lies in the debtor's paying an amount which he *bona fide* believes not to be owing.

PROMISES TO CHARITY

Are promises to charities and to other good causes binding? On the face of it, these are promises to make gifts; but the courts will generally enforce them on the grounds that the promisees are giving consideration by providing a service to the community or by completing a contemplated project. Also, on the strength of the promisor's "pledge," other persons will have been induced to commit themselves similarly and thus will have furnished the required consideration.

It has been suggested on good authority that even a promise to make an outright gift can be enforced against a promisor if the promisee can prove that, relying on this promise in good faith, he incurred legal obligations; and that he would, therefore, be prejudicially affected if the promise to make the gift were withdrawn. As an example, let us suppose that A promises B to give him an old special-purpose truck. On the strength of this promise, B contracts with C to make certain deliveries with this truck by stipulated dates, and to pay heavy penalties if he breaks his contract. A will probably not be allowed to break his promise to give B the truck under these circumstances. There is nothing, of course, to stop A from withdrawing his free offer if he can get notice of his intention to B before B commits himself to an obligation.

In the same vein, where a creditor voluntarily gives his debtor an extension of time (say, three months) in which to pay his overdue debt, and then changes his mind and sues his debtor after just one month of the period of grace has elapsed, the debtor will be able to set up as a good defense to the action the creditor's *waiver* of his rights.

NEGLIGENCE

The following point should also be noted: Where a person voluntarily and without consideration performs a service for another, he is still liable for any damage he causes through his negligence. Thus, if I promise to wash your windows for you, you cannot hold me to my promise to wash them if I received no consideration for it. But, if I did start on the job and broke a window in the process, I would be liable to make good its value to you—not for breach of contract, but for the tort of negligence.

QUESTIONS

1. Milton promised $35 to Nixon if Nixon would build a bird house in Nixon's own garden. Nixon thereupon did exactly what Milton asked. Explain whether Milton could avoid paying Nixon on each of the following grounds:
   (a) That Nixon had not properly accepted Milton's offer.

(b) That $35 was far too high a price to pay for a little bird house.

(c) That Milton had received no benefit.

2. Olga promised, under seal, to give her niece Nelly $1,000 next Christmas in exchange for Nelly's undying gratitude. Explain whether the promise is legally enforceable.

3. After passing his law examinations, Peters promised to give his fellow student Quentin $30 for having coached him successfully for the exams. In case of default, can Peters be legally made to pay Quentin? Explain.

4. Professor Rogers informed his twenty graduate students that he would cancel their classes a week before the final examinations so that he could take an extra long summer holiday. His students thereupon prevailed upon him to finish out his full teaching load by promising to pay him $25 each. Can Rogers legally enforce payment?

CHAPTER SIX

Form of Contract

ADVANTAGES OF WRITTEN CONTRACTS

Referring again to our definition of contract, we note that valid contracts do not, necessarily, have to be in writing. With a few exceptions, this is true in most cases; however, it is certainly more advisable to reduce all contracts of any importance to writing. Not only is it far easier to prove your claim (since it is much more difficult for your legal opponent to explain away a written contract than for him to deny having made an oral bargain with you), but there is less room for misunderstanding regarding the terms of the contract. However, if you reduce a contract to writing, be sure to include in the written contract all the points you verbally agreed upon—for once a contract is written, any verbal agreements in connection with it will seldom be enforceable.

SPECIALTIES

In the earliest days of common law, contracts were generally not enforceable unless they were couched in formal language, signed before witnesses, and imprinted in hot wax with the seal of the subscribing parties. While the simplest contract could, even today, be drawn up thus formally, the preparing of such a *specialty* contract or *deed* remains necessary in only a few instances. Even then, the deed has lost much of its glamour—the flowery language is, for the most part, gone (e.g., land is left "to X absolutely" instead of "to X and his heirs forever"); typewriting has taken the place of the scrivener's beautiful hand-written engrossments; except for a few situations (e.g., bills of sale, chattel mortgages, affidavits, and marriage registers), the legal requirement for witnesses is gone, al-

83

though they are still frequently used (note, that a will, which requires two witnesses, is not a contract); the sealing wax is usually replaced by a small gummed red sticker (and even this replacement can be replaced by a piece of stamp paper, or just the letters l.s., standing for "locus sigilli," Latin for "the place of the seal"); and the signer no longer has to place his finger on the seal and to utter the words, "I deliver this as my act and deed." Also, since copies can be made with carbons, photo-copying, etc., it is no longer necessary to prepare *indentures*; that is, matched sets of documents—off which the lawyer bit a corner, so that his tooth marks would identify the copies as genuine!

What, then, are the contracts that should be placed under seal? In Chapter 5 we learned that a person who has been promised something without consideration (e.g., a gift) can enforce such a promise only if it was made under seal. And in Chapter 13 we shall be told that, if the contract is under seal, the time limit for enforcing the claim at law is much longer, according to the Statute of Limitations. However, a document (a *conveyance*) transferring land, or any interest in it, is required to be under seal; the reason probably being that physical delivery of land is not possible, as in personal goods (i.e., moveable goods, or chattels). It is therefore considered fitting that the symbol of ownership should be of a formal nature. Ownership can be transferred permanently on a sale or a gift; or temporarily, as security for a mortgage. Leases over three years must also be under seal; except that a written lease will be valid without a seal if the tenant immediately takes physical possession of the premises.

SIMPLE CONTRACTS

All contracts that are not specialties are *simple* (or *parol*) contracts; as the name implies, these are valid contracts, even though made only by word of mouth.

CONTRACTS THAT MUST BE EVIDENCED IN WRITING

However, there are just a few among these contracts which various laws, such as the Statute of Frauds (first formulated in England in 1676), require to be evidenced in writing before they can be enforced by legal action. These are as follows:

Land contracts. As we shall see in Chapter 27, land deals are often involved and prolonged; and, long before the previously discussed conveyance under seal takes place, there will have been formed a preliminary contract between the parties concerned; and any contracts involving *real property* (land, or anything attached to it permanently, such as buildings) must be in writing. Even a real estate broker has no legal claim for his earned selling commission unless he obtained his "listing" from the seller in writing.

While leases over three years in length should be sealed, short leases (up to three years) require writing alone. This is excused where a tenant has paid rent and actually taken possession; for example, by leaving something of value on the premises, such as a suitcase or just a raincoat. However, leaving a National Geographic magazine in a rented room was held to be insufficient taking of possession, and the landlady in question was entitled to return to a prospective "verbal" tenant the rent he had paid in advance and to refuse to rent him the room.

One-year contracts. Contracts that *must* endure for more than one year or, more accurately, contracts that *cannot* be performed by *either* party within one year from the date of making the contract should be in writing; for example, a contract of employment for more than one year.

• Question: Should the following contracts be in writing?

1. On January 2, *A* contracts with *B* to hire him for three months as of next November 1. Answer: Yes, writing is required, because the contract will not be completed within one year from January 2.

2. *A* contracts with *B* to keep him supplied with certain goods for the rest of his life (whether "his" refers to *A* or to *B* is immaterial here). Answer: No writing is required because neither one's life need necessarily continue beyond one year. Even if after the expiry of one year both are still alive and well, the contract will not need to be placed in writing, since either one *could* have died before the year was up.

3. *A* promises to pay *B* $10,000 in nine months if *B* will work for *A* for eighteen months. Answer: No writing is needed because one of the parties, *A*, will have completed his part of the contract within the year.

4. On March 1, *B* agrees to work for *A* for exactly one year, begin-

ning the next day, March 2. Answer: No writing is needed because B's last day of work next year will be on March 1, which will be exactly one year and not "more than one year" from the date of making the contract.

Guarantees.[1] (Before discussing contracts of guarantee any further, please note that a manufacturer's promise to stand behind his product is incorrectly called a guarantee by the layman; it should be called a *warranty*.)

A's promise to C to pay B's debt if B should fail to pay C, can only be enforced by C against A if the promise was given in writing. In this guarantee A assumes a secondary obligation to pay C which is contingent on the debtor's, B, failing to meet his primary obligation to pay the creditor, C. This transaction must be contrasted to one of *indemnity*, where A tells C: "Supply certain goods to B and charge their price to my account." In this latter case A has assumed a primary obligation toward C which need not, generally, be in writing.[2, 3]

Promise by executor. Another contract that requires writing, probably again on the grounds that the question of consideration is rather tenuous (consisting, perhaps, of loyalty to a deceased person's reputation), is a promise by the executor of a deceased person's estate to settle, or to advance, out of his own personal funds, claims of creditors against the deceased.

Marriage settlements. A promise to pay a dowry or to make any other financial settlement in consideration of a marriage also requires writing to make it enforceable.

(Mutual promises to marry one another, of course, are legally enforceable even if oral. Before being awarded any damages, the jilted party—usually the girl—must be able to prove a loss, such as having given up a job or having bought some furniture in reliance on the other's promise to marry. A girl, who has been jilted after an unusually long engagement, may get compensation for her lessened marriage eligibility. An engagement ring is a conditional gift and ought to be

---

[1] For more particulars, see Chapter 21.

[2] A reader who wonders what consideration a guarantor receives for giving his guarantee need not be too concerned about this; for the other party to the transaction is giving consideration by extending credit on the strength of the guarantor's promise.

[3] Even where A does not expressly guarantee B's debt to C, A will be liable to make good for B's failure to meet his obligations if C extended credit to B at the request of A and on the strength of A's favourable credit report about B.

86

returned if the condition—the marriage—does not come about.)

Trusts (see page 11 and Chapter 26) must be established in writing.

Ratification. As will be explained in more detail in Chapter 8, an adult person who is to be held to a ratification of a voidable contract he entered into while under twenty-one years of age, must, in Ontario, make the ratification in writing.

Sales of goods. A section of the original Statute of Frauds which is now a part of the Sale of Goods Act of most of the provinces (but which has been repealed in England in 1954) requires executory contracts for the sale of goods priced at $40 or over to be evidenced in writing to be enforceable. Anticipating Chapter 16, the transaction must be a *sale* as distinguished from hire or exchange (barter); and it must be a sale of *goods* as contrasted to services. A purchase of a pair of items at $19 each plus $2 postage (totalling $40 exactly) would require writing.

WRITING REQUIREMENTS

In all the above situations it is not necessary for the original contract to be in writing; it is sufficient if the existence of a contract, originally made orally, is subsequently evidenced in writing; for example, by a letter written by the person trying to evade his obligations and signed by him. This writing may be quite informal, provided it contains all the essential elements of the contract; for example, a contract for the sale of goods would be evidenced in writing by an itemization of the goods and a statement of the price and the terms of payment, etc. (A sales slip or ticket issued to the buyer will bind the seller to his end of the bargain.)

The lack of writing does not render the above contracts invalid; it merely makes them unenforceable in a court of law. Therefore, if the creditor can enforce his claim in some other peaceable way, he is welcome to do so. For example, if he has already received payment, he need not return it; or, if he has been given something to hold as security for the debt, he can realize it (usually by selling it); or, he can withhold wages from a debtor who happens to be his employee.

Part performance. If the contract is executed in any way, no writing is required because the existence of the contract will then have been satisfactorily confirmed by its partial execution, called *part perform-*

ance. Part performance can take place:
- If all or part of the goods have been delivered and accepted.
- If full or partial payment has been made (e.g., if a deposit has been given).
- If the buyer has left with the seller some money or an article in "earnest"; that is, as a token of his sincerity.
- Or, if the buyer has authorized the seller to do some special alterations or other work on the goods.

OTHER TRANSACTIONS

It might be useful at this time to summarize the transactions discussed elsewhere in this book that are also required to be in writing; namely:
- An assignment of contract rights to be received; and notice thereof to the debtor. (Chapter 12)
- The extension or revival of claims barred by the Statutes of Limitation. (Chapter 13)
- Insurance contracts. (Chapter 20)
- Conditional sales (even if under $40), bills of sale, and chattel mortgages. (Chapters 17 and 18)
- Negotiable instruments; that is, cheques, drafts, and promissory notes; and notices of their dishonour. (Chapter 22)
- Notice by a landlord to his tenant to *quit* (to vacate the premises). (Chapter 29)
- A voluntary promise by a discharged bankrupt to pay the balance of his creditors' claims. (Chapter 25)
- Wills. (Chapter 30)

QUESTIONS

1. On November 17, 1964, Smith orally contracted with Thompson to sell him a certain stamp for $32 on December 16, 1965. Is either party entitled to sue the other if there is a breach of contract? Explain.
2. An advertising agent orally bought a half hour of air time from a local radio station owner for $500; payment was to be made in thirty days, just before air time. May either party, relying on the Statute of Frauds, safely break the contract? Explain.

3. Upton, while driving recklessly, is killed in a car accident; he slightly injures Vance in the process. When Vance demands $500 from Upton's estate, the executor of Upton's estate, Williams, personally promises before witnesses to pay Vance this amount. Is this promise enforceable? Explain.

4. A woman verbally buys a $100 hat in a salon. Having forgotten her wallet at home, she leaves her little daughter behind as evidence of good faith that she will come back for the hat and pay for it. May she, relying on the Statute of Frauds, safely break the contract?

5. Young orally promises Zane $100 if Zane will find a tenant for Young's house. Through Zane's services Young lets his house favourably to a suitable tenant. Can Young legally be made to pay Zane $100? Explain.

6. *A* signs his acceptance to *B*'s written and signed offer to sell him his house; but no seal (or substitute) is affixed to the contract. Is the contract enforceable? Explain.

CHAPTER SEVEN

Precautions to Take Before, and On, Entering into a Contract

BEFORE ASSUMING CONTRACTUAL OBLIGATIONS

Before proceeding any further with the theory of contracts, it may be useful at this stage to consider the basic precautions to take before ever entering into a contract, and the important points to check while drawing up a contract of your own or in a contract submitted for your signature by "the enemy."

Know the merchandise and the market. Before venturing into a deal in a new field you should, of course, familiarize yourself with the merchandise and with the market conditions concerning it. For instance, before buying your first house, it is a good idea to have several real estate brokers show you quite a number of houses for quite a long while. In this way you will learn a surprising amount—not only about house construction, but also how values vary according to style, location, and innumerable other factors.

Stay within your means. Be careful not to over-extend yourself financially. Everyone is familiar with the example of the small wage earner buying numerous items on the instalment system, who might lose them all because some unforeseen circumstance prevents him from keeping up the payments. Also, it may be tempting to buy an unnecessarily attractive house because it is a bargain and the down payment is very low; yet the carrying charges (mortgage interest, insurance premiums, taxes, utilities, and repairs) might come to more than you bargained for. Not only the small wage earner but even a wealthy business firm can fall victim to this pitfall: A few years ago a prominent Toronto real estate firm went bankrupt; while it had a fortune tied up in valuable real estate, it did not have enough liquid funds available to meet the current payrolls.

Deal only with reputable persons. Be sure to engage in business dealings only with people who enjoy a good reputation and who are financially responsible. A written "100% guarantee" is not worth the paper it is written on if the firm giving it is no longer in business, and a genuine claim for a refund is valueless if the firm in question has gone "broke." It is often worth paying a little more for the assurance that a firm wants to "stand behind its product" rather than risk tarnishing its good reputation. It has been said that contracts with honest persons are unnecessary (although this is going just a little bit too far!) and that, with crooks, they are useless, however carefully drawn up—because the crooks do not plan to keep their promises anyway. If you do not subscribe to a credit reporting agency (such as Dun & Bradstreet), convenient sources of reference are your bank and the local Better Business Bureau. A (perhaps over-conservative) slogan to observe when of two minds about someone's reliability is: "If in doubt, don't!"

Consult a lawyer. By all means consult a lawyer before entering into a contract of any importance, even with people you consider reliable. His experience will save you plenty of grief. Do not be put off by stories of the fabulous charges some fashionable lawyers make; a neighbourhood lawyer will probably not charge more for an office call than the neighbourhood physician will. In fact, lawyers traditionally render some services free, such as approving your offer to purchase a house before you sign the offer. Therefore there is no reason at all to allow a real estate agent to stampede you into signing an offer without first obtaining your lawyer's approval.

When conferring with your lawyer you must, of course, instruct him carefully; he cannot be expected to know the details of your particular business as well as you do. You must also be frank with him; you should disclose to him any weaknesses in your position that you are aware of, so that he may take the proper steps to protect you regarding them.

Read and understand everything before signing. If you decide not to consult a lawyer, be sure to take your good time before affixing your all-important signature. Read the entire contract, including the fine print; you are responsible for it, even if assured that it contains merely "the usual routine clauses." And reading, of course, is not enough; be sure you understand the meaning of unclear words and expressions, and that you are agreeable to their terms. There is nothing whatever holy about a printed contract form. If it says something you do not approve of, demand to have it changed and the change initialled by the other party.

On the other hand, many good deals have been lost by a person holding out stubbornly too long for trifles when the main features were obviously advantageous; and, conversely, sales have been lost by not promptly obtaining the signature of a customer whom you have already "sold" and thus giving him time to change his mind.

Be sure to include all the data. As was stated in the previous section, a contract can be formed by word of mouth alone; but, for the purposes of the following notes, we shall assume it to be in writing. With that in mind, be sure to get all the data into the contract, without leaving anything to guesswork, if possible. Beginning with the date, the place of the signing of the contract, and the names and addresses of the parties, you will want to describe accurately the quantity and quality of the subject matter, its price, its terms of payment and the delivery conditions.

Be specific—avoid vague expressions. Be specific and avoid like the plague any vague and ambiguous expressions; such as:

"Short" working hours,

A "fair" salary,

"Reasonable" working conditions,

"Satisfactory" living accommodations,

". . . will try" to obtain "in good time,"

"Liberal" holidays,

Time off "as conditions will allow," or,

Time off "at the employer's discretion."

In a written contract, put everything in writing. Where the contract is to be in writing, place no reliance on "gentlemen's agreements"; i.e., verbal promises which the other party does not wish to put in writing. As mentioned earlier, these are unenforceable. If he plans to keep such promises, he should not object to putting them in writing.

Do not leave blank spaces. On no account should you leave any blank spaces over your signature, whether accidentally or deliberately. Draw your pen through the blank spaces (particularly on cheques) and refuse to sign if any blanks are "to be filled in later." It may surprise the reader to learn how many people allow themselves to be tricked into this, for fear of being made to appear untrusting. If someone tries to shame you by saying, "Why, don't you trust me?" your automatic reply should be, "You're darn tootin', I don't!" Never forget that it is part of the stock-in-trade of sharp operators to possess a glib tongue and a trustworthy appearance and manner.

Provide for remote contingencies. Try to make provision in the contract against even remote contingencies. For example, an *escalator clause* is common as a protection against inflation; it provides for an automatic change in the rate of pay depending on changes in the periodically published Cost of Living Index. A *cost plus* quotation similarly protects a contractor and is frequently used in government contracts. Properly phrased *escape clauses* will help a person escape liability under a contract should he be unable to comply with its requirements due to unavailability of supplies, power, or labour because of natural disasters, strikes, or other causes. As mentioned once before, try to use protective clauses such as "subject to changes in price and to available stocks."

Provide for liquidated damages. Put an "if not" clause in the contract, providing for liquidated damages. While the contract may be quite specific regarding what the parties are to do or to refrain from doing, it may save troublesome litigation should the contract be broken if, instead of having to determine in court how much loss was caused to the one party by the other's breach of contract, this question had been regulated ahead of time in the contract. For example, the contract might have specified that a certain job was to be finished by a stated date for $100,000, but that the price was to be reduced by $2,000 for every day that the project was late in completion.

Nor is it unusual for a purchaser (particularly in building contracts) to be allowed to hold back a part of the purchase price for a stipulated time, as a safeguard that the vendor will honour the warranties he has given.

Check the local laws. Check the laws regarding minors before entering into business dealings with youngsters under twenty-one; and the Lord's Day Act before undertaking any business on a Sunday. As we shall hear later, there are many other technical illegalities that can be

93

unwittingly committed—which is another good reason for getting into the habit of consulting your lawyer.

Get receipts for goods or money. Let one term of the contract serve as a receipt for goods you have delivered or for money you have paid to the other party.

Include an arbitration clause. To avoid having to go to court in case of dispute, include an arbitration clause, as described on page 23.

Keep one signed copy of the contract. If the contract is in writing, be sure that you keep one copy, bearing not only your signature but also that of "the enemy." Make sure that the contract bears a seal, where required, and, perhaps, the signature of a witness.

AFTER CONCLUDING A CONTRACT

The following are precautions to be taken after the actual conclusion of the contract:

Cash all cheques immediately. Cash immediately any cheques that you accepted in payment. From persons you do not implicitly trust you would, of course, demand payment by cash or, at least, by certified cheque before irretrievably entrusting them with your goods.

Insure new property promptly. Taking out prompt insurance on newly acquired belongings is very important for obvious reasons. As we shall learn in Chapter 16, the transfer of technical ownership, and the risk of loss attached to it, will sometimes precede the act of taking physical possession, and the need for insurance under these circumstances might not become immediately apparent.

The above list of precautions is, naturally, not a complete and comprehensive one; it was started years ago by the author, and has since been added to by generations of students. It will doubtless grow longer in future years, and every reader will assuredly have additional points on a list of his own.

QUESTIONS

1. Briefly recount a personal business experience you have had in which you suffered a loss. Explain which (if any) of the precautions recommended in Chapter 7 would have been of assistance to you.

94

2. Make a list of any additional advice (legal or practical) that you would give to people contemplating a business transaction. This advice may be of a general nature or drawn from your particular field.

CHAPTER EIGHT

Legal Incapacity

PROTECTED GROUPS

Our definition of a contract requires all the parties to it to be legally *competent*; and, since most persons have the legal capacity to enter into contracts, it will be simpler to list and discuss the classes of persons who suffer under certain legal disabilities.

Usually found at the head of this list are two groups of people who are placed under no handicap by the law for contract-making purposes —in fact, they enjoy protection under it—namely the young and the mentally impaired. They are sometimes in the enviable position of being almost allowed to eat their cake and to have it too; that is to say, that while they are free to back out of certain contracts, they always have the power to enforce them against their opposite number. More technically, certain contracts are *voidable* at their option. Let us first discuss in detail the legal position of the young.

MINORS OR INFANTS

The two terms, *minor* and *infant*, are interchanged indiscriminately. In Canada these are people under twenty-one years of age, male or female, whether single or married. They become of age (or, they attain their majority) for contract-making purposes at the first moment of the day *preceding* their twenty-first birthday; the reason for this being that they complete their twenty-first year on that day, and because it is a legal maxim that "the law does not take into account any part of a day." One's twenty-first birthday is, actually, the first day of one's twenty-second year. (However, under other statutes one may still not vote or, in some provinces, consume liquor before one's twenty-first birthday. In Ontario it is illegal to supply "a child under eighteen" with tobacco or to permit him into a billiard parlour. For the purpose of entering into insurance contracts, a person is considered of age at sixteen by statute.)

Whether a contract is voidable by an infant or not will depend on whether it is still executory, or if it has been partly or fully executed. **Executory contracts** are those where neither party to the contract has done anything more positive than to promise to do something in the future. Executory contracts for the sale of goods are probably voidable by the infant, even if they involve the necessities of life. Thus, if an infant enters a store and picks out a serviceable, reasonably priced overcoat, and at his request it is set aside for him until he returns to pick it up and to pay for it, he is free to change his mind and to break the contract he has made to buy it. Conversely, the store keeper can be held to his end of the bargain, and he could be sued for breach of contract by the infant if he failed to keep the coat available to the infant for the stipulated time.

Partly executed contracts are contracts where only one party has performed his obligation; for example, where one party has delivered goods but the other party has not yet paid for them. In partly executed contracts we must distinguish between contracts for "necessaries" and for "non-necessaries."

NECESSARIES. Necessaries are goods or services which the infant needs to stay alive, healthy, and secure; such as, food, clothing, lodging, medical services (e.g., doctor, dentist, nursing, medicines), insurance, and favourable contracts of employment, apprenticeship and education. (Not so regarded are promises of marriage made by an infant.) So as not to scare off traders from providing infants with these essential commodities, partly executed contracts for necessaries are just about as binding on an infant as they are on an adult. However, what constitutes necessaries is construed very narrowly and, while some of the following situations are quite logical, others may surprise the reader.

Contracts even for the items listed above are not binding on the infant if they are not actually needed by him, his wife, or his children. Thus, an infant of moderate means may return, and will not have to pay for, a brown overcoat he had bought on credit if he already has a serviceable grey one. Also, an infant who is being fully provided for by his parents or guardian cannot really be said to be in need of any-thing—all such a one need do is "to ask (his parent) and he shall re-ceive." However, if suited to a youngster's "station in life," some items might be considered necessities for him that would constitute luxuries for less fortunately situated infants. For him, it would be necessary to have several suits of clothes to provide him with a wardrobe for every eventuality. In one case it was even held necessary for such a one to own a riding horse, and the court made him fulfil his contract to buy it. However, a Cambridge colleague of this young student was re-leased from his contract to buy a batch of eleven expensive fancy waist-coats, as being unnecessarily extravagant, even for such a wealthy young man. For such a person, a solid gold watch and a pearl tie pin might also be "necessaries"; but, contrariwise, an article used purely for luxury or ornament, such as a man's ring, would never be classed as a necessity, even if quite modest (although some jewellery would, surely, be considered an essential part of a well-to-do young woman's formal attire).

Other cases that have come up before the courts have involved a correspondence course in Steam Engineering: in that particular case, the youngster who signed up for it did not have to go through with it. On the other hand, a young man who signed up for a $1,200 course of dancing lessons with a well-known studio was held bound to the contract when the court learned that this course was to be the founda-tion for his contemplated career as a dance instructor.

Even when a contract is held to be binding on an infant, he cannot be made to pay more than a reasonable price for the goods or services he received, the reason being that such transactions by infants are considered not contracts but "quasi-contracts." While he is thus pro-tected from having to pay an exorbitant price, this does not mean that he can get away with paying the minimum prices charged by a "dis-count house" in a low-rent district; particularly if he bought the goods in a store furnishing substantial amenities and service.

NON-NECESSARIES.   Partly executed contracts entered into by an infant for non-necessaries are voidable by him, even if the contract would have been quite fair had it been made with an adult, with the following consequences:

- If he has made a payment in advance on some non-necessary

goods, but has not yet received the goods, he has the right to refuse to take delivery of the goods and the right to have his money refunded.

• If he has taken delivery of some non-necessary goods *on credit*, he may cancel the contract and refuse payment for the goods. In this case, however, he must return the goods; the reason for this is that the relief granted to infants has its origins in equity, and one of its maxims is, "He who comes to equity must do so with clean hands"; therefore, if an infant asks equity to relieve him of a legal obligation, he must be prepared to "play fair" himself. However, if the goods have accidentally disappeared or become damaged, he need only return whatever is left of the goods, if anything! If he has traded or sold the goods, he must give up the money or whatever else he received in exchange, or what is left of it.

If the goods he wants to return are damaged through the infant's negligence, he has to make good the loss or reduction in their value caused through this tort of his. But it should be noted that the courts are very watchful in guarding against an infant being held to a voidable contract indirectly by being sued in tort instead. Thus, while one infant was held liable in tort for injuring a mare by jumping her when expressly warned not to jump her, another infant was not so held liable when he injured a mare by riding her excessively hard. (It will be remembered that tender years do not protect a youth against the consequences of his torts.)

• A loan of money to an infant is not recoverable from him unless it was made for the purchase of necessaries and was actually spent on the purchase of necessaries.

• Since it has never been considered "necessary" for an infant to be a merchant or a trader (though in Quebec he can be "emancipated" at eighteen), he cannot be made to deliver promised goods or services for which he has received payment in advance. In other words, the young businessman will be excused the consequences of his careless quotations or rash estimates. But, as before, he will have to return whatever is left of the money he received or of the materials, etc., he bought with the money.

While these privileges may sometimes work hardship on people doing business with infants, it is considered better that this should be so, rather than having unscrupulous merchants take advantage of inexperienced youngsters (although some provinces are considering reducing the age limit below twenty-one, which is thought to be unrealistically high). After all, there is no obligation on a merchant to deal with an infant, and if he does so, he does it with his eyes open. And, since "the law is to be used as a shield and not as a sword," a youngster who persuades an adult to let him have goods on credit by pretending to be over twenty-one, can be made to return the goods he obtained by his fraudulent pretense. Also, "smart" youngsters, attempting to victimize traders with the aid of the infancy laws, may find themselves violating some criminal laws (such as obtaining by false pretenses) which are not voidable by him!

Incidentally, it is the author's experience that the average young person of today has healthy moral standards. He will (and certainly should) avail himself of the infancy laws to protect himself against sharp practice; but he generally realizes that it is unethical to use these laws to obtain unfair advantages and that, long after he turns twenty-one, his neighbours will still remember his actions while he was under twenty-one.

Fully executed contracts. If an infant has received goods and paid for them, whether necessaries or not, there is usually no relief for him unless:

1. The court considers that he has been victimized; and
2. The infant is still in a position to return to the other party *all* that he received (not only what he has left) in exchange for getting back his own money or goods.

To summarize: Most executory contracts for necessaries and non-necessaries and partly executed contracts for non-necessaries are voidable by an infant; while partly executed contracts for necessaries and all fully executed contracts for necessaries and non-necessaries are usually binding on him.

Note that any waiver an infant may make of his infancy privileges, even if in writing and under seal, is ineffective; he continues to enjoy these privileges even though he may appear to have relinquished them.

Also note that while an infant is entitled to repudiate a number of contracts, he must do so "in toto"; in other words, he cannot retain the portions of the contract he likes and repudiate the unfavourable portions. There can be no picking out of plums; it must be "all, or nothing at all."

REPUDIATION

What steps must an infant take (if any) to render void his voidable contracts?

In a purely executory contract (whether for necessaries or for non-necessaries), he need do nothing at all; it is sufficient for him to remain passive. The contract never becomes binding on him, *if he does not want it so*, even long after he becomes twenty-one. Of course, if he accepts something from the other party in the way of money, goods, or services, the contract becomes partly executed.

As we have learned, an infant is obliged to complete a partly executed contract for necessaries. However, when discussing partly executed contracts for non-necessaries, we must distinguish between two types:

1. *"One-shot" transactions.* The "one-shot" deal that a person entered into while an infant can be ignored, or repudiated by him at any time. Thus, if he paid a deposit on a non-necessary item while under twenty-one, he can change his mind about going through with its purchase at any time; and in that case he may demand his deposit back, even many years later. The only way in which the other party to a contract of this nature can hold the young person to his end of the bargain, is to get him to *ratify* it (to confirm it) *after* he has become of age. As we have seen on page 87, the Ontario Statute of Frauds requires such a ratification to be in writing, if it is to be legally enforceable.

2. *Contracts of continuing benefit.* Contracts of continuing benefit are transactions by which the infant acquires an interest of a permanent nature in the course of which he concurrently receives benefits and incurs obligations. Examples are the renting of non-necessaries such as a summer cottage or a power boat for several seasons at a stated sum per month; the buying of a non-necessary article "on time" (e.g., a colour T.V. set); becoming a partner in a business enterprise; or, buying dividend-bearing, non-fully paid-up company shares. In all these cases, the infant may terminate the contract at any time, even before the

expiry of the contract term, and he will not be liable for any rent, or other payments, relating to the time subsequent to his repudiation. However, he will not be entitled to any refund for amounts he has paid out during the time he was enjoying benefits from the contract. However, if he can prove that there was a failure of consideration, he will be entitled to a refund.

Contrasted to "one-shot" transactions, contracts of continuing benefit do eventually become binding on a young person, even if he does not expressly ratify them. If he does not expressly *repudiate* such contracts (no set form is prescribed for such repudiation) before or within a reasonable time after becoming twenty-one, he will be deemed to have ratified them by implication. Thus, if he continues to accept benefits under these contracts for more than a very short time after becoming twenty-one, he will have to abide by all the terms of the original contracts until their expiry date. What length of time is "reasonable" will vary, according to the circumstances.

PARENTS OF A MINOR

If a person is unsuccessful in obtaining payment of a debt owed to him by a minor, can he make the minor's parents pay the debt? The answer is "No," if the contract was purely between the minor and his creditor. A parent can be held responsible only if he guaranteed payment of his child's obligation to the creditor (e.g., by co-signing a contract or by "backing" a promissory note); or, if the minor dealt with the other party to the contract as the express or implied agent of his parent.

A minor who was instructed, or authorized to enter into a contract on behalf of his parent (e.g., by being told, or allowed, to charge a purchase to his parent's account) has, of course, been expressly appointed his parent's agent. In such cases (as we shall hear again when discussing *agency* in Chapter 15), the minor or *agent* is under no personal obligation to the creditor; while the parent or *principal* is alone liable for payment of the debt.

Under certain circumstances, persons with whom the minor had business dealings can regard the minor as his parents' *implied agent*. The creditors can do this if they have reasonable grounds for assuming the minor to be his parent's agent; this they are allowed to gather from the parent's previous conduct. According to the law of agency, if a person (e.g., a parent) has previously, *without objection*, honoured an obligation entered into by someone else (e.g., his child), it is implied that he is prepared to honour a similar obligation again in the future.

Therefore, a word of caution to soft-hearted parents of spendthrift children: when paying a bill which has been run up by the young sprout and which has been presented to you, the parent, make it clear to the creditor that you are paying him just this once as an act of grace, and that you do not intend to make a practice of it. Better still, give the money to your youngster and let him settle accounts himself.

Lastly, a parent might become liable for contracts entered into by his child as an "agent of necessity." Parents, generally, are under statutory obligation to provide for their children fully until age sixteen. If a parent fails in this obligation, he can be held criminally liable, and in some jurisdictions a neglected child contracting for the bare essentials of life can render his parents liable for their price.[1]

While on the topic of agency, it is useful to note that an infant who entered into these contracts through the services of an adult agent retains the right to repudiate executory contracts and partly executed contracts for non-necessaries. On the other hand, an adult and otherwise capable principal entering into contracts through the medium of an agent who is under age, cannot repudiate his contracts on that score. As an illustration, a store owner will have to honour the credit granted to a customer by one of his under-age salesmen.

In other words, it is the capacity of the principal and not that of his agent that is significant; if the principal is capable of being bound by contract, the incapacity of his agent is immaterial; and vice versa.

MENTAL IMPAIRMENT

Mental impairment may be due to a number of causes; such as, insanity, fever, drink, drugs, hypnosis, etc. People who have been certified insane or who have been committed to a mental institution will not, of course, be held to any contract that anyone may have influenced them to enter. In less obvious cases, a

---

[1] In Ontario a son or daughter can be made to pay up to $20 a week to a dependent parent.

mentally deranged person can escape liability under a contract he has entered, under the conditions outlined below. He must be able to prove, probably through his doctor and lawyer, that at the time of his entering the contract:

1. He was so deranged mentally (from any cause) that he did not understand the nature of what he was doing. This does not mean that a person can avoid liability under a contract just because his capacity to think clearly at the time was impaired because of fatigue, drinking, etc. If that were the case, all contracts made over a glass or two of wine might be voided! What it amounts to is that a person enjoys this protection only if he is virtually bereft of his senses. And—

2. The mentally impaired person must also be able to prove that the other party to the contract was aware of his handicap. In other words, the law will protect the person who was unaware of the debility of the other party to the contract.

If necessaries were supplied to him (e.g., needed food, clothing, shelter, or services), he must pay a reasonable price for them even though he was completely irrational and the supplier of the necessaries was fully aware of this.

Contracts made during the sane periods of a person who is subject to occasional spells of delusion are binding upon him; as are contracts made by a confirmed alcoholic during his sober intervals. But contracts made during the occasional lucid intervals of a person certified insane are never binding upon him.

A person who has been fraudulently doped or made drunk (e.g., by having his soft drink "spiked") can escape liability from any contract he enters into with the fraudulent party.

The impaired person has the privilege of repudiating the above-mentioned contracts only if he exercises this privilege at the first opportunity; that is, as soon as he, or his lawyer or other representative, realizes (usually after becoming sane or sober, respectively) to what he has committed himself while impaired. It is interesting to note that a minor, when allowed to repudiate a contract, generally need return only what is left of the goods he may have received (paying, however, for the goods that he used); whereas a mentally impaired person must be able to return *all* the goods he may have received from the other party if he is to be allowed to repudiate his obligations.

While, theoretically, the court makes no distinction between people whose impairment is due to medical reasons and those whose impairment is ascribable to drink and drugs voluntarily ingested, it seems safe to say that in practice the court's greater sympathy with the former will likely be reflected in its decisions.

UNENFRANCHISED NORTH AMERICAN INDIANS

Unenfranchised North American Indians, living on government reservations, are another group of people who can escape liability from any contract they enter into, even for items generally regarded as necessities. The explanation for this is that they are in the same category as minors living with their parents who supply them with all their physical wants—only in this case the parent is the Great White Father, namely the government who, through the Indian agents, supplies the reservation Indians with all their means of livelihood including treaty money.

Indians are free to leave the reservations at any time. They then become bound by their contracts, and they must pay taxes the same as everyone else; they also receive the franchise (i.e., the right to vote in elections) and the right to buy as much liquor as their white brothers.

MARRIED WOMEN

While today a married woman is as free to contract and as bound to her contracts as a man or as a single woman, this was not always the case. It is less than a century ago that the law stopped making the husband the owner of all that his wife possessed. In Quebec, unless the husband-to-be signs away this right in the marriage contract that is customary there, all the marriage property is controlled by the husband, and the wife is entitled to one half on his death.

However, a married woman can still make her husband liable to the same type of contract for which a child can make his parent responsible. For example, she can obligate him as his "agent of necessity" if he fails in his legal obligation to provide for her adequately; or, if she acted as his implied agent—that is, by pledging his credit in transactions of a nature he has previously honoured. Additionally, a wife is her husband's assumed agent when entering into reasonable contracts for household necessities, such as food, supplies, emergency repairs, etc.

This is a convenient place to summarize some of the points which make a married woman legally different from other people:

• As we shall learn when discussing real property, anyone buying land in Ontario from a man, even though that man is the sole owner of the land, must have the signature of that man's wife added to the deed of sale to "bar her dower." If the buyer omits this precaution, the seller's wife will acquire the right of *dower* in that land after her husband's death, against any future owner of the land. (Dower is the right to receive, for the rest of her life, one third of any income the land produces, or might produce if worked or rented.)

• As we have learned in the chapter on criminal law, a husband and wife cannot conspire with one another; and a wife cannot be an "accessory after the fact" to her husband's crimes.

• A wife cannot be guilty of theft from the husband she is living with.

• A wife cannot be compelled to give evidence against her husband (with certain exceptions).

• As we shall learn later in detail, many contracts entered into by a wife with, or for the benefit of, her husband are voidable by her on the grounds of undue influence.

OTHER PROTECTED PERSONS

Besides the groups of protected persons listed above, there are others who are under an incapacity to enter into contracts:

ENEMY ALIENS

Enemy aliens are residents of countries with which our country is at war. Any attempted contracts made with such people are illegal and therefore completely void, unless the Crown has granted a special licence to deal with them for certain specified purposes: for example, licence for the Red Cross to send parcels and mail to enemy aliens for delivery to prisoners of war; or for "mercy ships" to exchange wounded prisoners; or for needed preliminary acts to enable armistice negotiations, etc. Included under these exceptions are dealings with uninterned enemy non-combatants in this country.

Long-term contracts entered into with residents of a country against which we subsequently go to war are suspended during hostilities. Such contracts can be reinstated after the war; but usually bombings or other war activities make performance of the contracts impossible and specific legislation prohibits their reinstatement.

At the outbreak of war all property in this country belonging to enemy aliens is usually seized by the Custodian of Enemy Property and is disposed of, at the end of the war, as directed by the government.

Aliens are no longer prohibited from owning land outright in Canada as they were in some provinces until 1945.

While an enemy alien can institute no breach of contract action against a Canadian, he is allowed to sue for a tort that has been committed against him.

CONVICTS

While a convict confined in an institution can enter into numerous contracts of a business nature (e.g., to sell, or to raise a mortgage on his home), obviously there are some contracts he can not enter into; for example, those requiring his personal services outside his place of confinement. Nor can a penitentiary inmate be a candidate for public office.

LIMITED COMPANIES

Limited companies are created by acts of Parliament or by charters issued by the federal or provincial governments. These acts or charters determine specifically the types of contract into which the limited company or corporation may enter. Any other types of contract entered into by them are *ultra vires* (beyond their powers) and therefore void.

However, the Corporation Acts (or, Companies Acts) of each province and of the federal government grant the companies wide automatic powers to enter into contracts which are associated with, or incidental to, the powers which have been specifically granted to the companies by their charter.

It is also *ultra vires* for a provincial charter to grant powers to a company which the province has not the power to grant under the B.N.A. Act.

BANKRUPTS

A person who has been adjudged bankrupt and who has not yet received his discharge can enter into no contracts except for those of necessity. It is an offense under the Bankruptcy Act for him to enter into a contract involving more than $500 without his disclosing that he is an undischarged bankrupt.

QUESTIONS

1. Sober, sane, poor, blond Bill's twenty-first birthday is on Saturday, December 4, 1965. Explain why, or why not, each of the following contracts is voidable by him.
   (a) On December 2, 1965, he buys on credit and at a reasonable price some shoes which are badly needed by his nephew and takes them to him.
   (b) Also on December 2 he buys on credit two more pairs of the same shoes and takes them home for his own son.
   (c) Also on December 2 he makes a down payment on a canoe, to be delivered to him in the spring.
   (d) Also on December 2 he pays cash for some costume jewellery which he takes home to his wife.
   (e) On December 3 he buys on credit some more of this jewellery with instructions to have it sent to his cousin.
2. Black got White drunk and sold White a cheap gimmick for a huge price. After having used it for a month, is White entitled to return the gimmick and to get back the money he paid for it? Explain.
3. An insurance company buys the rights to an invention and starts to manufacture and to sell it. Are the sales contracts legal? Explain.
4. Two eighteen-year old boys, John and James, sign a contract to work for a non-union firm for two years at $40 per week. They later learn that their similarly qualified adult colleagues get paid twice as much for the same kind of work.
   (a) As soon as John learns this, he walks off the job. Will a suit against him for breach of contract succeed? Explain.
   (b) James appeals to the court to amend his contract by increasing

his salary. Will the court grant his request? Explain.

5. Fifteen-year old Tilly, having just lost her only winter coat, decides to buy one in a new store on its opening day. Tilly tells the store manager that her rich father (with whom she lives next door to the store) will pay for it. She thereupon gets the coat. Can Tilly's father be legally made to pay for the coat? Explain.

6. What points of legal difference are there between a married and a single woman?

CHAPTER NINE

Illegality

MEANING OF ILLEGALITY

Our definition of contract states that it has to be *legal*. Phrased another way, the contract must not be *illegal*—it must not involve the commission of an act which is contrary to the provisions of some law; if it does, the contract is *void*. Note that even if the defendant does not plead illegality as a defense, the judge will throw the case out of court should he "stumble upon" any such illegality, for he will not soil his hands with anything that is "tainted with illegality."

COMMON LAW ILLEGALITY

The broad common law principle declares illegal any contract which involves committing an act which is deemed to be contrary to "public policy."

Crimes. At the top of the list of such acts, of course, is the commission of a crime—whether a felony or a mere violation of the traffic laws. For example, if I promise a taxi driver a big tip if he will exceed the local speed limits in order to get me to my destination in time; and if he does so; then, if I fail to pay him anything, he will be unable to sue me in court not only for the tip, but possibly also for the fare.

Torts, dishonesty, and immorality. Nor will the courts enforce a contract which involves the commission of a tort (e.g., an agreement to spread a slander); or an act of dishonesty (e.g., an agreement to cheat in an examination); or an immoral act (e.g., renting a room to an obviously unmarried couple). Also considered immoral, and therefore unenforceable, is a promise by a married man to marry another woman after he obtains his divorce. It will be seen that an act need not necessarily be criminal for the courts to regard it as illegal for contract-making purposes.

Injury to the state. Any contracts which would result in injury to the state are, naturally, regarded as being against public policy. (That is the reason why contracts with enemy aliens are void.) This includes not only Canada but also other friendly states; thus, a contract which assists revolutionaries in overthrowing the government of a friendly country would be illegal.

Injury to the public service. Contracts involving injury to the public service are also illegal. An illustration of this would be the influencing of a public official in the manner of casting his vote or otherwise to act corruptly. Also so regarded is an undertaking to abstain from joining the country's armed forces.

Obstruction of justice. Compounding a crime (assisting a criminal or helping him to escape) is, of course, a crime in itself; any contract involving it is illegal because it results in an "obstruction of justice." Also belonging in this category is the "no questions asked" clause in an advertisement which offers a reward for a "lost" article—for this might amount to a contract to refrain from laying criminal charges.

Maintenance and champerty. Also illegal are contracts involving maintenance and champerty. *Maintenance* is the "promoting and/or financing of litigation or divorce" by persons having no legal interest in the action. There is, however, nothing wrong with giving advice or financial aid to litigants who are related to you, or who are needy, or from other disinterested motives. *Champerty* is "sharing in the proceeds of litigation"; for example, an unethical "ambulance-chasing" lawyer is prohibited by the Law Society from taking a case for a percentage of the recovered damages. Similarly, while paying a substantial fee to a *bona fide* expert witness is completely regular, a contract to reward him for his services with a percentage of the damages to be collected would be void as being champertous.

Unreasonable restraint of marriage. A clause in a contract whereby a person limits his right to get married is said to be in *restraint of marriage*. If this limitation is more than a reasonable one, it is against public policy and void; that is to say, the person giving the undertaking can disregard it without penalty. The RCMP had a regulation requiring recruits to give an undertaking to remain single for five years after joining up; this requirement was abandoned because it was dangerously close to being an "undue" restraint. Another example is the case of the baptized Winnipeg Jew who left a large inheritance to his daughter on condition that she marry no one but a gentile. When she married a man of the Jewish faith she was not made to forfeit her inheritance since the court held the stipulation in the will to be an undue restraint of marriage which she could disregard. However, a man has been held to have the right to enforce his wife's faithfulness beyond the grave, and therefore a stipulation in his will that a life income to his widow is to cease should she remarry is valid.

The law considers marriage brokerage contracts against public policy, and such a broker cannot sue for his fee or his commission (but a fee already paid need not be returned). Separation agreements between husband and wife are, of course, perfectly binding provided they are drawn up after the marriage has already "gone on the rocks." They are invalid, however, if drawn up ahead of time—making provision for a break-up which might never come about.

Undue restraint of trade. Nor will the common law enforce obligations a person undertakes which will result in an *undue restraint of trade*. It will uphold certain sensible or reasonable restraints; for example, where a person buys a business, the seller will be bound to observe the obligations he undertook in the contract to refrain from competing with the buyer within a certain reasonable area and within certain reasonable time limits. The area and time limits will vary, of course, in proportion to the importance of the business sold. For example, in the sale of a local tobacconist's store, the seller's undertaking not to operate a similar establishment within a radius of twenty miles for a period of ten years might be disregarded by him as being unduly restraining. However, when arms manufacturer Maxim Nordenfeldt sold his vast plant, he gave the buyers an undertaking not to manufacture arms again anywhere in the world for the next twenty-five years. A few years later he broke this undertaking, claiming that it was unduly restrictive. The court held that in an enterprise of world-wide scope, such as this, even a world-wide restriction was not unreasonable.

It should be noted that a servant's or apprentice's undertaking to his master not to compete with him after leaving his employ is not binding upon him; save that he can be prevented from using in direct competition with his former master any trade secrets or confidential information he acquired while working for him.

STATUTORY ILLEGALITY

In addition to the above examples of common law illegality, there are numerous statutes declaring certain contracts illegal.

The Combines Investigation Act is among the best known of such statutes. Its aim is to protect the public from exploitation through the formation of monopolies, price fixing rings, and other combinations which would serve to place an artificial restraint on free competition. It is now illegal for manufacturers to prevent retailers from selling their products below specified minimum prices, unless the product is clearly being used as a "loss leader" or is otherwise being misused. Today the only important monopolies of a legal nature are those enjoyed by the holders of patents and copyrights and by certain utilities corporations (hydro, telephone, public transport).

The Lord's Day Act, another well-known federal statute, declares illegal certain contracts during the "twenty-four-hour period beginning at 12 o'clock Saturday afternoon" (midnight, that is). With certain exceptions, it is illegal to buy or to sell anything, or to carry on one's ordinary business on a Sunday. One important exception refers to acts "of necessity or mercy": which is why hotels, restaurants, drug stores, street cars, police, blast furnaces, etc., can legally continue operating on Sundays. Seldom guessed is the exception that is listed first in the Act—namely the right to conduct divine worship! An older generation may recollect that, until the '20's, no street cars operated in Toronto on Sunday mornings. It is still illegal, strictly speaking, for drug stores to sell cigarettes on Sundays.

The other important exception consists of the right of the provinces to modify the federal Act; this is the explanation for the different manner in which the Lord's Day Act is observed in the various provinces. Most provinces have also delegated this right of modification to their municipalities; which is the reason why there are Sunday sports and/or entertainment in some cities and not in others.

It should be noted that, contrary to wide-held opinion, cheques and promissory notes issued on a Sunday are perfectly valid, provided they constitute payment of a contract that was concluded on a weekday. It is, undoubtedly, a fact that many important business deals (e.g., house purchases) are concluded on Sundays, and that the parties often try to "get around" the Act by writing a weekday date into the contract. In such a case, however, either party may escape liability under the contract if he can prove that it was actually entered into on a Sunday.

It is said that a special providence watches over children and drunks; and so does the law, as we have already seen. Others whom the law attempts to protect from exploitation are mortgagors, tenants, and borrowers; and it is the latter we shall discuss next.

Usury. There are several laws which protect a person who has to borrow money. The Bank Act of Canada (revised every ten years) restricts a bank from charging more than 6% per year interest on an ordinary loan (Section 91 allows this 6% to be "discounted," i.e., deducted in advance). Where special contracts are involved (e.g., Scotia loans) more interest is now being charged with no apparent authority.

It should be noted that no interest is ever payable on any loan, overdue account, negotiable instrument, or anything for that matter, *unless the contract provides for payment* of interest. The Dominion Interest Act provides that where the contract requires interest to be paid, but the contract omits to state the rate that is to be paid, then the rate is to be 5% per year—this is known as the "legal rate." This act also requires that the contract specify the yearly *rate* of interest that is to be paid; if the contract merely names amounts to be paid daily, monthly, etc., in the way of interest, any excess over 5% paid by the borrower can be recovered by him from the lender. This act imposes no other restrictions on the amount of interest that may be charged.

The Ontario Unconscionable Transactions Relief Act makes it illegal to charge more than a fair rate of interest. (In 1963 the validity of this act was unsuccessfully under attack in the courts on the grounds that the B.N.A. Act makes the charging of interest a matter of federal concern only.) What is "fair" depends on the circumstances (e.g., the amount of the loan, security if any, credit risk, money market, etc.). Used as a guide is the English case which stated that a rate exceeding 48% per annum is presumed to be unfair and the burden (onus) of proving otherwise is to be on the lender; consequently, the onus of proving an interest rate of 48% p.a. or less to be unconscionable still rests on the borrower.

While legislation is contemplated compelling sellers to inform instalment buyers of the actual interest rate they will have to pay, the only other major act now in force regarding the payment of interest (apart from the Pawnbrokers Act) is the federal Small Loans Act of 1956, which is designed to protect the "little man" from exploitation by loan sharks (note that it does not extend to purchase contracts with finance companies). It requires people whose business is the making of loans under $1,500 for 1% per month or more, to take out licenses as moneylenders; violations of the Small Loans Act are punishable by up to a year in prison and/or a $1,000 fine. Under this act no costs, expenses, or other sums must be added to the amount of the loan; it must be repayable in instalments not more than a month apart; the borrower is to be allowed to repay the balance of the loan at any time without penalty; and he must not be charged more than the following rates of interest *on the unpaid balance*:

2% per month on the first $300,

1% per month on the next $700,

½% per month on the next $500 after that.

Even so, only 1% of the unpaid balance may be charged if:

(a) The loan is for $500 or less and is to be repaid over a period of longer than 20 months; or

(b) The loan is for $501 to $1,500 and is to be repaid over a period of longer than 30 months.

Bets and wagers. There is no punishment for having a bet with a friend on the outcome of a sporting event (unless you operate as a bookmaker), or on anything else, for that matter. However, the law discourages such activity by seldom giving aid to a party to such proceedings. Thus, the loser of a bet cannot be successfully sued if he decides to "welsh" on the bet; in other words, it is purely a "debt of honour." For this reason, bets are seldom recorded in writing, since such writing has no legal value anyway.

Under the common law, a person who has paid a lost bet cannot sue the winner to get it back. The Ontario Gaming Act, however, permits such a suit if the amount lost was over $40, if action is brought within three months of payment, and if the bet was on a "sport or pastime"; for example, horse racing, billiards, cards, etc. No action can be brought on other wagers; for example, where the loser backed the wrong candidate in an election, or forecast incorrectly the sex of a new-born babe. Also, if both parties deposited their wagers with a trusted stakeholder anywhere in Canada, the latter incurs no legal liability to the winner if he returns the loser's share to him; in fact, the loser has the legal right to demand a return of his contribution from the stakeholder, provided it has not yet been given to the winner.[1]

Bets are technically illegal, even if they are disguised as other transactions. Examples are so-called stock exchange transactions that are not genuine investments but merely a gamble on the future behaviour of certain stock prices; or so-called insurance contracts that do not represent protection against genuine risk: e.g., attempting to make coin tossing legally enforceable by taking out insurance against a coin coming down "heads" or "tails" respectively.

Naturally, there are innumerable other statutes regulating or prohibiting our conduct: for example, in connection with the production and consumption of liquor, foods and drugs; hunting; the licencing of certain activities and occupations; etc. A contract in violation of any of these statutes would be void. Special mention should be made of the various anti-discrimination statutes, such as the Ontario Fair Accommodation and Employment Practices Acts, which prohibit an establishment from excluding, or an employer from refusing employment to, any person solely on the basis of his race, religion, etc.

Entire and severable contracts. If a contract contains several intermingled elements, some of which are legal and some of which are not, it is said to be an "entire" contract, and all of it is wholly void. However, a contract is said to be "divisible" or "severable" into legal

---

[1] A loser who issues his cheque (or promissory note) cannot be sued by the winner if he dishonours it. However, he will have to pay an "innocent holder for value"; that is, a person to whom the paper was transferred for a proper consideration and who was ignorant of its illegal origins. In fact, if the wager was *not* on a sport or pastime, the third party will be allowed to collect from the loser even if he knew all about the wager. If the loser is made to pay this third party, he is allowed to sue the winner for the amount involved, provided the bet was on a sport or pastime, but not otherwise.

and illegal portions if it amounts to a collection of several contracts, some of which are for a legal consideration and some of which are not. Thus, if a barman is to be paid, say, $250 a month for serving liquor during legal hours and another $350 a month for serving it during prohibited hours, he will be entitled to $250 for the legal portion of this "divisible" contract. However, if the contract had stipulated for him to get $600 a month for serving liquor at all hours, it would have been "entire," and he would have got nothing since the court shrinks from sullying its hands by picking out "clean," legal bits and pieces from a contract that is "tainted with illegality."

A person can recover money paid after the commission of an illegality, if he can prove that he did not know that he was paying for something illegal. For example, he may have paid an amount to a building contractor which he genuinely believed would be used to pay the regular fee for a legal building permit; while it was actually used to pay a bribe to a corrupt city official, to grant such a permit.

Promises to pay for contemplated future illegal transactions are unenforceable, even if they are under seal.

QUESTIONS

1. "All contracts in restraint of trade and in restraint of marriage are illegal and void." Give examples of exceptions to this statement.
2. What are the clauses in the Lord's Day Act that permit numerous business transactions to be carried on legally in Canada on Sundays?
3. Under what circumstances are cheques drawn on a Sunday illegal?
4. Under what circumstance may a chartered bank charge slightly more than 6 per cent interest per annum interest on an ordinary loan?
5. What rate of interest is payable on each of the following loans?
   (a) The contract made no provision for the payment of interest.
   (b) The contract provided for the payment of interest but did not specify its rate.
   (c) The contract was usurious.
6. Taking out fire insurance virtually amounts to a bet with an insurance company that one's house will burn down. Reconcile the legality of insurance contracts with the rules that make betting contracts illegal.

CHAPTER TEN

Lack of Genuine Intention

MEANING OF GENUINE INTENTION

The last item in our definition of contract stated that the agreement had to be entered into voluntarily. According to a Latin expression, the parties must have been *ad idem* (they must have had the same thing in mind), or there must have been "a meeting of the minds." If this has not been the case, there is no genuine agreement and, consequently, no contract.

DURESS

Obviously, the promise you made, or even the "contract" you signed with your right hand, while I was twisting and threatening to break your left arm, is void. Such a contract is said to be entered into under *duress*; which means that it was made while you, or a close relative:

• Were having an injury inflicted on you, or were being threatened with one; or
• Were being held prisoner, or were being threatened with deprivation of liberty; or
• Were being threatened with a criminal prosecution, whether on good grounds or on trumped-up charges; or
• Were being threatened with the publication of a libel or slander.

It has been held that if a coerced party is familiar with the contents of the agreement he is entering under duress, then the contract is voidable; if he does not know its contents, it is void.

A contract entered into under duress to fulfil one's existing obligations is valid; however, the party exercising the duress might be guilty of assault, of course.

UNDUE INFLUENCE

In some situations a person may have entered into an agreement with another, not because he was physically forced into it, but because he was unduly influenced by him. By this is not meant the pressure placed on a customer by a salesman, which is considered to be just normal influence.

The following are typical contracts that are voidable at the option of the injured party if he can prove that he was under undue influence of the other party:

• Where one of the contracting parties was suffering from feeble-mindedness or weakness of will due to senility or sickness; or

• Where he entered into a contract with someone in a position of authority; for example, his employer, teacher, prison guard, or a policeman; or

• With someone on whom he is dependent; for example, his nurse or housekeeper; or

• With someone who controls him emotionally. Note, that a woman who is acting on the advice of an independent lawyer (one who does not also represent her husband's interests) is bound by contracts she has made with her husband; or by contracts, such as guarantees, which she has signed on his behalf.

In some relationships the existence of undue influence is considered to be so obvious that the court will assume its existence, and then the onus (burden) of proof is on the "dominant" party to disprove its existence. The following relationships fall in this class:

• A parent, guardian, or trustee entering into a contract with his child, ward, or beneficiary, respectively, who has no business experience yet (e.g., a person in his early twenties).

• A lawyer, doctor, or spiritual adviser entering into a contract with his client, patient, or parishioner, respectively.

• A money-lender exploiting the immediate wants of an expectant heir (e.g., Jacob buying his brother Esau's birthright for the biblical mess of pottage).

These unfavourable contracts (often gifts) are voidable at the option of the injured party, and he must take appropriate action at the first opportunity to recover any loss he has suffered. Usually, however, undue influence will be pleaded as a defense by the dominated party when he is being sued to fulfil his alleged obligations.

Note that wills are often attacked (in Surrogate Court) by neglected relatives or other aggrieved parties on the grounds that the deceased testator made his will while under undue influence or duress, as above.

MISTAKE

Is a contract binding on someone who entered into it while suffering under a misunderstanding, or mistake, about the surrounding circumstances? The answer, normally, is *yes*—the Latin maxim covering this situation is *caveat emptor*, or "let the buyer beware."

COMMON MISTAKE

There are, however, some important exceptions to the above rule. The first exception is in cases where both parties to the "contract" make the same mistake regarding the subject matter of the case; this *common mistake* renders the contract void from its inception (*ab initio*, as the lawyers say).

VOID AND VOIDABLE. At this stage it might be well to consider the differing consequences of void and voidable transactions. Should goods have passed from *A* into the hands of *B* under a void transaction, and had *B* then sold (or otherwise transferred) them into the hands of a third party *C*, then *C* would have to relinquish them to *A* once the transaction had been declared void; *C* would, of course, be entitled to damages from *B*. However, had *A* (who might be an infant or an unduly influenced person) transferred goods under a voidable contract to *B* and *B* had then transferred the goods to *C* before *A* had repudiated the contract, then *C* could keep the goods; in this case it is *A* who would collect damages from *B* for any loss he may have suffered.

• An example of common mistake which will render a "contract" void is ignorance by both parties of the previous destruction of, or damage to, the subject matter of the agreement; for instance, the selling or insuring of a ship in distant waters, the ship already having sunk or been damaged. In this case both parties are mistaken as to the existence of the subject matter of the agreement. If the subject matter is accidentally destroyed immediately after the making of the contract, the loss will have to be borne by the buyer or insurer respectively, unless the contract contains a stipulation to the contrary. Marine insurance policies can contain a "lost or not lost" clause whereby the insurer agrees to pay compensation for a ship that might, unbeknownst to all the parties, have already gone to the bottom before the taking out of the policy. Generally, it is always wise for a purchaser to insure goods from the moment he acquires ownership of them, which frequently takes place before he receives delivery of them.

MUTUAL MISTAKE

Mutual mistake occurs where both parties make a different mistake about the subject matter of the agreement.

The following are examples of mutual mistake which will render a "contract" void:

• Where both parties are genuinely mistaken about the identity of the subject matter of the agreement. Thus, in the case of two ships called "S. S. Peerless," sailing with cargoes of cotton from Bombay to England at about the same time, where the seller and the buyer proveably had different ones in mind when negotiating the sale of the cargo, the "contract" was held to be void—since the parties were not *ad idem*.

• In contracts involving a personal element (such as the rendering of personal services or the granting of credit terms), a mutual mistake regarding the identity of the party being contracted with renders the transaction void. For instance, if on receipt of an order from "Cosmos Traders" you agree to ship them goods on ninety days' open credit and then learn that ownership of this business had changed from your old business friend, Joe White, to an unknown, Ben Black, you will not have to fill the order under the generous credit terms. Therefore, it is a wise precaution when buying a business to send a notification of the change in ownership to all business associates of the previous owner.

• Mutual mistakes rendering a contract void can also arise through unclear writing (e.g., a hand-written O might look like a 6). There might also be genuine misunderstanding about the units of currency and measurement between contracting parties in different countries (e.g., U.S. and Canadian dollars and gallons), or about the units involved (e.g., $1 per lb., per piece, or per square foot?).

• The mutual mistake might also have been brought about by the intervention of some outside party, either through that party's negligence, or deliberately. An example could be the changing of a cabled price quotation by a cable company clerk.

Note that a contract is not void but is valid if both parties have independently arrived at a mistake regarding the value or quality of the goods involved. Thus, if I find a large piece of stone streaked with yellow which I think is gold worth $1,000, and I show it to you silently, and if I then accept your offer to pay me $800 for it, the contract is binding on you even though the stone turns out to be worthless. (Similarly, the contract would be binding on me if the stone turned out to be worth $5,000.) There is no mistake as to the subject matter since both parties knew they were dealing with a stone streaked with yellow.

Nor would a contract be void if both parties were mistaken regarding the law governing the circumstances. Thus, if both you and I mistakenly thought that smoking had recently been declared illegal and you therefore bought my warehouse of tobacco at distress prices, I could not have the contract declared void by claiming mutual mistake.

The following situation, however, illustrates not a mutual mistake of value or of law, but one regarding basic facts rendering the transaction void: Suppose that I agreed to buy from you an article that was among the effects you had inherited from your father, and it turns out that the article was on loan to him by my father (who has since also died and whose belongings I have inherited). I have, in effect, purported to buy from you an article that already belongs to me. Consequently, because there is mutual mistake about the basic facts of our agreement, I could have the contract declared void.

UNILATERAL MISTAKE

Where the mistake is not mutual to both parties but is *unilateral*— that is, where only one of the parties is mistaken—the principle of *caveat emptor* applies: the mistaken party must suffer the consequences of his error in judgment, *unless* this one-sided mistake was brought about by the other party's *negligence* or *dishonesty*. In the latter cases, the contract is voidable by the mistaken party (never, of course, by the party who induced the mistake) if he takes action at the first opportunity after he realizes his mistake. The court must find that the defendant knew (or ought to have known) of the plaintiff's mistake.

Palpable clerical mistake. Just as accepted offers by me to buy goods at too high a price or to sell goods at too low a price are binding on me if I made these offers through an error in judgment, similarly such offers will be binding on me if I made them through a slip of the pen or carelessly proof-read typewriting. The only exception is where the clerical error was palpable; that is, where it *must* have been obvious to the other party. Thus, if in the course of negotiation about the price of an article, I write you a letter stating: "I am sorry that I cannot afford to sell you the article at the $1,200 you offer me for it, but I will reduce my asking price from $1,300 to the cost price of $250"; it is obvious from the context that $250 is a misprint for $1,250, and I shall therefore not have to sell at $250.

Quasi warranty. Where the seller sees that the buyer is mistaken about the value of the article he wants to buy, the seller has no duty to warn the buyer of his mistake (in other words, *caveat emptor*), and he is entitled to keep the inflated price he received. However, if the seller sees that the buyer has come to the mistaken conclusion that a warranty is being given with the article under discussion, it is the seller's duty to clear up the buyer's misunderstanding of the situation. If he fails to do so, the buyer will have a *quasi warranty*; that is, he will enjoy the warranty benefits which he thought went with the article—always provided, of course, that the seller knew that this was in the buyer's mind.

Non est factum (it has not been done). A mistake can also be caused in the mind of a blind, illiterate, or gullible person by a swindler or confidence trickster who represents the paper to be signed by the victim as one of an entirely different nature; for instance, where the pretended will the victim was asked to witness turned out to be an unfavourable contract that he was unwittingly induced to sign. It is said that the mind of the signer did not accompany the signature. However, if one fails to read carefully before signing a document which one knows to be a contract, the signer is bound by the unfavourable terms of that contract, even though the other party deliberately talked him out of reading it.

INNOCENT AND FRAUDULENT MISREPRESENTATION

Probably the most frequent reason for avoiding contracts is the claim by the injured party that his mistake was caused by the other party's *misrepresentation* of the goods or circumstances. While the general rule is *caveat emptor* (according to which a buyer has no cause for legal complaint if a false description has been given him of goods which he has examined, or has had a chance to examine, where such examination could have disclosed to him the falsity of the description), the buyer does have the right to place reliance on the seller's statements regarding goods which the buyer has had no opportunity to inspect. In other words, in the latter case the goods must conform to the seller's description of them. If they do not so conform, the contract is voidable by the buyer on the grounds of the seller's misrepresentation, provided that all the following circumstances exist:

1. The statement was false.

2. The statement was "material"; that is, substantial rather than insignificant.

3. The statement was one of fact and not just one of opinion. If a car manufacturer's catalogue states that a certain car weighs 4,000 pounds and is 220 inches long, he is guilty of misrepresentation if it weighs only 3,000 pounds or if it is only 200 inches long. On the other hand, if the catalogue just states that the car is "very heavy and very long," the dissatisfied buyer would be a victim of what is called salesman's "puffing" and would have no legal redress for his disappointment.

4. Nor will he have a remedy if the misrepresentation was not an inducing factor of the transaction. Thus, if a car buyer plans to tear out and burn the car's back seats in order to make extra room for his sample cases, he could not sue for misrepresentation if it turned out that these seats were not filled with expensive foam rubber, as advertised.

Contracts can be avoided on the grounds of misrepresentation even if the misrepresentation was made unintentionally. The seller, who has falsely described the goods through his unintentional mistake or

124

carelessness will have to take back the goods and make a full refund to the buyer. Similarly, the injured party will be entitled to the return of any goods with which he may have parted, provided they have not yet reached the hands of an innocent third party. However, the victim of an innocent misrepresentation can only obtain a refund if he is still in a position to return all the goods he received from the other party; and he will never be awarded damages for any consequential loss he suffered from the transaction.

If, however, the misrepresentation was "fraudulent"—that is, made either deliberately, or knowingly, or with reckless disregard for the truth, or as the intentional statement of a misleading half-truth—the victim will be entitled to damages in addition to having the contract annulled. If there is no criminal prosecution arising out of these circumstances against the offender, the court might award punitive damages to the victim even if he suffered no great material loss.

CONTRACTS "UBERRIMAE FIDEI"

Normally, a person is under no obligation to disclose to the other contracting party anything to his disadvantage or any special knowledge he may have on the subject matter of the contract. He will be, however, guilty of *non-disclosure of material facts* (with the same consequences as misrepresentation) in the very few *contracts of the utmost good faith* (or contracts *uberrimae fidei*) listed below if he does not volunteer to the other party any relevant information he may possess. These are contracts involving trust and personal elements to a high degree, such as:

Insurance. The applicant for insurance must not only answer truthfully all questions asked of him on the application form, but he must also volunteer any other relevant facts; for example, in the case of an application for fire insurance, that his little boy is a budding pyromaniac. If the house burns as the consequence of this youngster's proclivities, the insurance company can refuse to pay on the grounds of non-disclosure; and the house-owner will not be able to successfully defend his withholding of the information on the grounds that there was no specific question on the application form regarding the number of firebugs in the applicant's household.

On the other hand, when taking out life insurance with a company that does not enjoy an established reputation, it is advisable to submit to an examination by that company's doctor rather than being tempted by advertisements which state that no such examination is required, that your word is good enough for them. The absence of a doctor's certificate makes it very easy for such companies to avoid payment of claims by asserting that the insured was guilty, in his application, of a non-disclosure of material facts.

Agency and partnership contracts. Again the parties must be scrupulously open with each other and must hold back nothing that is "material." What has been held to be material? Just about anything which might dissuade the other party from entering into the contract.

Company prospectuses. When an incorporated company wishes to finance itself through public subscriptions, it must issue a *prospectus*; that is, a description of the company's business. This document must be exactly correct; and, it is to be hoped, misleading statements of half-truths will soon be made illegal also—so that, for example, a mining company's prospectus will not be allowed to state that its property adjoins a famous rich mine, without adding the equally true fact that it adjoins that portion of the rich mine which has turned out to be valueless.

Licences. Generally, most application forms for licences for all sorts of activities contain the requirement that the applicant list all and any information not specifically asked for that might affect the granting of a licence to him; if such information is withheld, the licence can be invalidated.

QUESTIONS

1. Which of the following statements are *true*, and which are *false*?
   (a) Fraud by one party to a contract makes it voidable by the other party.
   (b) Mutual mistake as to the identity of the subject matter renders a contract void.
   (c) Puffing makes a contract voidable.
   (d) Duress and undue influence are the same.
2. In cases involving undue influence, the influenced party must generally prove it. Name four groups of people in whose case the onus is reversed.

3. On a Monday morning, Carr offered his car for sale to Kerr. On Monday afternoon, Kerr mailed payment for the car to Carr. On Monday evening, Carr wrote a letter to Kerr, repeating the offer and adding some fraudulent misrepresentations about the car. When Kerr discovers the fraud, will he be able to avoid the contract? Explain.

4. Before her death, John's wife, without John's knowledge, had sold the family jewels and had substituted imitations for them. After his wife's death, John sold the jewels to his friend James. What exactly are James's rights when he learns that the jewels are not genuine?

5. Brown offered some goods to Gray for $1,000, and Gray accepted the offer. Actually Brown had made a mistake: he had intended to ask for $2,000. Under what circumstances will the contract be voidable by Brown?

6. A publisher advertises a text book and, among other things, describes it as containing 600 pages. May a customer refuse to accept the book he ordered on the grounds that it contains only 595 pages? Explain.

7. Name three contracts of the utmost good faith and contrast these with "at arm's length" contracts.

CHAPTER ELEVEN

Termination and
Discharge of Contract

WAYS OF EFFECTING TERMINATION AND
DISCHARGE OF CONTRACT

There are, of course, several ways in which a contract can come to an end and/or in which the contracting parties will be released from further obligations under it. The main ways are by mutual agreement, by repudiation, by operation of the law, by impossibility of performance, by performance, and by breach of contract, as described below.

BY MUTUAL AGREEMENT

Examples of terminating a contract by mutual agreement are:

• The arrival of a previously agreed-upon expiry date or event. For example, a contract might stipulate that certain lessons are to continue until December 31; or, until the student passes certain examinations; or, until the earlier of the above two events takes place.

• The arrival (or not, respectively) of specified contract conditions which call for the cancellation of the contract. Thus, a dancer's long-term contract may be subject to her not exceeding certain weight limits; or, a television show may be subject to cancellation by its sponsors if viewer ratings fall below a certain figure.

• Mutual release, or *waiver*. This takes place when both parties agree to cancel, or to alter the terms of, a contract they have entered. The consideration for this new contract is the release of the other party from the obligations he undertook in the original contract. It is interesting to note that a contract, for which writing was required by

128

the Statute of Frauds, can be mutually cancelled (but not altered) by word of mouth.

 • *Novation*; that is, substituting new parties for the old ones in a contract which, otherwise, remains the same—with the consent, of course, of all the parties involved.

 • Merger into a higher form. If an oral contract is put into writing, the oral contract expires. Similarly cancelled is a rough draft that is replaced by a formal deed. It is a wise precaution in such situations, however, to mention in the new document that it replaces an already existing agreement; otherwise there is the chance of a person finding himself burdened with two sets of obligations.

BY REPUDIATION

Repudiation of the contract by a person who is entitled to repudiate it (e.g., one who obligated himself while legally incompetent or without genuine consent) is another way of terminating a contract.

BY OPERATION OF THE LAW

Contracts can be brought to an end by operation of the law as follows:

 • If a person makes a *material alteration* in a contract that is in his keeping, without the other party's express or implied consent (i.e., if he makes an unauthorized change that amounts to substantially more than the rectification of a clerical error), then the victim of the "forgery" is entitled to have the contract declared void.

 • In a bankruptcy, all of a bankrupt's contract obligations devolve on his trustee in bankruptcy. When the trustee has made the necessary distribution of the bankrupt's assets among his creditors and after the bankrupt has received his official discharge, he is freed from all further obligations under his contracts (with a few specified exceptions).

IMPOSSIBILITY (OR DIFFICULTY) OF PERFORMANCE

Traditionally, a subsequently intervening impossibility (or difficulty) of performance does not serve to excuse a person from the consequences of his failure to perform his contract obligations. It used to be held that a person entering a contract should have the wisdom to foresee all possibilities that might prevent him from fulfilling his obligations and to insert appropriate "escape clauses" into the contract; or, alternatively, to take out insurance against these risks.

Today, however, the Frustrated Contracts Acts of most provinces have crystallized the principles established in the many cases tried during the last war-torn half-century, according to which it is recognized that there is an implied condition in all contracts that all fundamental factors will remain unchanged. A contract shall, consequently, be terminated if there occur unanticipated changes as follows:

• If a new statute or government regulation renders the performance of the contracted-for act illegal.

• If a party to a "personal service" contract dies or is physically disabled from rendering this service. Note that an undertaking to perform a contract obligation that can be performed equally well by another is not ended by death or disability, but devolves on the representative of the deceased or disabled person.

Also, a long-term contract for personal services is not terminated due to, solely, a temporary incapacity. Thus, a singer's contract is "frustrated" should he suffer laryngitis on the night of his big concert; but a contract would continue were he merely incapacitated for a short time during the long run of a show.

• If a mutually anticipated event fails to occur. For example, many contracts were entered into for the anticipated coronation festivities for Edward VII after Queen Victoria's death. When the coronation had to be postponed due to the monarch's appendicitis, all leases for choice viewing space along the coronation route, banquets, etc., were "frustrated." Moneys paid in advance had to be returned (less any expenses that had been properly incurred), and undertakings to pay at a later date were forgiven. Similarly, if I agree to sell you "50 bushels of apples from the crop of my orchard" this fall, I shall not be liable for breach of contract if there is a crop failure in my orchard this year. However, I would be liable for failure to supply them had I contracted simply to sell you "50 bushels of apples" this fall.

• Performance is also excused if a *vital* subject matter of the contract is destroyed or made unavailable by an Act of God (i.e., a violent

130

upheaval of nature, such as earthquake, flood, hurricane, accidental fire, etc.), or by enemy action or war activities. Connected contracts are consequently frustrated if fire destroys a large auditorium; or a special-purpose factory; or an apartment house, etc. Also, if I promise certain goods to you by a certain date "come what may," I will not be allowed to plead Act of God, etc., as an excuse for non-delivery.

PERFORMANCE

Of course, the most frequent way for contracts to be terminated is by the parties fulfilling (or "performing") their obligations under it. If both parties perform to the hilt they are, naturally, released (or "discharged") from any further duties. It sometimes happens that one party to a contract falls just a little bit short of fulfilling his obligations completely. In such a situation, he will still be regarded as freed from further obligations; he will, however, have to submit to a corresponding reduction in the other party's obligation; for example, a slight price reduction. What amounts to "substantial" performance and what conduct falls short of satisfactory performance is often a tricky matter for the courts to decide.

In some contracts it is stipulated or implied that two events are to take place simultaneously, or almost so; for example, that goods are to be delivered or services rendered against immediate payment. In such situations one party cannot sue the other for non-performance unless he, himself, has actually performed his end of the obligation or, at least, has offered to do so by making a *tender* (attempted performance) to the other of the required payment, goods, or services. Thus, I cannot demand delivery of such goods unless I can show that I have paid for them or that I am willing to pay for them. Conversely, I cannot demand payment for such goods unless I can show that I have delivered them to the other party or that I am prepared to deliver them.

If my tender (of the contract) is refused by the other party, the consequences are that I am discharged from any liability for non-performance of the contract (though I am not released, of course, from liability to pay the right price for received goods), and that the other party has committed a breach of contract for which he, in turn, might be held responsible.

For the tender of goods, services, or money to be legally effective, it must be made exactly according to the terms of the contract. If goods are being tendered, the exact quality and quantity must be delivered at exactly the right time and place; if services, the worker must appear at the right place and time with the proper equipment; if money, the following additional requirements apply:

1. It must be the exact amount. If too large a bank note is offered and change is demanded, the tender is ineffective.

2. It must consist of *legal tender*. That is, the money must be in one of the following forms:

(a) Bank of Canada notes (of any denomination); or

(b) A limited amount of Canadian coins: not more than $10 in silver; $5 in nickles; or 25¢ in "bronze" pennies. (There is now no such limitation on coins in the U.S.A.); or

(c) Minted British, U.S., or Canadian gold coins at face value.

Note that *nothing* else need be regarded by the other party as legal tender (not even cheques—whether certified or not—nor traveller's cheques, money orders, foreign money or unused postage stamps), unless the contract provides for it.

Payment into court is also a valuable procedure available to a defendant after a suit for damages is commenced. If he notifies the plaintiff that he has paid into court, say, $1,000, the plaintiff may accept this in full settlement of his claim, and will be entitled to his costs only to the time of payment into court. However, if the plaintiff proceeds with his action and is then awarded $1,000 or less by the court, then the defendant is entitled to court costs from the time of payment into court.

Note: When negotiating for an out-of-court settlement of a dispute, you should protect yourself against your compromise proposals being construed as an admission of liability in whole or in part. This can be achieved by heading up all letters containing such proposals with the words "Without Prejudice." Such correspondence cannot be produced in court as evidence against you by the other party.

BREACHES OF CONTRACT

A less pleasant way of terminating a contract than any of the above is by breaking it, or any part of it; that is by committing a breach of contract. Generally the consequence of such a breach is that the injured party is absolved from further obligations under the contract and that the contract breaker becomes liable for any loss occasioned to the other party thereby.

WAYS OF COMMITTING BREACHES OF CONTRACT

A contract can be broken in several different ways:

By making it impossible for oneself to fulfil the contract; for example, if I contract to sell you an antique and then deliberately smash it before the delivery date, or if I previously sell and deliver it to an "innocent" (literally: "unknowing") third party.

By making it impossible for the other party to fulfil the contract. Thus, if I contract to pay you a stipulated amount for doing a repair job in my house by a certain date, and if I then fail to let you into my house, it is I, of course, who have broken the contract.

By renunciation; that is, by a previously announced refusal to perform. For example, if you contract to sell me an article or to give me a job in three months, and if after one month you inform me that you are not going to let me have the article or job, then I may regard myself as freed from further obligation. I am then safe in immediately buying a similar article or taking a job elsewhere; and I can, in fact, immediately thereupon sue you for any loss your action has caused me.

Curiously enough, if, on your announcement after one month of your intention to break the contract, I do not "change my position" (i.e., enter into other commitments), or do not start legal proceedings against you, it remains open to you to change your mind about your refusal and to fulfil the contract within the original deadline, by letting me have the article, or the job, respectively, provided that I agree.

By actual failure to perform substantially: meaning that, at the due date, one party simply fails to fulfil his obligations; for instance, he does not supply the required goods, money, or services. If, however, in the course of a long-term contract small portions of it are performed unsatisfactorily, the contract will not be terminated but will continue (subject to adequate compensation to the injured party for the unsatisfactory portion). Thus, if I contract to supply a builder with ten truckloads of cement every Monday for a year, and I supply him with

133

only nine (or eight, or seven) on one particular Monday, the contract will (probably) continue for the balance of the year. If, however, I miss a delivery altogether (or I supply only one truckload, or two) the builder will (probably) be entitled to regard the contract as completely ended. Note that even a relatively insignificant short-shipment will serve to terminate the contract altogether if I had previously been warned expressly of the need for complete shipments.

CONDITIONS AND WARRANTIES.

What amounts to "substantial" performance will, of course, vary from case to case (which explains the presence of the word "probably" in parentheses in the example above). Whether or not the performance was substantial will often depend on whether the broken contract term amounted to a condition or to a warranty. A condition is a term so vital to a contract that its non-fulfilment results in a termination of the contract. Thus, sellers of refrigeration equipment that was promised to keep certain foods from spoiling in tropical conditions and which allowed it to spoil in even a moderate climate, have obviously violated a condition and will have to take back their equipment for a full refund. If, however, the equipment performs its refrigerating functions adequately, and merely broke down occasionally, then the sellers will be liable for only a financial adjustment (or, free service) for the malfunctions: in such a case, the sellers have violated a warranty.

While unpunctuality, even the slightest, always used to be regarded as a breach of condition, it is today regarded as such only if time is expressly specified in the contract to be "of the essence"; or, where the need for punctuality is obviously implied. Thus, a florist who delivers flowers to the dock for a ship's passenger just seconds after the ship has sailed will have committed a breach of condition.

Where goods are sold with "satisfaction unconditionally guaranteed," the customer is entitled to return them without argument (undamaged and within a reasonable time, of course) if a question of personal taste (such as colour or shape) is involved. Other types of goods, however, may be returned only if the buyer has some reasonable grounds for dissatisfaction.

Naturally, the injured party always has the option to waive a breach of warranty, and even of condition. This, in fact, is common practice in today's business world; it is only in a tiny percentage of cases that late deliveries, short shipments, etc., form the basis of court actions. Such mistakes are usually forgiven in the anticipation of similar favours from the other party at some future time. The injured party also has the option to treat a broken condition as a breach of warranty; that is, he may permit the contract to continue, provided he receives adequate compensation.

REMEDIES AND CONSEQUENCES

The remedies for and consequences of breach of contract can be summarized as follows:

Release (or exoneration). When one party breaks a contract, the other party is thereupon released (or exonerated) from any further performance.

Compensation for incurred losses. If one is prevented by the other party from fulfilling his contract obligation, he becomes entitled to payment for the work he has done until the moment of stoppage, even if this is of no value to the other party (the lawyers call this a *quantum meruit* claim).

Litigation. If the party injured by the breach of contract is given no compensation for incurred losses, he can sue for the following remedies:

DAMAGES. As explained on p. 51 ff., damages are designed only to compensate the injured party and not to punish the contract breaker—regardless of whether he broke the contract deliberately, through carelessness, or through the unfortunate force of circumstances. The successful plaintiff usually will obtain compensation only for losses resulting naturally from the breach of contract. Thus a buyer who has not received contracted-for goods will be compensated for loss of "normal profit," and a worker who has been improperly dismissed will receive compensation for his lost wages.

The defendant will not be liable to make good an unusually large loss the plaintiff may have suffered, unless the possibility of this was clearly contemplated by both parties when entering into the contract. Contemplation of this kind is illustrated in the following example. Manufacturer to supplier: "I need these materials by this deadline;

otherwise I shall suffer heavy damages for not fulfilling my contract with the customer in time." Supplier: "I understand; you can rely on me!"

The injured party must try to hold the loss down to a minimum: he must try to mitigate the damages and not make them worse deliberately, or negligently. For example, if a contracted-for repair part is not received in time, a factory owner must try to get one elsewhere and then sue for the difference in price of the repair parts. If he fails to do so and his machinery breaks down for lack of this repair part, he will not be awarded compensation for his needlessly damaged machinery and loss of profits.

To avoid time-consuming litigation, the parties may, in their contract, determine ahead of time the amount of compensation to be paid for the breach of any particular term. Thus, if a building is to be erected for $10,000 within six months, a reasonable sum of, say, $100 may be agreed upon as *liquidated damages* for each week's delay beyond the six months. However, if instead of $100 this figure were $1,000 a week, the court would not regard it as liquidated damages but as a penalty; and the $1,000 would be disregarded, even if the contract had stated that "this amount is to be regarded not as a penalty, but as liquidated damages." The court would then figure out the actual amount of compensation to be awarded.

Under principles of equity it was felt that in some circumstances the common law remedy of awarding damages to the plaintiff did not do him sufficient justice; consequently two additional remedies were originated which are now awarded in all the higher courts as alternative or in addition to damages. These remedies are specific performance and injunction, as described below:

SPECIFIC PERFORMANCE.   Specific performance by the defendant of the actual contract terms will be ordered where money damages alone would not properly compensate the plaintiff. For example, a seller who breaks his contractual obligation to deliver some item that cannot be duplicated (e.g., a work of art, or collector's item; some scenic land, or custom-built house; a copyright or patent; controlling shares in a company), will be made to transfer the item to the buyer.

This equity order will be made only if the court considers it to be in the best interests of justice and only if it can supervise the carrying-out of the order. If the defendant refuses to sign a deed of land over to the plaintiff, a court official is empowered to sign it instead.

Specific performance of personal services is never ordered, since the courts feel that forcing a person to work for someone else smacks of slavery. While a contract-breaking artist could, conceivably, be physically forced onto a stage, the court could hardly make him sing or dance his best, and a clerk who had wrongfully left his employ can hardly be chained to his desk.

INJUNCTION. As in tort, an injunction can also be granted to prohibit someone from breaking his contract. While our artist cannot be compelled to appear in a certain theatre, it is sometimes possible to prevent him, by an injunction, from performing for a direct competitor. Or, a dealer holding an exclusive franchise can have his manufacturer "enjoined" (stopped) from supplying a competitor in his territory, while the manufacturer could have the dealer enjoined from carrying a competing line of goods. Similarly, a buyer who learns that a seller is about to sell certain unique goods to a third party in violation of his contract with the buyer, can get an injunction against the seller to stop him from doing this; for, once the innocent third party has received the goods, he need not deliver them to the original buyer, who would then be left only with a claim for damages against the contract-breaking seller.

QUESTIONS

1. List the circumstances under which the law will discharge a person from his contract obligations on a plea of "impossibility of performance."
2. Contrast a termination of contract due to the operation of the law with one due to a change in the law.
3. Generally, when will physical incapacitation be grounds for terminating a contract?
4. Of what does legal tender consist in Canada?
5. On February 1, Thompson agrees to do something for Meyer on April 1. On February 26, Thompson tells Meyer not to expect performance until April 30. What is the earliest date on which Meyer can take action? Explain.
6. Glynn places an order for some goods with Grant, consenting to

pay a premium for early delivery, within three days. What attitude is Glynn entitled to take if Grant delivers the goods to him on the fourth day?

7. (a) What are liquidated damages?

   (b) Under what circumstances might the courts refuse to enforce the liquidated damages clause in a contract?

8. (a) Under what circumstances will the courts grant an order for specific performance?

   (b) Why will the courts not grant this order to enforce personal services?

CHAPTER TWELVE

Privity of Contract

MEANING OF PRIVITY OF CONTRACT

If I, in a contract with A, promise him that I will pay a sum of money by a certain date to B, can I be sued by B if I break my promise?

If I, in a contract with C, promise him that he will receive a sum of money by a certain date from D, can D be sued if C fails to receive that money?

In both cases the answer is *no* because there is no *privity of contract* (contract relationship) between me and B in the first case; or between C and D in the second case. In the first case I could, of course, be sued by A, and in the second case I could be sued by C.

The rule to be drawn from these examples is that a person who was not an actual party to a contract can generally derive no rights or duties under it. Another example of this rule is that a manufacturer is not liable to a consumer for the breach of warranty that an enthusiastic retailer made for his product. (The manufacturer is, of course, liable in tort for any injury suffered by a consumer through negligent manufacture of the product.) However, the manufacturer is liable for breach of a warranty that he issued generally to persons who will logically become users of the product.

Exceptions are the beneficiaries under insurance policies or trusts; they can enforce proper payment from the insurance company or trustee, respectively, even though there was no direct contract relation between them. (Other exceptions are undisclosed principals and principals by ratification to be discussed under Agency.)

NOVATION

In this chapter we want to discuss how new parties can be introduced into an existing contract. One method has already been discussed in Chapter 11; namely, *novation*—whereby, by mutual consent of all the involved parties, one contract is cancelled, and a new one, with different parties, is formed (with no change, usually, in any of the terms of the previous contract).

ASSIGNMENT

Is a person allowed to transfer his contract to someone else? The answer is that, with the consent of the other party to the contract, such an *assignment* is always possible. Consent may be obtained just before it is desired to make the transfer, or the original contract may have reserved this right to the parties by use of the words ". . . and his agents, heirs, representatives, and assignees." Sometimes such a transfer is expressly prohibited; for example, by the words "not transferable" on season tickets, bus transfers, and similar items, or by special clauses in leases which prohibit a tenant from sub-letting or assigning his lease without permission.

Liabilities. Is an assignment possible without the other party's consent? The answer will depend on whether a liability or a right is to be assigned. While a liability can be transferred by novation, it can never be assigned by a debtor without the creditor's consent. This is quite logical because otherwise situations similar to the following could arise: A bank, after careful investigation, might grant a loan to a trusted customer, only to be informed later by this customer, "out of the blue," that he has made a deal with some financially weak friend whereby this friend is now to become the bank's debtor in his place.

Similarly, a person with special skills (e.g., an artist or craftsman) may have undertaken to do or make something for the other contracting party. He is not allowed to delegate his task to another without the consent of the other party to the contract. Of course, if a person has undertaken to perform a run-of-the-mill job, he is at liberty to sub-contract this job to someone else; however, he retains full responsibility for the proper performance of the contract.

Personal services. Nor can the right to receive personal services be assigned without the consent of the other party. Thus, a person who has contracted to have his portrait painted cannot, by an assignment of this right to someone else, force the artist to paint the other person's portrait. Nor can I sell my share of a partnership to another without my partner's consent, or, as an absurd example, inform my fiancée that I have traded off to another man my right to marry her.

Rights. However, rights to receive money or property *can* be assigned by a creditor (assignor) to an assignee without the debtor's consent; and, provided certain requirements have been met, the debtor then becomes as liable to the assignee (the new creditor) as he was to the original creditor, and he can be sued for any non-performance directly by the assignee. These requirements are:

1. WRITING. The assignment must be in writing.

2. UNINCREASED BURDEN. The burden on the debtor must not be increased in the slightest degree by reason of the claim on him having been assigned to someone else. The assignment must not result in the debtor having to pay more money or to deliver more goods; or, to have to do so earlier; or, to be involved in additional expense or inconvenience. If this should turn out to be the case, the debtor will be released from further obligations if he pays his original creditor on the original contract terms.

3. NOTICE. The debtor cannot be expected to know of any assignment unless he is notified of it. Such notice must be in writing and it will usually be in the assignee's interest to inform the debtor of it. To allay any doubts in the debtor's mind about the genuineness of the assignment, the assignee should ask the assignor to supply him with a carbon copy of the assignment for forwarding to the debtor (today it can be photo-copied).

In case a creditor has dishonestly or negligently assigned the same claim to two different assignees, it is the assignee who first gets notice of the assignment into the debtor's hands who becomes entitled to payment by the debtor; the other assignee is then left with a claim against the fraudulent or careless assignor.

In case there is a dispute between the assignor and the assignee(s) and the debtor is unclear about whom to pay, he will be wise to pay the money into court and to notify all concerned parties. Otherwise he runs the risk of paying the wrong party; in which case he might be made to pay the right party all over again (with a subsequent claim to a refund, of course, from the incorrectly paid party).

When a person has a negotiable instrument (cheque, draft, or promissory note) properly assigned to him (by endorsement or, sometimes even, delivery) he need not notify the debtor; obviously, you need not notify the Bank of Canada every time you receive a $1 bill—which is a promissory note issued by the Bank of Canada.

DEBTOR'S DEFENSES

It should be noted that a debtor retains against his new creditor (the assignee) any defense he may have possessed against the original creditor (the assignor), such as incapacity, lack of genuine intent, or breach of warranty. Thus, if creditor *C* assigns to assignee *A* the $1,000 debt owed him by debtor *D*, *D* can refuse payment of all or part of this sum to *A* by claiming any of the following: that *D* was under twenty-one when he received this credit from *C*; or, that he entered the contract with *C* under duress; or, that the goods in question which he bought were misrepresented to him, or that they failed to live up to *C*'s warranties for them. Also, *D* might reduce his payment to *A* by the amount of any set-off he had against *C*.

When assignee *A*, on any of these proper grounds, does not receive from debtor *D* as much as expected, *A*'s remedy is to recover the deficiency from the assigning creditor *C*. Note that the regular assignee of a negotiable instrument (a "holder in due course") or of a mortgage (a *bona fide* purchaser for value without notice) takes it free from any of the above defenses, and *D*'s only remedy would be against *C* and not against *A*.

GENERAL ASSIGNMENT OF BOOK DEBTS

If a businessman sells or puts up as security all or a block of his Accounts Receivable (claims on his customers), he must comply with additional formalities. Such a *general assignment of book debts* must be registered (usually within twenty-one to thirty days at the local County Court) with accompanying affidavits (statements under oath) by a witness and by the assignee (often a collection agency) that the assignment is a *bona fide* business transaction and was not designed to defeat the interests of the assignor's creditors.

When a person dies, or is adjudged bankrupt, or is certified insane, all his contracts (rights, as well as liabilities) by law automatically devolve on others: his administrator, trustee, or committee, respectively.

QUESTIONS

1. List the different ways in which new parties can be introduced into existing contracts.
2. Describe the circumstances under which new parties can be introduced into existing contracts without the previous consent of all involved parties.
3. Johnson buys some goods from Robarts and, in his contract with Robarts, Johnson agrees to make payment of the invoice directly to Pearson, who is Robarts' wholesaler. If Johnson fails to pay Pearson on the due date, who has the right to sue Johnson? Explain.
4. Famous sculptor Michael Angels contracted with Liza Lovely to sculpt her portrait.
   (a) Is Michael Angels entitled to delegate this task to a substitute?
   (b) Is Liza Lovely entitled to demand that Michael Angels sculpt a portrait of her sister instead? Explain.
5. An exporter contracts to ship some goods, all expenses paid, to an importer at his address in an overseas seaport town. Just before making shipment, the exporter is informed that the importer has sold his right to receive the goods to a customer who lives fifty miles inland. Explain whether the exporter must follow the importer's instructions to ship the goods to the inland customer.
6. McInnis receives a letter from his creditor, Bythell, instructing him to make payment of a $500 invoice to Tait instead. In each of the following situations explain how much McInnis must pay Tait.
   (a) It so happens that Tait still owes McInnis $100.
   (b) Bythell has not yet satisfied a $75 judgment awarded against him for having damaged McInnis's car in an accident.

CHAPTER THIRTEEN

Limitation of Actions

MEANING OF LIMITATION OF ACTIONS

"The law will not help him who sleeps on his rights." Since the earliest days the courts have felt that anyone who has delayed overly long in enforcing his legal claims should be deprived of them. Such a person's right to sue is "barred" (or, his claim is "outlawed") if a writ of summons is not issued within the time limits set out in each of the provinces' Limitations Acts or in the Limitations sections of other statutes. The reasons for this policy are quite logical: after too great a time lapse witnesses may have died, moved away, or have had their memories fail them, and evidence will have become lost.

It should be noted that, *except for land*, it is only the right to *sue* that is eventually lost by the creditor—the debt itself is not extinguished. (The debtor may waive the protection afforded him by the Statutes of Limitation and may defend a claim against him on its merits alone.) Thus, if the creditor can obtain satisfaction by legal means, without having to go to court, he is fully entitled to retain it. For instance, if the debtor pays the creditor all or part of his outlawed claim, it is the creditor's to keep. And, if the creditor, by chance, incurs a debt to the original debtor, the creditor may "set off" (deduct) the outlawed debt owed to him when making settlement. Or, an employer may deduct from his employee's wages the amount of an outlawed debt owed to the employer by the employee. Or, a creditor may realize a lien or security left with him to cover a debt, even after it has become outlawed.

CRIMES

With regard to crimes, the rule is uniform throughout Canada that "time does not run against the Crown"; in other words, it is never too late to indict a person for a serious crime except that a treason charge must be laid within three years; certain sex offenses must be prosecuted within one year, and prosecutions under the Lord's Day Act within sixty days. Summary conviction cases must be begun within six months.

SIMPLE CONTRACTS AND TORTS

In most of the provinces (including Ontario) actions for breach of *simple* contracts, for promissory notes, and for tort damages must be instituted within six years. Again, there are numerous exceptions: Under the federal Copyright Act, the period of limitation for plagiarism actions is three years. Under the Ontario act, actions for assault, etc., must be begun within three years; claims arising out of motor vehicle accidents on a highway and claims against insurance companies must be lodged within one year; claims against the Motor Vehicle Accident Claims Fund (formerly the Unsatisfied Judgment Fund) by hit-and-run victims must be begun within three months; and slander (*not* libel) actions must be instituted within two years. The claim of the holder of a bank note against the bank issuing the note (today this is only the Bank of Canada) is never outlawed.

REAL PROPERTY

A person's claim to real property without registration is extinguished completely after ten years in Ontario and after varying periods in the other provinces. Note that all of such a person's rights regarding the property are lost, not only his right to sue. Thus, if a usurper enters upon vacant land and openly and without anyone's permission stays on it for ten years uninterruptedly, he will have the right to keep the original owner off the land.

It takes twenty years to obtain squatter's rights by moving in on, and developing, Crown land that was granted to someone else who failed to occupy and to develop it according to government requirements. While ownership of ungranted Crown land can never be obtained by long-term possession of it, anyone (or his successors) who has occupied it for sixty years without paying rent for it will be exempt from back rent payments. As we have heard earlier, easements over land (rights of way, etc.) can be established by the right of prescription after twenty years of open, uninterrupted, and adverse use.

SPECIALTIES

The right to sue on specialties (contracts under seal) is lost after twenty years in most provinces, including Ontario. Also, the successful party to a law suit has twenty years in which to enforce the judgment that was awarded to him.

DISABILITIES

The starting point for these varying periods of limitation is not the moment when the credit was granted but the time when payment fell due and the creditor's right of action first arose. However, if at that particular time the creditor is "under a disability," the starting point is postponed until he ceases to suffer from such a disability. For example, he might have been suffering from unconsciousness, insanity, or infancy, or the debtor might have placed himself beyond the court's reach by going into concealment or by leaving the jurisdiction (the province); or the debtor's fraud may have prevented or delayed the creditor from instituting proceedings. Note, that if such disability begins *after* the creditor has had a chance—even a short one— of serving the debtor with the writ of summons, it will not stop the time of limitation from running. Thus, if I go into hiding one month after my simple contract debt to you fell due and I do not emerge for six years after that, the Statutes of Limitation will protect me from legal action by you.

EXTENSIONS

Note that there is no extension of time if the last day of the period of limitation falls on a Sunday or some other day on which court offices are closed. However, all claims are extended for further six, ten, and twenty year periods, respectively, whenever the creditor receives from his debtor a written acknowledgment of the debt, or a written promise to pay the debt (including a request for an extension of time in which to pay); or if he receives a part payment which can be construed as an *implied promise* to pay the balance. Of course, a part payment which is accompanied by a declaration of the debtor that he will pay nothing further, cannot be regarded as such an implied promise, and it will not serve to extend the period of limitation.

REVIVAL

While claims to land can, as we have just seen, be extended before their expiry, they cannot afterwards be revived. However, a revival of outlawed debts is possible, provided the claims do not involve land; an express written promise or a part payment by a debtor who was protected by the Limitation Acts can eliminate that protection, even though the debtor received no new consideration for his promise.

APPLICATION OF PAYMENTS

If a creditor has granted credit, at different times, to a debtor for several items, what should be done with a payment on account that the debtor sends to the creditor? The first thing to remember is that where there are several items in an account, each of them constitutes a distinct and separate debt. Then, the application of payments is made according to the following rules:

1. When the debtor sends a payment, it is his privilege to allocate his payment to the debt of his choice. (If the debtor allocates to an outlawed debt, it will be revived.)

2. If the debtor neglects to make such an allocation, but the amount of his payment coincides exactly with the amount of one of his debts, that is the debt assumed to be paid. For example, suppose a debtor has incurred the following debts to one creditor. (The debts above the dotted line are outlawed.)

YEAR DEBT INCURRED	AMOUNT OF DEBT
1956	$100
1957	125
1958	150
1959	175
1960	200

If the debtor remits $175 without designating its purpose, the creditor will have to apply it in satisfaction of the 1959 debt in our illustration.

3. If the debtor sends in an odd amount, without saying how it is to be used, the creditor has the right to allocate it wherever he pleases—even to an outlawed debt. Thus, a sum of $50 received in early 1964 could be applied to any of the five debts, including either of the then outlawed debts of 1956 and 1957. But note that, since there was no implied promise by the debtor to pay, an allocation by the creditor to an outlawed debt will not automatically revive or extend the balance of it.

4. If neither the debtor nor the creditor made an allocation of the odd remittance at the time it was sent and a dispute afterwards arises in this connection, the court will apply the remittance to the earliest non-outlawed debt; in our illustration, to the late 1958 debt.

One might ask why any creditor would voluntarily wait a long time before deciding to enforce his claims? Under certain circumstances, the reasons are obvious: One example might be financial transactions within the family circle or between close friends which will need regulating after a rift in the relation or when successors inherit claims after a death or bankruptcy. Another example might be a claim against an indigent person who might not have appeared worth suing for a long time but who unexpectedly comes into some money at a later date.

QUESTIONS

1. In Ontario, generally, what are the periods of limitation for initiating court action
   (a) For simple contract debts?
   (b) For claims in tort?
   (c) For contract debts under seal, other than land?
   (d) For contracts involving land?
   (e) In criminal prosecutions?
2. "Toronto, May 10, 1965. Dear Mr. Smith: I admit that I borrowed $100 from you twenty-one years ago and that I have not yet repaid you anything because, as you will remember, I repaired your roof. (Signed—by hand) J. Brown." What legal use can Smith make of Brown's letter? Explain.

3. (a) What circumstances will serve to extend the periods of limitation?
   (b) What circumstances will serve to revive outlawed claims to
      (i) Personal property?
      (ii) Land?
4. What circumstances place a creditor "under a disability" for Statute of Limitation purposes?
5. Mr. Robinson's private secretary fraudulently converted to his own use some of his employer's valuables, replacing them with deceptive substitutes. After seven years Mr. Robinson discovers the swindle. Will the Statute of Limitations prevent him from suing his secretary? Explain.
6. "No gentleman ever takes advantage under the Statute of Limitations." Discuss this statement.

Special Contracts

CHAPTER FOURTEEN

Employment

INTRODUCTION

We have now finished discussing the basic principles of contract, and the rest of this book will be devoted to specialized types of contract. Each of these will continue to be based on the general rules already set out but will also contain additional ones which appertain particularly to it. We begin with a consideration of employment contracts.

This field of law is so old that instead of referring to "employer and employee," lawyers still use the traditional terminology of "master and servant." Still, "a rose by any other name would smell as sweet," and by using the antiquated expressions we avoid mistakes arising from unclear nomenclature.

FORMATION OF EMPLOYMENT CONTRACTS

A contract of "hiring and service" (employment) is formed in the same way as all other contracts. It need be in writing only if some statute requires it to be; for example, written form is required for contracts that cannot be ended by either party within one year, per the Statute of Frauds). Otherwise, employment contracts can be formed orally or be implied by conduct. To illustrate: It might be my custom to put my lawn mower on the front porch whenever I want my grass cut by the first person who wants to do it. After performing that service, the person will, of course, be entitled to payment, either of an expressly stipulated amount; or, failing that, of the customary "going rate"; or, failing that too, of a reasonable amount. Note that a fee is payable to a near relative for his services only if previously agreed upon expressly or by custom; but other people (e.g., friends and neighbours) are entitled to make reasonable charges for their services unless they were clearly rendered gratis.

In some provinces, contracts of apprenticeship and employment can be entered into only for limited periods; for example, in Ontario any such contract for over nine years is reduced to that term.

DUTIES OF THE MASTER

The duties of the master to the servant are:

• To adhere to the terms and conditions of any express contract entered into with the servant or of any collective bargaining agreement with his union.

• To reimburse the servant for any expenses he has properly incurred in the course of his duties (i.e., to honour his "swindle sheet") and to honour any liabilities he has so incurred.

• To provide a safe place of work; safe machinery, equipment, roadways, elevators, etc., and to issue warnings of dangerous situations. Most provinces have a Factory Act with regulations which specify certain safety requirements and a system of government inspection.

• To establish rules and regulations and to issue instructions.

• If the safety or efficiency of the worker is in any way to depend on the competence of fellow workers, to make reasonably sure that the workers possess the necessary skills.

• It is customary to pay a salaried worker even during a temporary illness. (This is in contrast to a worker being paid an hourly wage, who does not get paid for any time off but who, in compensation, customarily gets extra pay for overtime.) "Temporary illness" can extend from one to three days for a recently hired employee to several months for a valued old-timer. However a salaried worker is seldom paid anything but "supper money" for overtime.

• Provided there is nothing in the agreement to the contrary expressly or by custom (as in banks, Hydro, and the Civil Service), the servant is allowed to "moonlight"; that is, to take a second job in his off hours; provided also that his second place of employment is not of a competing nature with the first place. The reason why an employee is often contractually prohibited from taking a second job is to conserve his energies, attention, and loyalty for the one employer.

• In some occupations, the master is under an obligation to supply the worker with work to do: For example, in jobs where the lack of activity would result in the worker losing his skills (stenographer); or commissions, tips and bonuses (salesman, waiter, piece-worker); or opportunities or popularity (actor, athlete).

RIGHTS OF AN INJURED WORKER AGAINST HIS MASTER

First we shall consider the worker's or servant's rights at common law, and then his statutory rights.

RIGHTS AT COMMON LAW

There are still many classes of workers who are not protected by Workmen's Compensation (discussed below) and who must, therefore, seek redress for their injuries under the common law. These are the workers in domestic employment; on the farm; in banks; in trust, loan and insurance companies and other financial institutions, and in casual or occasional employment.

Stated briefly, at common law a worker can collect damages from his master for his injuries only if he can prove that they were caused by his master's negligence. Till as late as the beginning of this century, this situation was aggravated by the fact that a worker forfeited all claims against his master if he was guilty of the slightest contributory negligence. That situation is now remedied, but a servant still loses all claims if he failed to report to his master any defect in machinery, etc., which had come to the worker's attention and which subsequently injured him.

The rule of *volenti non fit iniuria* (see Torts) applies with particular force to employment. According to this rule, a servant is deemed to accept the risks incidental to his particular type of employment. If a worker is injured on an inherently dangerous job, he can hold his master liable at common law only if he can prove that his injury was caused by the master's negligence independently of the job's dangers, or that the master needlessly exposed the servant to danger.

The Workmen's Compensation Acts of most provinces have abrogated the master's common law defense of "common employment," according to which a master was not liable to his servant *A* who was injured by the negligence of fellow-servant *B*. The only chance servant *A* had of winning was to prove that the master was negligent in hiring a fellow-worker *B* who was incompetent to begin with; or to prove that *B* was not, strictly speaking, a co-worker but a safety officer or other representative of the master.

STATUTORY RIGHTS

The Fatal Accidents Act has been discussed under Torts. In brief recapitulation, it entitles the surviving dependant of a deceased person to sue, in his place, the person responsible for his death.

The Workmen's Compensation Act is the other important instance of legislative relief to large classes of workers (the chief exceptions were listed earlier).

Introduced in Great Britain in 1906, it was soon adopted by all common law countries. (Ontario accepted it in 1915 and now has a system that is regarded as a model by all the world.) In brief, by what virtually amounts to a governmentally supervised system of compulsory insurance, it provides compensation to a worker—or, if dead, to his surviving dependant(s)—for any injury or occupational disease received through *accident* in the *course of work*. Thus, ordinary sickness (such as appendicitis, hemorrhaging ulcers, heart attack) is not covered even if occurring at work, nor are accidents that occur off the job. As a rule of thumb, compensation is paid for all accidents occurring at the place of work, even if on the worker's free time. Examples of industrial diseases are silicosis, inhalation of fumes, or a diver's bends.

The worker receives compensation even if he was injured entirely due to his own carelessness and even if his employer (or anyone else, for that matter) was entirely free from blame. The only exception is where the worker was injured because of his own flagrant recklessness (virtually bringing on his injury deliberately) and if he was not injured very severely thereby. Even in this situation compensation will be paid if the accident results in severe injury or death. "Accident," under an amendment to the Act, is deemed to include the deliberate injury of the worker by someone else.

All employers of labour (except those listed above) are required to make contributions to the provincial Workmen's Compensation Board according to a levy imposed on them by the Board's assessors. The assessment is arrived at by combining the size of the employer's payroll and the accident rate in his particular industry. (If the accident rate in that industry increases, so does the assessment, and vice versa.) Note that *nobody* makes contributions to the Board except the employers (this is frequently confused with federal Unemployment Insurance, five-sixths of whose cost is borne equally by the employers and the workers, the balance being subsidized by the government).

While the previously listed excepted occupations cannot be compulsorily assessed by the Workmen's Compensation Board, any of them may apply to join the scheme voluntarily. And, while it is only accidents to employees that are normally covered by Workmen's Compensation, employers can also apply for coverage for themselves, provided, of course, that they pay a proportionate extra "premium."

The victim of an accident must immediately notify his employer who, in turn, must promptly notify the Board. In case of a disputed claim, the Board conducts a hearing and then makes its decision. If the decision is favourable to the worker, it is the Board which compensates him. It must be noted that an injured worker on a job that is covered by the Workmen's Compensation Act has, by this statute, lost his right to sue his master or anyone else at common law, however negligent they may have been.

Compensation consists of:

1. Full coverage of all medical expenses: doctors, hospitals, medicines, nursing, X Rays, physiotherapy, etc.

2. Compensation for loss of earnings. In Ontario, during the worker's *total* disability, this amounts to 75% of the worker's average earnings (with maximum payments of $4,500 per year). If the worker's earning capacity has not been completely lost, he receives a proportionately lower percentage. If the worker's disability does not last beyond two days, he receives no compensation for lost earnings; if disabled longer, he receives compensation also for the first two days.

3. Benefits to his dependants, should the accident result in the worker's death. In Ontario these consist of a $400 lump sum payment to his widow plus a monthly payment to her, till she dies or remarries, of $75 for herself and of $40 for each child. (Widow now includes a common-law wife.)

Other legislation. In addition to the statutes already discussed, many

157

other types of legislation have been enacted by most provinces for the additional protection of the worker. Some of these are:
- Vacations with Pay Acts.
- Minimum Wages Acts (often restricted to females or to specified areas).
- Maximum Hours of Work Acts, and One Day's Rest in Seven Acts (restricted to certain age groups or to specified occupations; e.g., to hotels in Ontario).
- Labour Relations Acts, which legalize trade unions and collective bargaining.
- In some provinces a Master and Servant Act provides for quick settlement of wage disputes by having them heard in the police courts.

LENGTH OF TERM AND TERMINATION OF SERVICE

Employment for a fixed term. The contract of employment may expressly provide for a clearly specified length of time or for the duration of a clearly specified job or project. At the end of this specified period or project, the contract is automatically at an end, *without either party having to give or to receive previous notice to (or from) the other.* Nor is either party justified in unilaterally breaking off this fixed-term contract before the expiry of the stipulated time—*not even by the giving of notice*—except for proper cause, such as: mutual agreement; breach of contract by the other party; or impossibility of performance (e.g., the employee's physical incapacitation). It is a curious point to note that the employer is released from long-term employment contracts by going out of business.

Employment for an indefinite term. Far more common than contracts for stated terms are contracts of employment for indefinite periods (sometimes called *hirings at will*). The length of these periods is implied from the rate of pay: whether it is quoted as an hourly, weekly, monthly or annual *rate*, even if the actual payments are made at different intervals. For example, a worker at $6,000 per annum may be paid $250 gross twice a month and yet be considered as on a yearly basis; or a worker at $2 an hour might be paid $80 gross at the end of a forty-hour week and yet be considered as on an hourly basis.

Termination with notice. Contracts of this nature can be terminated by either party for any of the above reasons; or by the giving of *notice* by one party to the other of his intention to end the contract. The length of notice to be given may have been expressly specified in the contract; if not, there might be a length of notice that is customary in certain enterprises; failing which, the notice should be of *reasonable* length. This is generally, but subject to exceptions, *one clear rate period*. However with workers on annual salary a three-month notice period is usual. By "clear" is meant one week, one month, etc., from the payday.

A master, but not the servant, has the privilege of demanding a servant's instant departure provided he pays the servant in full for the required notice period plus the value of any free board and lodging, etc., the servant may have lost thereby. (This is called *payment in lieu of notice*.)

Termination without notice. In case either party commits a serious breach of any of the express or implied conditions of the contract of employment, the other party is at once released from the contract and is allowed to terminate it without the giving of any notice. The following are some of the implied conditions violation of which by the master will entitle a servant to quit without notice:

- If the master gives the servant unreasonable or unlawful orders *and tries to enforce them* (e.g., by making an accountant scrub the floor).

- If the master requires the servant to continue work on unsafe machinery, etc., after having been informed of the existence of such dangers.

Quitting in the middle of a pay period under such justified circumstances entitles the servant to at least proportionate pay (*quantum meruit*) for his services until the moment of severance; and, probably, to damages for the employer's breach of contract according to the rules set out below.

The following are some justifiable grounds for "firing" a servant without notice (if this is not done promptly after the servant's misbehaviour, the master loses this right).

- If the servant is persistently unpunctual or absent without leave (except, of course, for Sundays or other agreed-upon days off).

- If the servant wilfully disobeys orders that are not unreasonable or illegal.

• If the servant is dishonest, disloyal, or clearly incompetent.

• If he is grossly immoral or habitually drunk, on the job or else-where; or if he is convicted of a crime involving moral turpitude (something disgraceful).

• If he is habitually negligent or destructive.

• If he is prolongedly disabled, either through sickness or accident. (This can be justified logically, if not morally, by the worker ceasing to fulfil his contract obligation to do work. Impossibility of perform-ance will, however, excuse the worker from having to pay the master damages for breach of contract; and, we trust, that the worker is covered by Workmen's Compensation and/or group insurance or by a pension scheme.)

Even if a servant is justifiably fired in the middle of a pay period, he is entitled to pay on a *quantum meruit* basis to the time of firing. On the other hand, the master may be justified in making reasonable deduc-tions from the servant's pay to compensate for any deliberate damage caused by the servant.

REMEDIES FOR WRONGFUL QUITTING OR DISMISSAL

A worker who leaves his job in breach of contract cannot be forced back onto it since, it will be remembered, the courts will not issue an order for the specific performance of personal services. However, theoretically, he is subject to damages for breach of contract. In prac-tice, damages are usually enforced only against "key" employees; but even "the little man" may have some of his salary contractually with-held to the end of his term to ensure that he completes it. A valuable employee may also have an injunction issued against him, preventing him from working for the injured party's competitor for the balance of the contract term, or in violation of the terms of the original con-tract, or from revealing "trade secrets" (as contrasted to "special skills").

An improperly dismissed servant cannot get his job back (except with his union's assistance); he is only entitled to damages to compen-sate him for his actual loss (not for his hurt feelings or injured pride). This loss is computed on his lost pay, plus any lost bonuses, etc. In the case of employment for a fixed term or job, the improperly dis-missed employee is entitled to pay for the balance of such term; and in the case of an indefinite term, until the end of the required period of notice, *less* what the servant earned elsewhere in the meantime or what he could have earned had he immediately started looking for *suitable* other work (under the rule that requires an injured party to "minimize the damages"). Incidentally, the onus in such cases is on the sued employer to prove the availability of such suitable employment.

There is *no* basis by a worker for a claim to a reference from his previous employer. (Such a forced reference would probably not be worth much to the worker, anyway; e.g., "I have nothing to say against Joe Doakes.")

SERVANT'S TORTS AND VICTIM'S RIGHTS

As will be remembered, anyone who commits a tort (e.g., negligence, fraud) can be made to compensate the injured party. This includes a servant who commits a tort against someone while working for his employer; and it should be noted that the servant cannot escape liability by pleading that he was merely carrying out his master's instructions. But in addition, for historical reasons,[1] a master is burdened with *vicarious liability* for losses caused to others by any of his servants *while in the course of his employment,* even though the master is completely free from any blameful act personally.[2] The point most frequently in dispute in cases of this nature is whether the servant caused the injury while in the scope of his employment or on, what has variously been called, an "independent frolic" or a "jaunt of his own." So long as the servant commits the tort "on the job," the master is liable to the third party even though the servant deliberately flaunted his master's instructions; for example, by disobeying safety rules or by unauthorized giving of fraudulent warranties to customers. The dividing line is not hard and fast; therefore, the following decided cases are briefly given as a guide:

---

[1] In olden days an indentured servant was virtually a serf. He owned practically nothing; whatever his efforts earned from the outside, inured to the benefit of his master. It was consequently considered but fair that the master should be held accountable for any losses occasioned by his servant's actions.

[2] As a practical consequence of this rule, injured third parties frequently voluntarily "bypass" the impecunious servant who actually caused the injury and choose to concentrate on suing only the financially stronger master.

161

• Brewery workers lowered casks of beer from the loft to the waiting drays by means of a single loop of chain around the casks. A passer-by was severely injured when a cask worked loose and fell on him. When sued, the brewery owners had to pay damages even though they had issued strict instructions for double loops of chain to be used on all casks.

• A bus driver assaulted a passenger over a political disagreement. The bus company was held not responsible.

• Another bus driver enforced his request that passengers move to the rear of the bus by driving his elbow into a passenger's ribs. This assault was held to be committed as a manner of carrying out his job; even though it was an improper manner, the driver's employers had to compensate the victim. (In such cases, technically, the employer is entitled to eventual reimbursement by the actual wrongdoer.)

• The driver of a gasoline tanker caused an explosion because he violated strict instructions against smoking. His employers were held responsible for the resulting damage to the service station whose gasoline cisterns were being refilled.

• When, one day in 1946, the driver of a truck deliberately let go the controls because he suffered the delusion that the entire fleet of trucks was being electronically operated centrally by remote control from headquarters, the truck smashed into a Toronto streetcar. In the resulting action by the streetcar company it was held that the truck driver's hallucination placed him outside the scope of his employment and released his employers from liability.

• A similar decision was rendered when a truck driver unexpectedly fell unconscious at the wheel, thus causing an accident.

• A trucker, causing an accident while on an insignificant detour (in order to visit his girl friend) was held to be on a "jaunt of his own" and did not involve his company in liability.

• Another trucker, causing an accident while on a slight detour (in order to eat lunch at a favourite restaurant, rather than at the one designated by his company) rendered his company liable to the victim.

A master is held responsible for the consequences of any tort that he actually instructed or authorized a servant to commit, or if he subsequently "ratified" the servant's unauthorized tort; that is, if the master approved of it either expressly or by implication (e.g., by accepting any profits resulting from the tort).

On the other hand, a master is not liable to third parties who are injured by someone to whom a servant delegated his duties without the master's consent.

QUESTIONS

1. Crosby is employed by a firm at a salary of $12,000 per year and receives a "take-home" pay cheque of about $400 twice a month. He started work with the firm on March 1, 1965; on January 2, 1966, he decides to leave the firm and gives notice. What is the earliest date on which he is entitled to leave?

2. At his request, you paint your father's house (with his paint), without payment having been discussed at any time. If a professional painter had quoted $200 for the job, how much can you legally make your father pay you? Explain.

3. What exactly are the legal rights of a worker who has been improperly dismissed?

4. Mr. Giggins accidentally steps on the tender corns of his employee, Hobson. Thereupon Hobson calls his employer some rude names; Hobson's friend, Jarvis, backs him up and also calls Mr. Giggins some insulting names. Explain whether Mr. Giggins can, without notice, dismiss (a) Hobson; (b) Jarvis.

5. Complete the following sentences with either "always," or "sometimes," or "never"; also give the reasons for your answers.

   (a) Legally a servant may .... quit or be dismissed without notice.

   (b) An employer must .... endeavour to maintain a safe place of work.

   (c) If injured at work purely by your own carelessness, you can .... collect damages from your employer.

   (d) If injured at work purely by your own flagrant recklessness, you can .... collect Workmen's Compensation.

6. Under what circumstances would it be important for an outside party to know whether two persons are employer and employee, or independent contractors?

7. A company has strict rules against smoking which it enforces daily

by posters, announcements, and inspectors. A company worker sneaked in a smoke; this caused an explosion which injured a stranger passing by. Whom may the injured person sue, and on what grounds?

CHAPTER FIFTEEN

Agency

THE THREE PARTIES INVOLVED

An *agent* is a person who is employed by a *principal* for the purpose of entering into contracts on behalf of his principal with others, or *third parties*. Usually, the principal is fully bound to, and enjoys full benefits from, the third party with regard to contracts entered into for him by his properly appointed agent, while the agent is under no such obligations and has no such rights.

In business, agents are generally appointed by contract and are entitled to payment for their services. But there are many situations where the law presumes an agency relationship to exist without the parties realizing it. If you, as a favour, do his shopping for a busy friend, you are actually acting as his agent with all the legal consequences which this relationship entails and which we shall now discuss.

People often have to transact their business through intermediaries for a variety of reasons; for example:
- To save themselves a journey.
- Where the principal is physically incapacitated through illness, accident, etc.
- Where the size of the enterprise prevents the principal from doing everything himself.
- Where it is desirable for certain transactions to be delegated to specialists.
- When the principal takes a vacation (or is just congenitally lazy).
- When the principal wants his identity kept secret (e.g., the president of a temperance association wishing to invest in a distillery).
- Limited companies, by their nature, operate only through agents.

Who may appoint, or act as, an agent? "What one can do himself, he can do through another." This means that any legally competent person can enter into a contract through an agent. Conversely, a contract entered into by a legally incompetent person (e.g., a contract for non-necessaries by a minor) through an agent is voidable by the incompetent principal. As long as the principal is competent, it does not matter if the agent is not, provided the agent is a rational human being (i.e., not an immature child, an imbecile, or a trained chimpanzee). Thus, a contract entered into with a customer by a sales clerk who is under twenty-one is binding on the firm employing this minor.

Some typical agents (many of them independent; i.e., not necessarily in the employ of one particular person only) are the following: the real estate broker (or realtor) who is purely the seller's agent; insurance brokers, stockbrokers, debt collection agencies, and employment agencies; lawyers; banks, when acting as collecting or paying agents of cheques, drafts and promissory notes. Auctioneers after effecting a sale become not only the seller's agent but also the buyer's agent to the extent of being authorized to sign the memorandum of sale for the buyer, as is required by the Statute of Frauds. Another person acting for two parties is the stakeholder or *escrow holder* to whom valuables or documents are handed in *escrow* (or in trust) with instructions to transfer them to another person after that other person has performed a particular undertaking satisfactorily.

A *factor* is usually a seller's commission agent with quite wide powers; apart from frequently preparing the contracts with the customers, he often has control of the goods (sometimes with the power of selling them "on consignment"), and he often effects collections from the customers. A *broker* finds a buyer for a seller, or vice versa, without handling the goods himself.

As we shall subsequently learn, every partner is a fully authorized agent of the other partner(s).

FORMATION OF THE AGENCY RELATION

When discussing contracts in connection with agency, one should never lose sight of which of two contracts is under discussion. It can be either the contract between the principal and the agent creating the agency; or, it can be the contract that an agent brings about by his endeavours between his principal and a third party.

Discussing first the creation of the agency relationship between principal and agent, a person can become an agent by the following methods:

Express contract. In most cases an express contract may be oral. Important contracts are often reduced to writing, frequently by an exchange of letters. Some will have to be in writing because of the requirements of various statutes; for example, the Statute of Frauds requires writing for agencies that are to endure beyond one year or that involve land (e.g., a house sale).[1]

A *power of attorney*[2] is the agent's written evidence of his authorization. Examples would be the *proxy* that a stockholder sends to a company director authorizing him to vote in his stead at a meeting; or the power that a man deposits with his bank, authorizing his wife to draw on his bank account either freely or to a limited amount; or a sick man issuing an absolutely unlimited power to his trusted son. If the agent is to execute deeds on behalf of his principal, the power has to be under seal.

Implied agency. An agency can be implied to exist from the conduct of the parties. The principle is that, when a person (the principal) puts another (the agent) in a position where he carries the authority that is usual to that position, or "clothes" the other with facts that appear to give him authority, then such a person (the principal) is bound by the acts of the other (the agent), unless the third party has notice of the defect in authority.

Even without intending to create an agency, a person may conduct himself in such a manner as to make people believe that someone else is his agent; for example, by having honoured in the past, obligations incurred in his name by this other person. The other person becomes an *ostensible* agent, and his principal is thereupon, by the doctrine of *estoppel*, estopped (prevented) from repudiating the agency. Thus

---

[1] A *del credere* agent (for an extra commission) guarantees to his principal the creditworthiness of customers whom he procures for him. While the Statute of Frauds requires guarantees to be in writing, *del credere* agencies, curiously enough, need not be created in writing. Overseas factors often act as *del credere* agents.

[2] Attorney means agent. Therefore an attorney-at-law is one's legal representative.

a man who has previously paid without complaint the accounts charged to him by his child, wife, servant, protegé(e), or purchasing agent must continue to do so, provided a sensible third party can reasonably conclude that the purchaser continues to have this authority.

If a principal wants to escape further liability from such contracts made in his name, he must send direct notice to this effect to everyone to whom he has honoured his agent's obligations in the past. To protect his credit from being pledged to others in the region who might reasonably regard him as a responsible principal, he should publicize the termination of the agency; preferably by inserting an "ad" in the provincial Gazette. This constitutes "constructive notice" to everybody in the province, while an "ad" in the local press constitutes notice only to those whom the principal can prove to have actually read it. In business it is particularly important for a principal so to publicize the fact of an agent ceasing to be in his employ.

APPARENT AUTHORITY. An agent with certain limited powers (e.g., a purchasing agent who is not to place orders exceeding $1,000 independently, or a newspaper editor who is not to accept liquor or tobacco advertising) should not, of course, exceed such powers (to do so constitutes a breach of the contract with his principal). Yet if he does so, the resulting contract will be binding on the principal provided the agent acted within his *apparent authority*; that is, provided his action appeared reasonable to a third party who was not aware of any such unusual restriction of the agent's powers. (Subsequently, the principal can recover damages from his agent as compensation for any loss caused by the agent's unauthorized activities). Where an agent enjoys less than the usual amount of authority, or where his powers have been curtailed, the principal should give notice of this as in the previous paragraph.

It should be noted that a travelling salesman who merely books orders for later delivery of goods by his principal, normally has no authority to collect payment from the customer. If he does so and absconds with the money, the customer will have to make payment all over again to the supplying principal.

The terms *special* and *general* agencies are sometimes used. A special agent is employed for one transaction only (e.g., a realtor to find a buyer for your house) or for a narrow type of transaction (e.g., a sales clerk). A general agent has unrestricted powers over all the principal's affairs or, at least, over a specified sphere of activity (e.g., he might be a general manager or a branch manager of a chain operation).

The distinction is only important for determining the amount of apparent authority that can reasonably be attributed to each. Obviously, the apparent authority is far wider in the case of the general agent.

Agent by necessity. In a very limited number of situations a person can become another's *agent by necessity*. We have previously discussed the neglected child and the deserted wife who can charge their purchases of necessities to their parent or husband, respectively. In a similar category would be a good samaritan summoning an ambulance for an unconscious accident victim; a person finding himself in charge of animals and ordering feed for them in their owner's absence; or a ship's master, unable to obtain the owner's instructions, incurring charges for emergency repairs to valuable cargo to prevent its deterioration or destruction. None of these agents of necessity should, ultimately, be out of pocket.

Ratification. If a person represents himself to be someone's agent without, in fact, having any authority to do so—express or implied or apparent or by necessity—and enters into a transaction on his behalf, no contract arises between anybody. (The third party can sue the so-called "agent" for damages for his deceit, in this case called a *breach of implied warranty of authority*; i.e., an implied undertaking that he was a properly authorized agent.)

But if this completely unauthorized person makes it clear to the third party that he is not acting for himself but as an agent for a clearly identified principal who enjoys full legal competence (i.e., he is sane and of age; and, if a company, it is properly incorporated with a charter that permits this particular type of transaction), then that named principal (but no one else) may subsequently *ratify* (adopt, approve, legitimize) the previously unauthorized contract by the unauthorized person. Ratification can be express, or implied (e.g., by tacitly accepting the business or benefit). Such a ratification is retroactive to the date of the original, unauthorized contract. If a principal chooses to ratify such a contract, he must do so within a reasonable time, and he must ratify the entire contract; he is not allowed to ratify merely the favourable portions and to reject the portions he dislikes.

Note that such a ratification may give rise to the implication that the principal will, in future, ratify all similar transactions with the same party; if he wants to avoid this, he must be careful to give contrary advice to all the parties involved.

LIABILITY TO THIRD PARTIES IN CONTRACTS

Where an agent acts with authority. Let us first consider the situations where an agent acts for his legally competent principal with actual authority; or at least with apparent or usual authority (i.e., activities that are normal for an agent of this type and that are not known to the third party to be beyond the agent's actual authority).

• The most common situation is where the contract is brought about by the agent *as an agent* for a *named principal*. In other words, the agent lets the third party know that he represents a principal. In this case it is only the principal who is fully liable for the proper performance of the contract entered into on his behalf; and similarly, he is the only one with the right to enforce proper performance of the contract by the third party. The agent has no contractual rights or duties with respect to the third party.

To protect himself against the possibility of being regarded as contracting for himself, the agent should take certain precautions. For example, the letterhead or contract he uses should indicate his position as agent; or a term of the contract should explain his position; or he should sign contracts as follows:

Principal Company

By

or Per   A. Gent

or Per Pro (*or* p.p.)

If he signs his own name first, he should sign: "John Smith, as agent for (or, on behalf of) Jones Company." Merely signing "John Smith, Purchasing Manager" might expose him to personal liability for the contract since the third party (unless otherwise informed to the contrary) may justifiably think that "Purchasing Manager" was added to John Smith's name only for the sake of distinguishing him from other worthy bearers of the same name.

Naturally, the agent is liable for any personal obligations he may volunteer to the third party in furtherance of his principal's interests.

• Sometimes an agent will appear to act on his own behalf and does not reveal to the third party that he is actually acting on behalf of someone else; namely, for an *undisclosed principal*. Since the third party does not know of the existence of a principal, the agent has the right, in his own name, to sue the third party for breach of contract. Of course, the third party can also hold the agent personally liable for breach of contract. The principal, at any time, may reveal his identity and may himself sue the third party. Conversely, if the true principal's identity becomes known, he, instead of the agent (not both), can be sued if the third party so chooses.

• The rules are similar where a person admits that he is an agent but does not wish to reveal the identity of his principal: where he is acting *as an agent* for an *unnamed principal*. Either (but not both) the agent or the revealed principal can sue the third party for breach of contract or be sued by him. However, in this situation the agent avoids personal liability (and rights) if the agent (with the third party's consent) signs the contract "as agent only."

Where an "agent" acts without authority. If a so-called "agent" enters into a contract on behalf of a person who is not really his principal, we have already explained under Ratification that no contract comes into existence between anybody unless ratified: however, the agent can be sued by the third party for breach of implied warranty of authority. The agent can also find himself exposed to such a suit if his principal dies (or becomes insane or otherwise legally incompetent) without the agent's knowledge; or if the company he is working for is incompetent by reason of not being properly incorporated, or by reason of the subject matter of the contract being *ultra vires* according to the company charter. The reason for this is that he would be acting without authority. The agent can protect himself against the latter eventuality by checking the company before working for it; and against the former by keeping in regular touch with his principal and thereby assuring himself of his continued existence and sanity. Incidentally, the agent can protect himself against his principal's death, etc., still further by obtaining from him a sealed power of attorney which expressly absolves him from liability for such breach of warranty actions; the deceased's estate becomes liable in his stead.

LIABILITY TO THIRD PARTIES IN TORT

Where an agent commits a tort while furthering the interests of his principal. If the agent commits a fraud, assault, negligence, or any other tort, it is primarily the agent who is responsible to the injured third party. More important to the injured third party, though, is the fact that a principal has vicarious liability for an agent's torts. That is to say, if the agent commits a tort while furthering the interests of his principal (e.g., by committing a misrepresentation), the principal can also be held responsible. A blameless principal who has had to make good to a third party the losses caused by his agent has the legal right afterwards to demand reimbursement from the culpable agent (the right of *subrogation*).

If the tort in question was a fraudulent misrepresentation by the agent which induced a contract, the third party is entitled not only to damages but also to repudiate the contract in question. If the agent committed merely an innocent misrepresentation, the third party's only right is to have the contract rescinded, without being entitled to damages.

At this point it is worthwhile to consider the *independent contractor*. He is neither a servant or agent but someone in business for himself who contracts to do a certain job, usually at a stated price, within a definite time and according to certain specifications. He alone, and nobody else, is responsible for injuries inflicted on third parties by himself or by those working for him. Only where the job to be done is one of an inherently dangerous nature (such as the handling of explosives, wild animals, etc.) might the person engaging the services of the independent contractor also be held liable to the third party.

Where the agent commits a tort beyond the scope of his employment. In such cases, the principal is free of any liability to the injured third party; unless, of course, he subsequently ratifies the agent's tort expressly or by implication (e.g., by taking a benefit resulting from the agent's tort). Of course, any contract resulting from such an independent tort of the agent can be repudiated by the third party, and the agent alone is responsible for damages to him.

LIABILITY TO THIRD PARTIES IN CRIMES

A principal is not liable to punishment for any crimes committed by his agent, on or off the job, unless he can be proven to have been an accomplice. An exception is the violation by the agent of minor traffic regulations while driving his principal's motor vehicle.

DUTIES OF A PRINCIPAL TO HIS AGENT

An express contract of agency (whether written or oral) between principal and agent may spell out the terms between them very concisely. However, many agency contracts come into existence quite informally; in which case the following rules take the place of a formal contract between the parties:

1. The principal is to abide by the terms and provisions (whether express, customary, or implied) of the contract.

2. The principal is to pay the agent whatever remuneration (often in the form of a commission) has been agreed upon between them; or failing which, a rate that is customary in that field of endeavour; or failing which, an amount that is reasonable under the circumstances. At common law, the agent becomes entitled to his reward as soon as he has performed his share of the bargain (e.g., by introducing to his principal a "willing and able customer"—a financially responsible buyer who has placed an order on the selling principal's terms). It is common practice, however, for clauses to be included in contracts according to which the agent becomes entitled to his commission not when he books the order but at a later stage, which might be:

(a) When the seller accepts the order; or

(b) When the seller ships the goods; or

(c) When the seller has received payment from the buyer.

3. The principal is to indemnify the agent for all his expenses, losses, and liabilities properly incurred in the performance of his duties—in others words, he is to honour the agent's expense account.

4. Where appropriate, the principal must render accounts to the agent. This is of particular importance to a selling agent covering a

173

particular territory, from which customers frequently place orders directly with the principal.

A reputable firm will not "short-circuit" its agents; that is, it will credit each agent with commissions for all orders originating from his territory, even though they were placed directly and not through him. The agent should be supplied with copy invoices of all shipments made to his customers; and with regular "commission statements" indicating in detail with how much he has been credited in the way of commissions; also, commission payments should be made to him at regular intervals.

For the protection of the agent, he has a common law right of *lien* on *all* goods of his principal that are properly in his possession. This means that he can withhold all such goods from his principal until the principal has met his financial obligations to his agent. As a last resort, the agent may even sell these goods in satisfaction of his claims against his principal. While the right of lien certainly covers any expenditures the agent has incurred on behalf of his principal, it is not completely established whether it extends to his claims for any unpaid commissions.

DUTIES OF AN AGENT TO HIS PRINCIPAL

The overriding point to keep in mind in this connection is that an agency contract is one of the *utmost good faith* and that a *fiduciary* relationship exists. In ordinary contracts the parties are said to be dealing with one another "at arm's length"; which means that they are legally (though not morally) entitled to get away with almost murder, as long as they violate no law. In other words, they are entitled to take advantage of legal loopholes. An agent, on the other hand, must be completely loyal to the principal he serves, and he must take no action that might harm his principal's interests in any way. Thus, the following rules of conduct apply, which can be changed by an express contract term only where specifically indicated:

1. The agent is to carry out his duties and follow the instructions contained in the express or implied contract or in a customary manner. Conversely it follows that he is not to act contrary to the authority entrusted to him nor to exceed the extent of this authority. If the agent

violates this condition and by use of his "apparent authority" thereupon burdens the principal with an unfavourable contract with a third party, the principal can look to the agent to make good any loss his conduct has occasioned.

2. The agent is expected to possess and to exercise the skills he claims to possess. Thus, a professedly expert salesman can be let go at once if he produces no results; as can a broker who is unfamiliar with the commodity in which he deals; or a lawyer who knows no law. The latter, in fact, can be sued for losses resulting from his professional negligence.

3. The agent must exercise the care and skill that can reasonably be expected from a normally conscientious person. Even if an agency is undertaken gratuitously (without reward), the agent exposes himself to a negligence suit if a violation of this requirement results in loss to his principal.

4. Since notices sent to an agent are constructively held to be notices to the principal, it is the agent's duty to keep his principal promptly advised of any such notices he has received. As an example, an apartment house supervisor must inform the owners promptly whenever a tenant gives him the required amount of notice of his intention to vacate his apartment. The agent must also keep his principal informed of any other developments which could be to his interest.

5. An agent must not delegate his duties to anyone else except:
(a) With the principal's consent; or
(b) Where this is customary (e.g., a lawyer will obviously delegate many of his routine duties to clerks); or
(c) In an emergency.
The reason for this restriction is that a contract of agency is typically one of personal services which, it will be remembered, may generally be assigned only with the other party's consent.

6. Just as the principal must render accounts to his agent, so the agent must make an accounting to his principal for all moneys that have been advanced to him or which he has received on his principal's account. Agents who habitually receive moneys on behalf of their principals (lawyers, realtors, collection agencies) should, and sometimes must, open separate "clients' bank accounts" into which to deposit such receipts, in order not to be guilty of *intermingling*

their own funds with those of their principals. The agent must advise his principal even of "windfalls"—receipts which are only remotely connected with his principal's interests. An example might be a $100 prize which the branch manager of a chain store wins from the local chamber of commerce in a "most original window display" contest. The agent must also make prompt remittances to his principal of moneys received on his account.

7. Since agency contracts are of the utmost good faith, an agent's own interests must never conflict with those of his principal. If there ever arise such conflicting interests, the agent must immediately inform his principal of them. The following are important examples of conflicting interests:

(a) If the agent has been instructed to purchase something for his principal, he must not sell to his principal, *without full disclosure of the surrounding facts*, goods which actually belong to the agent or to a person or company in which the agent has a personal or financial interest. This rule applies even if the goods to be sold are, in the agent's belief, the best and the cheapest available; the reason is that what is best for the principal is to be decided not by the agent but by the principal. It is against human nature (unfortunately) for an agent to do his very best for his principal if he has a personal ax of some sort to grind. Similarly, the agent for a selling principal must not buy from the principal for himself, or any associate, without disclosing particulars of the transaction to his principal.

(b) An agent (e.g., for a manufacturer) must not carry a competing line of goods without his principal's consent. However, trade custom may allow an agent to "round out his line" with goods from another manufacturer; for instance, by carrying another manufacturer's cheap line along with his principal's quality goods (e.g., a luxury car dealer perhaps also selling English small cars).

(c) The agent must not make any secret profits; such as, utilizing his principal's business premises to carry on a profitable side line of his own.

(d) The agent must not accept what is called a "second commission"; namely, a secret payment, tantamount to a bribe, from the third party. The receiving of such payment by a purchasing agent from an eager seller is popularly called a "kickback"; while an eager purchaser of scarce goods is said to "slip something under the counter" to the seller's agent.

CONSEQUENCES OF VIOLATING THE DUTIES OF AN AGENT

The consequences of an agent's violating any of the above provisions are as follows:

1. The principal can at once terminate the agency contract, as on any other breach of contract.

2. The agent forfeits any commission in connection with such dealings.

3. The principal becomes entitled to any secret profit the agent made or any bribes he received.

4. The principal can repudiate any contract with third parties closed under these circumstances. Alternatively, he has the choice of letting the contract stand and suing the agent and/or the third party for any loss suffered; for example, if the principal bought at too high a price, he can sue for the excess he paid over the market price.

5. Since taking a bribe is illegal, the agent cannot take to court a third party who breaks his promise to pay the agent his second commission.

6. The agent and the third party are exposed to a criminal prosecution for offering and receiving a secret commission.

TERMINATION OF AGENCY

An agency contract comes to an end in the same manner as other contracts: namely, by performance or by mutual agreement (e.g., at the end of a stated term or project; at the end of a stipulated notice period; after a breach of contract by one party; or by impossibility of performance). Since agency is a personal matter, death or insanity of either party ends the contract automatically; so does the bankruptcy of the principal and also the bankruptcy of the agent unless his financial strength is completely irrelevant.

It will bear repeating here that an agent, who continues to act for his principal after the latter's incapacity or death, renders himself liable to the third party under the agent's *implied warranty of authority*, even if ignorant of the unfortunate event, unless protected by a

177

properly worded power of attorney.

It should be noted that, contrasted to a contract of employment, an agency contract can be terminated by either party *at once,* without either party having to give the other any notice, *unless*:

1. The agency contract expressly stipulated a certain period of time for the agency or a specified length of notice to be given; or

2. A power of attorney under seal declared the agency to be irrevocable by the principal for a specified period of time; or

3. The agent had given the principal valuable consideration to receive the agency; or

4. The agent is still unabsolved from some personal liability he undertook in his capacity as agent (e.g., to pay to one of his principal's creditors a debt he was to collect from one of his principal's customers).

At this final point the importance should again be stressed of notifying third parties by mail, in the *Gazette,* or in the press of the termination of an agency, or of the limitation of an agent's powers. Otherwise, as we have learned, the ex-agent can continue to bind his principal by implied authority.

QUESTIONS

1. (a) Make up an example of an agent acting with apparent, rather than with actual, authority.
   (b) What is the effect on the parties involved?
2. Make up an example of an agent being appointed by ratification.
3. What is meant by, and what are the consequences of, an agent's breach of warranty of authority?
4. O'Keefe has some land for sale. His competitor, Molson, wishes to buy it, but he knows that O'Keefe would not sell it to him. How could Molson use an agent to acquire the land from O'Keefe?
5. An agent receives 5% commission on all sales that he makes for his firm. During one month he books $20,000 worth of orders, and his firm ships $15,000 worth of goods to the customers. Of these, $1,000 worth of goods are taken back by the firm from a dissatisfied customer. Explain how much commission the agent will probably receive.
6. State whether each of the following statements is *true* or *false*; also

give the reasons for your answers.

(a) If a principal revokes the contract with his agent, the agent should at once notify interested third parties.

(b) If an agent makes a secret profit, the principal's legal claim is to 50% of such profit.

(c) A minor is entitled to act as an agent for an adult.

(d) A minor is bound by all contracts entered into for him by his adult agent.

(e) *Del credere* contracts must be in writing.

(f) A power of attorney is an agent's written authority.

(g) If an agent has worked double time, he is entitled to a second commission.

(h) An agent is allowed to sell his own goods to his principal without the latter's consent if the goods are exactly what the principal required.

(i) The powers of a special agent are greater than those of a general agent.

(j) An agent is entitled to deduct his unpaid expenses from the proceeds of a sale before remittance to his principal.

(k) A principal may legally repudiate all contracts made for him.

(l) An agent can be held personally liable to third parties for some contracts made by him.

(m) An agent can be held liable personally for all torts and crimes committed by him.

CHAPTER SIXTEEN

Absolute Sales
of Personal Property

SALE OF GOODS ACT

More frequent even than contracts of employment are the transactions known as sales, whereby ownership is transferred from one party to another on payment of a price or a money consideration. Many things can be sold: land, securities, services, and goods. This chapter is devoted purely to the sale of tangible moveable goods (or chattels), the law regarding which has been codified in all common law territories in virtually identical Sale of Goods Acts. None of the Sale of Goods Acts covers transactions involving any of the following:

- Real property (land, houses, etc.).
- Barter; that is, the exchange of goods. Since, as will be remembered, writing is required for *sales of goods* of $40 or more, lack of writing is no hindrance to bringing actions involving the barter of goods of far greater value. However, the Sale of Goods Acts cover transactions where part of the consideration consists of money; for example, when trading in your old car for a new one and paying for the difference in cash.
- Consignment sales; that is, the shipment of goods to a retailer (often one's factor, or mercantile agent) with instructions to sell as many of them as possible. Although this retailer has no title to the goods, he has the right to pass title to the person who buys from him. (In fact—see footnote on p. 181—with his apparent ownership he has the power to pass title even to unauthorized persons.) The retailer will eventually return to his supplier the goods he has not been able to sell. He must, of course, make payment for the goods that he has been successful in selling.

180

- Mortgages and pledges: where the article changing hands is not intended to change ownership permanently.
- Bailments: where only possession, but not ownership, changes hands (discussed in more detail later).
- Paper money, bonds, and other securities that have no intrinsic value.
- Materials that are supplied incidentally to fulfilling a contract of labour. Thus, $100 worth of parts used in doing $300 worth of repairs to a wrecked car is not regarded as a sale of goods under the Act.

TITLE

According to the Sale of Goods Act, a sale takes place the moment *title* (or legal ownership, as contrasted to mere physical possession) to the goods passes from the seller to the buyer. The question of who has title is very important because:

1. Unless it is expressly otherwise agreed between the parties, the *risk of loss goes with the ownership*; that is to say, if an article is lost, stolen or damaged, its owner will have to suffer the loss.

2. Only the owner can pass ownership to another;[1] and if two parties claim ownership to an article, he will prevail who obtained title from the true owner. Thus, an unwitting buyer from a thief of a stolen article can be made to return it to the person from whom it was stolen. (In England, but not in Canada, a person buying a stolen article in *market overt*—an establishment customarily trading in goods of that nature—obtains good title to it as against the true owner. The only reason why Canadian pawnbrokers are not generally made to return to their true owners, without charge, stolen articles of small value that have been pawned with them is because the owners usually cannot give positive identification of their belongings—such as the serial number of a watch, camera, etc.)

The above two points seem to be labouring the obvious; and so they

---

1 This rule is subject to an important exception: if the true owner has vested apparent ownership in another, without taking proper safeguards (as will be discussed later), the buyer from such apparent owner will obtain good title. Examples of "apparent owners" are a mercantile agent, a mortgagor, a buyer under a conditional sale, or a seller with whom possession had been left—not, however, a thief: the owner did not vest him with ownership of anything; the thief *took* it.

would, if the question of ownership were always clearly determinable. A contract of sale can, and often does, state expressly at what particular moment title is to pass. Frequently this is done by commercial jargon, or by abbreviations such as *F.O.B. cars point of origin,* or *C.I.F. RR station of destination.*

The first quotation means free on board the train in the seller's town: that is, as soon as the goods have been loaded, the buyer becomes the owner, unless the contract expressly provides otherwise. He becomes responsible for any losses suffered, and he is entitled to compensation against the party responsible for damage to the goods. He is liable henceforth for any transportation and other charges in connection with the goods. He is now entitled to pass title of the goods to others (e.g., by endorsing a bill of lading made out to his order).[2]

The C.I.F. quotation means that ownership is to pass at the seller's freight depot as above, but that the seller will also pay the freight charges to the buyer's town, will take out insurance coverage on behalf of the buyer, and will make an all-inclusive charge to the buyer for the cost (of the merchandise), insurance, and freight charges.[3]

Where the buyer arranges for his own insurance, he will request the seller to make him a C. & F. quotation.

On an F.O.B. point of destination quotation, the seller would bear all risks and be responsible for all expenditures until the buyer took ownership in his own town.

Just as often, however, the parties fail to stipulate expressly when and where title is to pass. In such cases the Sale of Goods Act sets out the following rules to cover the many various situations:

Where the goods are "specific"; that is clearly identified, and—

1. If the goods are in a deliverable condition. In this case title passes at the moment of the *closing of the contract*; in other words, as soon as the valid offer is unequivocally accepted. This is the law, even if payment and delivery do not take place immediately. Thus, if I contract today to buy some goods which are to be delivered next week

---

[2] This quotation is one of the lowest a seller makes; the buyer must calculate on his own the freight and insurance costs.

[3] A C.I.F. quotation by the seller is obviously much higher, but the buyer then knows exactly what his "laid down" cost for the goods will be.

and to be paid for next month, *I become their owner today*. If they are stolen or damaged without the seller's negligence, I shall have to suffer their loss; that means I shall have to pay the seller for them next month (if I was wise, my insurance policy will cover me); though reputable firms will have their own insurance policy cover such customers' goods free of charge. On the other hand, I shall be entitled to sell the goods for cash to someone else as soon as I obtain them on credit next week. (It should be emphasized again that the above rules apply only if the parties neglected to make an express agreement to the contrary.)

2. If the specific goods have yet to be put into a deliverable condition (e.g., the tailor has to adjust the cuff lengths on a pair of slacks he has just sold). In this situation title passes as soon as the goods have been put into proper deliverable condition and have either been sent to the buyer, or the customer has been informed that the goods were ready for delivery or to be picked up.

3. If the price of the specific goods has yet to be determined by weighing, measuring, counting, valuation, etc. Then title does not pass until such weighing, measuring, counting, valuation, etc., has taken place. For example, suppose that a rich philatelist has fallen in love with a friend's stamp, and the sale is to take place at catalogue value; title passes when a catalogue is obtained and the price looked up in it. Or, a housewife picks out a nice turkey, priced at 50 cents a pound. If a dog makes off with it before it has been weighed, the butcher will have to stand the loss; if after, the housewife will. The same would be true for a bunch of bananas priced at 5 cents each or a remnant of cloth at $10 a yard.

4. If the goods at the seller's suggestion have been taken by the buyer on *approval*. In this case title passes when the goods have been approved by the buyer. Such approval can be either express or implied:
(a) Express approval takes place when the buyer tells or writes the seller that he approves the goods and will keep them, or if he pays for them.
(b) Implied approval is indicated in one of two ways:
  (i) By some positive action of the buyer: such as placing the article into use; or by consuming it; or by selling or pawning it; or by giving it away; or even by dismantling or de-

183

stroying it—this being something a person would not do except to goods he regards as his own.

    (ii) Approval is also implied if the buyer keeps the goods beyond the agreed upon (failing which, a reasonable) trial period. The following situation is a common example: if goods are taken on a ten-day "approval or return" basis, the buyer must return them within the ten days if he does not want them; otherwise he will have to pay for them. Note, that these rules apply only if the buyer wanted to take the goods on this basis (e.g., by filling out a coupon). If they were sent to him without his request, the buyer falls under no obligation if he fails to return the goods.

    This method of purchase is not as common as it used to be in retailing, due to the general policy of most reputable stores to accept the return of sold goods on a virtual "no questions asked" basis.

Where the goods are as yet "unascertained." Examples of unascertained goods are goods that have not yet been manufactured, grown, or bought; for instance, a suit to be made to measure, or the future crop of a certain field, or goods that the seller is importing. Ownership to these unascertained "future goods" passes as soon as they become ascertained or specific by their being manufactured, grown, or acquired by the seller—without, be it noted, notice of these events having to be sent to the buyer.

    Another large category of unascertained goods is goods bought by description (e.g., from a catalogue and/or price list), or by sample. As an example of buying by sample, suppose that you compare radio sets in a store and decide on a Commodore table model No. XYZ-1234. You will expect to receive not the floor model (the sample) but a brand new one just like it, still in its original carton. Ownership passes when the unascertained carton (or other goods) has been made specific by:

    1. Separating it from the bulk (i.e., from its identical mates); and

    2. Doing something final to it so that it will be impossible to replace it with another. Such irretrievable conduct takes place if:

(a) The buyer selects one article which he likes better than the others; or

184

(b) The seller, at the buyer's request, makes such a selection; or

(c) The buyer's name is engraved on the article, or some other custom job is effected on it; or

(d) The article is entrusted to a public carrier (the mails, or a freight company) for delivery to the buyer.

The seller's unilateral action of tying or sticking a "sold" tag with the customer's name on the article is not sufficient ascertainment since there is nothing to prevent the seller from removing the tag afterwards and letting the customer have another identical article. Thus, if the article is stolen, or damaged without anyone's fault, the seller of the, as yet, unascertained article will have to bear its loss.

DELIVERY AND PAYMENT

Once the sale has been completed, the seller must "deliver" the goods (he must let the buyer have them), and the buyer must accept the goods and pay for them. If there is an express contract, it will provide for the time and place of delivery and payment. If there is no express contract, the Sale of Goods Act makes the following provisions:

Place of delivery. The buyer must pick up the goods at the seller's place of business (or home, or wherever else they are known to be) and make his own transportation and insurance arrangements. (It is well known, however, that most large stores customarily make free delivery to the purchaser's address within specified limits.)

Time of delivery. Goods must be delivered by the seller and taken up by the buyer within a reasonable time. If delivery or acceptance is delayed through the fault of one party, any damage to the goods is at his risk, even though he is not their owner. Any clearly specified delivery time is of the essence of the contract, and the buyer is technically excused from accepting late deliveries; but this stringent requirement is frequently waived among business friends.

Unless specifically otherwise agreed upon or customary, shipment should be made of the whole order at once. In other words, the seller may not make shipments in instalments (by constantly "back-ordering" items), nor may the buyer call for delivery in driblets.

Right of disposal. We have heard that ownership of unascertained goods frequently passes when they are delivered to a carrier. To protect himself against poor credit risks, a seller can retain the right of disposal (postpone the passing of title) by the following means:

1. Shipping the goods by his own truck, instead of by a public carrier.

2. Shipping the goods C.O.D. (collect on delivery). (Incidentally, a customer who refuses to accept a satisfactory C.O.D. shipment he has ordered, technically commits a breach of contract.)

3. Shipping the goods under a bill of lading made out to the order of the seller himself or of his agent, who is often a branch or a correspondent in the buyer's town of the seller's bank. By this method the order bill of lading (which is not only a contract between the shipping seller and the carrier, but also a document of title) is not endorsed (like a cheque) over to the buyer until he has made satisfactory arrangements for payment of the goods; for example, by paying cash or by signing his "acceptance" to a draft (see Chapter 22, Negotiable Instruments).

This method is called variously a *documentary draft* or an *order bill of lading* with draft attached. The terms of payment would be quoted *S/D-D.O.P.,* meaning Sight Draft, Documents to be endorsed to buyer On Payment; or *S/D-D/A*, meaning Sight Draft, Documents against Acceptance (of draft by buyer).

By thus retaining his right of disposal over the goods until they are paid for, the seller retains title to them and may sell them to someone else if the original buyer will not pay for them.

Improper delivery. What happens if the seller sends the buyer too many, or too few, of the ordered goods, or if he sends him the wrong goods? In that case the buyer is "in the driver's seat." He may accept the shipped goods, or he may send them all back; or he may pick out the contracted items and return the others. He must, of course, pay the contract price for all the goods he decides to accept.

Payment. Unless credit or prepayment is expressly otherwise agreed upon or customary, cash payment should take place simultaneously with taking delivery of the goods.

If no price has been expressly fixed, the customary or a reasonable price must be paid. To avoid dispute as to which party is to pay the costs of special packing, postage, insurance, customs duties, etc., it is strongly recommended that these points be specifically dealt with by

186

the parties when reaching an agreement on the price.

Time of payment, incidentally, is *not* of the essence of a contract of sale. If a buyer makes payment later than he has promised, the seller may not terminate the contract by taking back the goods; all he can do is to charge the buyer interest and to be more careful when extending credit terms next time, or sue for payment.

CONDITIONS AND WARRANTIES

We have previously learned that any contract may be avoided that was entered into as a result of the other party's previous misrepresentation, whether innocent or fraudulent. A sales contract may further be rescinded by the buyer if the seller breaks an important promise he made to the buyer at the time of the sale regarding the goods in question. This is called the *breach of a contract condition,* as we learned in Chapter 11 under Breaches of Contract; while the breach of a less vital contract term is called a *breach of warranty.* Many such conditions and warranties can be expressly placed in a contract; but there are others that are impliedly present in all contracts of sale, unless expressly negatived in the contract.

Express conditions and warranties. These are incorrectly called "guarantees" in popular language (e.g., "these articles are guaranteed not to shrink or fade"). The following points should be noted regarding express conditions and warranties:

1. If a contract is in writing, a verbal warranty is ineffective.

2. A warranty (even if in writing) given *after* the closing of the contract, is ineffective unless it is under seal, or unless some fresh consideration is given.

3. If a warranty is given even after the buyer drew the seller's attention to an apparent defect in the goods ("This harness looks pretty weak to me." "Don't worry sir. It will do the job satisfactorily.") such a warranty is binding on the seller; he will not be allowed to plead *caveat emptor.*

Implied conditions and warranties. The conditions and warranties implied by the Sale of Goods Act are the following:

1. There is an implied condition that the seller is the true owner of the goods and has the right to sell them; or at least that he will have

187

that right when it comes time to pass title. In other words, if the true owner of stolen goods (which you bought from the thief) makes you return the goods to him, you can sue the thief for breach of this implied condition.

2. There are implied warranties as to *quiet enjoyment* and *possession*. In other words, the seller undertakes that he will not become a nuisance to you in connection with the sold goods and that he has not given the right to use your goods to anyone else.

3. The implied warranty as to *freedom from encumbrance* means that there is nothing owing on the goods sold to you.

4. An implied condition as to merchantable quality exists only in special cases. Normally, particularly if the buyer has an opportunity to inspect the goods he buys, there is no such condition, but the rule of *caveat emptor* applies. The following are the circumstances where the condition of merchantable quality is implied:

(a) Where the buyer explains to the seller what goods he requires and the exact purpose for which he requires them, and intimates to the seller that he is relying on the seller's judgment, then the goods recommended by a regular dealer in such products must be reasonably satisfactory and fit for the specified purpose. In other words, if a dealer knows that his judgment is being relied upon, the goods he sells must do a fair job.

However, if the buyer exercises his own judgment without asking the seller's advice, he has no claim against the seller if the goods prove unsatisfactory; for example, if a buyer buys a light car which fails to pull a heavy trailer up a steep hill. Similarly, the seller is under no liability if the buyer asks for an article by its brand or patent name. Thus, a druggist is under no liability if a customer bought aspirins which failed to remove his corns, as he had hoped.

Of course, the manufacturer of faulty goods bought by brand name can still be held accountable for the tort of negligence if they injure the user.

In many circumstances it is not necessary for the customer to indicate the purpose of the goods. For example, if I buy food from a regular dealer in groceries, it is taken for granted that I am buying it to be eaten, and it is implied that it is not spoiled and that it contains no foreign substances (e.g., nails in cakes; mice in bottled drinks).

(b) If goods are bought by description (e.g., from a catalogue or an advertisement) and/or by sample (e.g., the floor model of an appliance; the fruit displayed in the showcase of a store), there is an implied condition that the goods will correspond with the description and sample and that they will be of merchantable quality (i.e., be reasonably suited for what is normally expected of them). An article shown to a buyer must be clearly stipulated as a sample for this rule to apply.

RIGHT OF INSPECTION.   Before having to accept the goods, the buyer must be given the opportunity of comparing the goods supplied to him with the previously furnished description and/or sample. If they do not match both, he may reject the goods. On inspection the defects must, of course, be discoverable. If they are latent (coming to light only later), the buyer regains the right of rejection when the defects become apparent.

REMEDIES OF THE BUYER FOR BREACH OF SALES CONTRACT

For non-delivery of goods by the seller the buyer's remedies are:

1. Naturally, the buyer need not pay for non-delivered goods (nor, as we have seen, for non-accepted late-delivered goods).

2. In the case of non-delivered specific goods that are unique and non-replaceable, the buyer may sue for specific performance.

3. He can sue the seller for damages.

(a) If he has a chance of buying similar goods elsewhere, he can sue the seller for the difference between the contract price and the actual price he had to pay in the "available market"; that is, the going rate if he "bought in" promptly plus any necessary expenses incurred thereby.

(b) If there is no "available market," he can sue the seller for the loss of the normal profit he would have made on reselling the article. Furthermore, if he had previously informed the seller of some unusual profit he stood to make as a consequence of the sale, he could recover even this.

For breach of warranty. If the buyer has already paid the seller, he can sue for damages to compensate him for any loss he has suffered

189

by the breach. This includes restitution to the buyer of any damages he may have had to pay his customers for a similar breach of warranty committed by him.

If the buyer has not yet paid the seller, he can use the loss suffered by the breach of warranty as a defense (set-off) against the seller's claim for the price of the goods.

The injured buyer cannot rescind the contract for breach of warranty.

For breach of condition. The buyer may refuse to accept the goods (sometimes he may even return them), and he may sue for damages as above. Alternatively, as we have previously learned, he may decide to accept the goods and to treat the broken condition as a breach of warranty.

After acceptance of the goods, it is too late to reject them, even if there has been a breach of condition. If defective goods could have been inspected but were not, and the defect is afterwards discovered, the buyer must treat the breach of condition merely as a breach of warranty. Acceptance, in this sense of the word, means "showing satisfaction" with the goods by:

1. Using them; or
2. Reselling them; or
3. Keeping them beyond a reasonable time, without notifying the seller of dissatisfaction with them.

REMEDIES OF THE SELLER, NOT WHOLLY PAID

Having both title and possession. Where the seller still has title to the goods and also has them in his possession, his remedies are as follows:

1. If the buyer wants delivery of the goods before the contracted date, the seller may, of course, withhold delivery.

2. If the buyer refuses to accept the goods and to pay for them, he can be sued for damages.

Having neither title nor possession. Where the seller no longer owns or possesses the goods, his remedies are as follows:

1. If the buyer has the goods and refuses to pay for them on the due date, he can be sued for their full price. Having lost the ownership, the seller has no right to get the goods back, unless this right was expressly reserved to him in the contract. If the seller voluntarily

agrees to take back the goods from the buyer, he can sue the buyer for damages as above, instead of for the full price.

2. If the goods have not yet reached the buyer's place of business or home but are in transit to him, the seller—although he no longer owns or possesses the goods—has the ancient right of stopping them in transit, if the buyer *has become insolvent*. If the carrier's contract was made with the seller, the seller can demand the return of the goods to him. If the original contract was made by the carrier with the buyer, the seller still has the right to instruct the carrier to stop delivery to the buyer. If the carrier disobeys these instructions, and loss results to the seller thereby, the carrier will be responsible to make good the loss. On the other hand, if the seller issued such stoppage instructions improperly (e.g., the buyer was not actually insolvent) and loss resulted to the buyer thereby, the seller would have to make good such loss to the buyer.

Insolvency means an actual disability to meet one's payment obligations as they fall due. Therefore a seller is not entitled to stop goods solely on the grounds that the buyer is suspected of becoming insolvent; nor, if he learns too late that the buyer has very poor payment habits.

This right, as has been said, may be exercised only if the goods are still "in transit." This does not mean that they have to be actually in motion; if they are standing on a siding or warehoused en route, they are technically in transit. They cease to be in transit as soon as the buyer has been sent notification by the carrier that the goods are ready to be picked up by him.

After receiving orders to stop the goods, the carrier need not unload the goods in the middle of a haul. He is entitled to carry the goods to their point of destination (and to make his regular charge for this carriage) as long as he does not let the goods fall into the hands of the buyer.

Having possession, but no title. Where the seller is no longer the legal owner but still has physical possession (e.g., where specific deliverable goods have been sold for later delivery and payment), his remedies are as follows:

1. If the buyer changes his mind about the goods and does not wish to accept them or to pay for them, he can be sued for their full price;

the seller must, of course, have tendered delivery of the goods to the buyer at the agreed-upon time and place.

2. If the buyer wants to take the goods without paying for them, the seller has the *right of lien* on the goods (title to which goods technically rests in the buyer); that is, he need not let the buyer have them if:

(a) The contract specified payment on delivery; or

(b) The agreed-upon credit deadline had expired; or

(c) The buyer, though granted credit terms originally, had become insolvent.

This right of lien is lost and cannot be recovered by the seller once he has delivered the goods to the buyer or to a public carrier; even if he later happens to get possession of them again. He does not lose this right if the buyer takes the goods forcibly or secretly.[4]

3. The seller also has the *right of resale* over the goods which he retained under his right of lien: if the goods are perishable, he may resell them at once. In other cases he must first give the buyer notice of his intention to resell and then wait a reasonable time for the customer to pay the price and all accrued expenses occasioned by his tardiness. On reselling the goods, the seller must try to obtain the best possible price from the new buyer (who becomes the true owner of the goods); while the defaulting first buyer can be made to pay damages for any loss suffered by the seller.

The seller naturally also has the right to resell goods in the following circumstances:

(a) Goods which were not accepted by the buyer.

(b) When the right to resell was expressly reserved to the seller in the contract.

(c) When the goods were stopped in transit.

(d) After the seller has exercised his right of disposal.

4. Where the seller has been asked to delay delivery of sold goods, he can start charging the buyer storage if the goods are not picked up

---

[4] In a curious case it was held that a buyer has no right of lien. A buyer wanted a refund from a store for goods which he claimed were unsatisfactory. The store was willing to entertain his claim, provided the customer let them have the disputed goods for examination. The customer insisted on retaining them as security until his demands were met. The court found that he was entitled to no refund unless he complied with the store's very reasonable request.

within the agreed-upon, or within a reasonable, length of time.

Having title, but no possession. Where the seller is still the legal owner but has given up possession of the goods, his remedies are as follows:

1. *Sale on approval.* At the expiry of the stipulated trial period, the seller is entitled to full payment of the goods sent out on approval.

2. The other important instance under this heading, namely the *conditional instalment sale*, is dealt with in the next chapter.

QUESTIONS

1. Explain when title passes to the buyer
   (a) On an absolute sale of deliverable, ascertained goods.
   (b) On an absolute sale of ascertained goods, not yet in a deliverable state.
2. List and explain the important conditions and warranties that are implied in an absolute sale of goods.
3. A stamp company sends a collector $100 worth of stamps on eight days' "approval or return." As soon as the collector gets the stamps, he pawns them for $60. When the stamp company learns of this, it wants to get the stamps back from the pawnbroker. Explain the stamp company's legal rights.
4. "Ownership of unascertained goods passes to the buyer when the goods have become specific." Explain this statement.
5. Discuss the rights and remedies of the unpaid seller in an absolute sale of goods.
6. Allgood sold goods to Nogood on credit. On hearing of Nogood's insolvency, Allgood immediately instructed the railroad company not to deliver the goods to Nogood. As Nogood had already been notified of the arrival of the goods, the railroad company took no action, and Allgood eventually received 70 cents on the dollar from Nogood's trustee in bankruptcy. Explain to what extent Allgood can make the railroad company liable for his loss.

CHAPTER SEVENTEEN

Conditional Sales

THE INSTALMENT SYSTEM

Buying on the instalment system has become a way of life today all over the world. In England they call it buying on the "never-never plan" or more officially, under a *hire purchase agreement*: that is, the buyer is regarded as renting an appliance, car, etc., until he has made a certain number of specified payments; after which, the seller transfers ownership of the article to him. The purpose of this proceeding is to protect the seller by leaving him with title to the goods until he has been paid in full and entitling him to get his goods back if not paid in full.

STANDARD CONTRACT TERMS

The same result is achieved in North America under an almost identical contract called a *conditional sale,* the usual clauses of which are as follows:

No. 1 gives a full description of the goods and an acknowledgment of their receipt by the buyer.

No. 2 states the price and contains a promise by the buyer to pay it: (a) either at a certain future date; or (b) far more commonly, to pay it in specified instalments at stated future dates. Time is usually declared to be "of the essence," and the buyer is usually made to sign a *lien note*—a promissory note payable in instalments for the amount involved. An *acceleration clause* provides for *all* payments becoming payable forthwith, should any one payment be missed.

The above two clauses are obvious ones, common to all sales contracts. Breach by the buyer entitles the seller only to the stock remedy of suing the buyer for the price of the goods. It is the following clauses that give the seller additional privileges. Note that the seller is not automatically entitled to these; if he wants their benefit, he must reserve them in the contract, as follows:

No. 3 states that ownership of the goods is to remain with the seller, until the goods have been fully paid for. (Without this condition, after which this particular type of sale is called, ownership of goods would pass to the buyer at delivery, at the latest.)

No. 4: A person who is not the owner of the goods, but who is entitled only to their legal possession, is responsible for taking "reasonable care" of the goods in his possession. By this clause, the seller protects himself against accidental loss by placing full responsibility for the goods on the buyer, often making the buyer take out insurance for them, with the policy naming the seller as the beneficiary.

No. 5 states that the buyer, in case of non-payment, agrees to return the goods to the seller.

No. 6 gives the seller the important right, in case of non-payment, to enter the buyer's premises without rendering him liable to a trespass action, and to repossess the goods; that is, to take them away. It should be noted that, regardless how strongly the contract is worded in favour of the seller, the principles of common law will not allow a seller to repossess the goods forcibly. If the buyer resists him, the seller must request a *replevin* (recovery) order from the court which, when granted, can be carried out by the bailiff or sheriff's officer with as much force as is necessary under the circumstances.

No. 7 gives the seller the right, even after he has repossessed the goods, to keep in their entirety all the payments the debtor has so far made on them. This is not always as unfair as it seems, for it would probably have cost the buyer just as much to pay rental for the goods in question.

No. 8 gives the seller the right to resell the repossessed goods. Most of the provinces have a Conditional Sales Act, which usually requires the seller to wait twenty days before reselling in order to give the buyer that much time to redeem the goods; that is, to get them back by paying all the arrears together with interest and all the necessary expenses incurred by the seller in effecting repossession, etc.

No. 9 gives the seller the right to sue the buyer for any deficiency, provided the resale of the repossessed goods has not fully compensated the seller. (A fair contract will reciprocally entitle the buyer to receive from the seller any excess that the resale has realized over and above the seller's full claim to the unpaid balance and expenses as above.) Even then the seller will only be successful in his claim for the deficiency if:

(a) He made reasonable attempts to obtain as good a price as possible for the goods when reselling them; and

(b) (Applying only to goods costing over $30) he complied with the requirements of most provinces, according to which the buyer is entitled to receive a written notice of the contemplated resale five days before its occurrence, accompanied by an accurate, itemized break-down of the buyer's indebtedness.

No. 10 prohibits the buyer from removing the goods from his premises, without first notifying the seller or, in some cases, without first obtaining his consent. In the case of automobiles, this restriction usually extends to the province instead of to the buyer's premises.

PROVISIONS OF THE CONDITIONAL SALES ACT REGARDING TITLE

The conditional sale contract affords adequate protection to a seller should the buyer fail to keep up his payments. But it should be recalled that, by the act of entrusting the buyer with possession of the goods, the seller has *vested the buyer with apparent ownership* (see footnote 1 in Chapter 16, page 181); with the result that should the buyer—in violation of his agreement—sell or mortgage these goods to a genuinely innocent third party (one who has no knowledge or intimation of the antecedent conditional sale), then that third party would obtain title to the goods. The only remedy available to the original seller would be to sue the original buyer for the price of the goods.

To remedy this unsatisfactory state of affairs, all the previously referred to Conditional Sales Acts reserve title to the original seller as against the innocent third party, provided certain requirements are complied with. In Ontario they are as follows:

• The conditional sale agreement must be in writing and signed by the buyer. (A copy of it must be furnished to the buyer within twenty days. To comply with this requirement of the Act, a typical contract

196

contains an acknowledgment by the buyer that he has duly received his copy.)

• A copy of the agreement must be registered; that is, filed (for a small fee) in the offices of the buyer's County Court within ten days (and renewed every three years if necessary). If the seller has a good excuse for registering late, he is granted an extension of time.

• In spite of nonregistration, the seller of manufactured goods and of musical instruments enjoys protection provided he has affixed his name on the article prominently.

• Household furniture does not need even this last safeguard for its seller to be protected.

• Conditional sellers of goods to buyers who are in the business of selling them to retail customers do not enjoy any protection of this nature, even if they register.

The logical conclusion to be drawn from this legislation, by buyers at second hand of articles that are commonly the subject of conditional sales, is to check carefully that nothing is still owing on the goods. This can be done:

1. By checking (for a small fee) the Conditional Sales Registry in the County Court of the area in which the seller resides. Or

2. By checking with the person or firm whose name is imprinted or attached to the article, to find out whether it is fully paid for. The Act inflicts a penalty ($50 in Ontario) on such a person or firm, and on the person described in 3. below, if he refuses to give the desired information within five days. Or

3. By requiring the seller to show the buyer a receipt in full from his seller and then checking back with that original seller. If none of these investigations proves satisfactory, the rule of *caveat emptor* applies with a vengeance!

SUMMARY OF BUYER'S RIGHTS AND DUTIES

Any waiver by the buyer of his rights under the Conditional Sales Act is void and ineffective.

The buyer has the right to the full use of the goods so long as he keeps up his payments. He is responsible for taking only ordinary care of the goods, unless the contract imposed unrestricted responsibility on him for their safety.

He must not part with the goods irretrievably; for example, by selling or pawning them, or by changing them unrestorably (e.g., by converting a dining room suite into firewood, or a set of toy soldiers into lead bars). Nor may he take them elsewhere in breach of contract. If he does any of the above, he can be held criminally guilty of *fraudulent conversion*—a form of theft.

On full payment, the buyer becomes the absolute owner of the goods and is entitled to get from the seller a final receipt, release or discharge and the return of his honoured promissory note(s). Upon request, the seller should then also cancel any registration he effected against the buyer. If he neglects to do so, the buyer may cancel the registration by producing the discharged contract at the registry office.

SELLER'S RIGHTS

No other creditor of the buyer has a stronger claim against the goods than their seller; the only exception being the lien of an unpaid innkeeper into whose hotel the buyer brought these goods as a guest.

As soon as the buyer moves into another county, the seller should effect registration in its County Court to enjoy protection there too.

Fixtures. As we shall hear in the section on real estate, anything firmly affixed to the land becomes a part of it, and is known as a fixture. Even so, the owner of land to which a delinquent tenant has affixed goods bought "on time" does not become their owner until their seller has been fully paid (by the landlord, if not by the tenant). The conditional seller has the right to enter on the land and remove his fixture provided he has registered a notice of his conditional sale[1] against the real property and provided he repairs any damage he might do.

QUESTIONS

1. In a conditional sale contract, discuss the importance of inserting the following clauses:
   (a) That the buyer is to bear the full risk for any damage to the goods.

---

[1] In Ontario, there are presently studies being conducted into the revision of the Conditional Sales Act, including the possibility of province-wide registration rather than on a county basis.

   (b) That the seller is not to use any force in repossessing the goods.

   (c) That the seller is to wait twenty days before reselling the repossessed goods.

2. You have bought (and paid for) a new television set from a small appliance store. Several weeks later the set's manufacturers demand payment from you all over again, claiming that the set had been sold by them to the store under a conditional sale agreement which had been properly registered. Explain your legal position.

3. Explain how the Conditional Sales Act affords protection to the true owner against the person vested with apparent ownership of goods.

CHAPTER EIGHTEEN

Bills of Sale,
Chattel Mortgages,
and Bulk Sales

BILLS OF SALE

The piece of paper a buyer generally receives when making a purchase is a sales slip, sales ticket, or a receipt. The more formal *bill of sale* (often, but not necessarily, under seal and witnessed) is only required where the buyer needs official proof that he is the owner of the article he bought. This might be the case where the buyer leaves physical possession of the goods with the seller, for one reason or another.

Since this non-owning seller has been vested by the buyer with apparent ownership of the goods, the danger arises that the seller might try to sell or mortgage these goods to some third party. If this party is "innocent" (i.e., unaware of the surrounding circumstances), he would obtain title to the goods, as against their true owner. Most of the provinces have statutes (mostly called Bills of Sale and Chattel Mortgages Acts) which afford protection to the non-possessing true owner as follows. If:

1. The contract is in writing and signed by the seller.

2. A copy of the contract is registered in the offices of the County Court of the area in which the goods are. (In Ontario this must be done within five days and renewed every twelve months, if necessary.)

3. The document is accompanied by two affidavits:

(a) An affidavit by a witness attesting to the due execution of the bill of sale; and

(b) An affidavit by the buyer, swearing to the *bona fides* of the transaction; that is that he bought the goods for genuine consideration and that the transaction was not a mock one, entered into for the purpose of defeating the seller's creditors (by placing out of

200

their reach goods subject to execution, pursuant to a court judgment they may have obtained against the seller).

Thus a person who buys from the apparent owner an article against which a bill of sale has been properly registered, can be made to return it to its true owner. His only remedy will be to sue the apparent owner for damages for breach of the implied condition given by him that he had the right to sell the goods.

CHATTEL MORTGAGES

A *chattel mortgage* is a document given by a borrower (mortgagor) to a lender (mortgagee) which transfers ownership of goods to the mortgagee as security, until such a time as the loan is fully repaid. The mortgagor usually retains full physical possession and use of the goods and is thus their apparent owner. To protect himself against possible purchasers of the goods from the mortgagor without knowledge of the mortgage, the mortgagee must go through exactly the same registration procedure as the buyer under a bill of sale.

The clauses of a chattel mortgage are essentially the same as the ones in a conditional sale contract. The debtor agrees to make certain payments; and the creditor has the right, in case of nonpayment, to enter on the debtor's premises, to seize the goods, to sell them, and to sue the debtor for any deficiency. However, the Bills of Sale and Chattel Mortgages Acts impose no twenty-day waiting period on the creditor before selling the goods; instead, the debtor must be given a reasonable opportunity to redeem the goods. Further, the debtor can be sued for any deficiency resulting from the sale, without first having been given five days warning of the impending sale.

A standard clause in the chattel mortgage of a trader who mortgages his stock-in-trade, gives him permission to sell to customers in his normal course of business. However, he is required to replenish these stocks from his suppliers; the "substitute" stock is then automatically included in the mortgage.

Assignment. A mortgagee is allowed to sell (assign) his mortgage without the debtor's consent. In fact, it is standard practice for traders who sell on conditional sales and persons who grant credit against chattel mortgages to assign their claims to the so-called finance companies.

Similarly, the mortgagor may assign the mortgaged goods; that is, he may sell the goods to a third party, subject to the mortgage, of course. This means that a third party, buying mortgaged goods, must continue the payments on them or face the possibility of their being seized. He will have to make these payments even if he was unaware of the mortgage, provided a search of the Registry would have revealed its existence.

By selling the mortgaged goods, the original mortgagor does not completely become rid of his liability to the creditor; he remains liable under his *personal covenant*—his direct promise to the creditor to make payment.

Only under exceptional circumstances (e.g., if there is no market for the goods) will the Acts allow a mortgagee to keep seized goods. He must sell them as advantageously as possible; and to ensure this, he must not buy the goods at the sale himself or through a nominee.

Repayment. When the debt has been fully satisfied, the mortgage terms will entitle the mortgagor either:

1. To have the mortgage cancelled; or
2. To have ownership of the mortgaged goods retransferred to him.

The creditor will also have to arrange for the mortgage registration to be cancelled.

An important point regarding registrations should be noted here. Should a borrower mortgage his property to several different persons, *the one who registers his claim first has first claim against the property.*

Thus if debtor D borrows $500 on his car from A on Monday, $300 from B on Tuesday, and $100 from C on Wednesday—each creditor not knowing of the other's claim; and if C registers his claim on Wednesday, while B delays doing so until Thursday, and A until Friday, then C will have his claim satisfied first. Thus if the sale of the mortgaged car realizes but $350, C will get his $100, B will get $250, and A will be left with nothing but his claim against D under D's personal covenant.

BULK SALES

A bulk sale is not merely a sale in large quantities. It is said to take place when a merchant sells his entire inventory, or at least a large part of it, otherwise than in his normal course of business; or if a store sells its equipment or fixtures, or a plant its machinery. Also regarded as a bulk sale is the sale by a firm of an interest in its business (but not the sale by a partner of his own share in a business).

The Bulk Sales Act of most provinces affords protection to the creditors of a merchant who might make a bulk sale at ridiculously cheap prices and then run off with the proceeds, leaving the creditors with nothing concrete out of which to satisfy a court judgment they might obtain.

If, as the result of such a bulk sale, the creditors are not paid all their claims in full, they may, within six months from the sale, have the sale annulled by the court as fraudulent (with the consequence that, in effect, the creditors receive a mortgage on the goods that the buyer bought from the seller), unless certain procedures have been observed as set out below:

1. The buyer may safely pay the purchase price to the seller if a judge is satisfied that the sale is in the best interests of the creditors and issues a court order to the seller to that effect.

2. Otherwise, the buyer must obtain from the seller a list (sworn to by the seller in an affidavit as being correct in all particulars) of all his secured and unsecured creditors and full details of his indebtedness toward them.

(a) The buyer is then safe in paying the seller if:

    (i) The list shows that there is a total indebtedness of no more than $2,500 to all his unsecured creditors and a similar amount to all his secured creditors, and the buyer has no knowledge from his own sources of any larger indebtedness; or

    (ii) The seller swears in an affidavit that all his creditors have been paid in full; or

    (iii) The seller has made adequate provision for the full payment of all his creditors immediately after the sale; or

    (iv) All creditors sign waivers of their rights (i.e., authorize the buyer to pay the price to the seller).

(b) Under the following circumstances the buyer, while not safe in paying the seller, may pay the purchase price to a trustee[1] if:

(i) The seller delivers an affidavit to the buyer stating that he has delivered to all his creditors full particulars of the contemplated sale and also a true statement of his affairs; and

(ii) The formal consent to the sale is obtained from at least 60% (in number and value) of those unsecured creditors whose claims exceed $50.

3. In any case, the buyer is safe in paying the seller a deposit of not more than 10% of the purchase price without observing any of the above formalities.

The important thing to remember for a person who is about to buy a business as a going concern, is that the burden is on him to see that the seller's creditors are safeguarded, as above. If they are hurt by the buyer's failure to do so, ultimately he may have to suffer the loss.

QUESTIONS

1. (a) Under what circumstances should a bill of sale be required by a buyer of goods?

   (b) What formalities should accompany the receipt of a bill of sale?

2. A seller, wishing to retain the title to sold goods, can sell them either under a conditional sale contract, or he can sell them absolutely and have the buyer sign a chattel mortgage for them. Explain the advantages and the disadvantages of the two methods.

3. What are the principal remedies of the unpaid holder of a chattel mortgage?

4. (a) What is a bulk sale?

   (b) Whom does the Bulk Sales Act principally protect?

   (c) What are the principal duties imposed by the Act on the buyer?

---

[1] The trustee is appointed by the seller, with the approval of at least 60% (in number and value) of those unsecured creditors whose claims exceed $50. If this cannot be done, the judge appoints a trustee who is bonded and receives a fee (ranging from 5% to 2½%) for his services. The trustee then distributes the proceeds of the sale rateably, among the creditors as on a bankruptcy.

CHAPTER NINETEEN

Bailments of Personal Property

NATURE OF A BAILMENT

In a contract of *bailment* the owner of goods, the bailor, temporarily entrusts possession of them for some reason to another person, the bailee; but ownership in the goods does not pass to the other person.

Some transactions that look like bailments may be something else: for example, the pound of sugar a housewife "lends" her neighbour will not be returned in the original—therefore this deal was really an exchange, or barter. However, if grain is stored in a public elevator, the transaction is still a bailment even though the self same goods will not be returned; this rule applies to all "fungibles," or readily interchangeable commodities such as oil, pulp, etc. (all of the same grade, of course).

While the risk of loss or damage to goods normally falls on their owner, common law generally requires the person who has been entrusted with their possession (the bailee) to take "reasonable" care of them; that is, as much care as a normally prudent person (not a fussy one nor a sloppy one) would take of his own goods. The principal forms of bailment are treated separately below, and the bailor's and the bailee's common law duties in each are respectively listed. They are all, of course, subject to change by any special contract terms the parties choose to include.

HIRE OR RENTAL

A contract of this nature can extend from the rental of a student's typewriter for a month, to the lease by a manufacturer of an entire fleet of delivery trucks and salesmen's cars, or by an insurance company of a battery of computers. Leasing of equipment is becoming very popular lately because the entire rental can be properly deducted from income as an operating expense for income tax purposes; because the user always has the latest type of equipment; and because there are no unforeseen repair bills.

There are no repair bills because the bailor warrants the article to be reasonably fit for the purpose for which it is rented, throughout the length of the hire term. In addition, he is liable to the bailee for any damage caused to him as the result of any defects in the rented goods, where the bailor knew of the defects or where he could reasonably be expected to know of them. The bailor is not liable for hidden defects—defects which a careful inspection could not reveal.

This rule applies even though the bailee had an opportunity to inspect the goods, or if he actually examined them. A hire or rental is not a sale but a bailment, and therefore the rule of *caveat emptor* does not apply. In fact, the bailor is under a duty to warn the bailee of possible dangers in the use of the article in question—to the extent of the gratuitous bailor of an automobile jack having to draw the bailee's attention to the normal risks in its use!

Even though the bailor is the owner of the goods, he has no right to get them back from the bailee before the expiry of the rental term; unless the bailee, by committing some breach of contract, had terminated the contract earlier and given the bailor this right thereby.

While the bailee must exercise reasonable care in the use of the articles, he is not responsible for their "normal wear and tear"; that is, their aging and suffering damage through regular use.

If the rented article should need repairs, it is the bailor's duty to make them. Therefore the bailee should not have the repairs done himself: apart from not being entitled to recover the cost of the repairs from the bailor, he would be responsible to the bailor if unskilled repairs resulted in further damage to the goods. The only exceptions are where the bailor's consent is first obtained to having the repairs done, or where the bailee would be guilty of negligence for failing to have emergency repairs done promptly—in other words, where the bailee acts as an agent of necessity.

The bailee must not sub-let the goods to anyone else, or use them in any other way than agreed upon. If he does, he becomes *absolutely* responsible for the safety of the goods, even if they are damaged through no fault of his. He must not, of course, attempt to sell or pawn the goods, whereby he could be guilty of the crime of fraudulent conversion. A common contract clause will prevent him from removing the goods to a different locality without the bailor's consent.

The bailee must pay the rental fee as agreed upon; failing agreement, he must pay a customary or a reasonable amount. He must pay rental for the entire rental period, even if he returns the article earlier; unless the bailor voluntarily makes a concession in the price. At the end of the rental term, the goods must be returned to the bailor or be made available to him, depending on the terms of the contract. If the goods are so made available to the bailor, but he is late in picking them up, the bailee is not liable for additional charges, provided he does not continue using the goods.

GRATUITOUS BAILMENT

Where the bailee is given the free use of goods as a favour by a friend (the law calls this a gratuitous bailment for the sole benefit of the bailee), the courts have always felt it "reasonable" for such a borrower to take particularly good care of the article entrusted to him (e.g., a book or a lawnmower).

Conversely, in the case of a gratuitous bailment for the sole benefit of the bailor, a bailee who has kindly undertaken to look after or to deliver someone else's goods gratis can "reasonably" be expected to take just a little bit less care of them.

REPAIR, SERVICE, PROCESSING OF RAW MATERIALS, ETC.

The bailor's responsibilities are:

• To pay the agreed-upon charges. If none were agreed upon, the bailor must pay the customary or reasonable charges. For example, if I took my shoes or my watch to be repaired without first asking the price, I would have to pay the standard fee charged for this service. Unless the bailee agreed to grant credit to the bailor, the bailor must pay for the services before he is entitled to receive the goods back. The bailee has a lien on the bailor's goods until then (liens are discussed in full at the end of this chapter). In Ontario the Unclaimed Articles Act specifies the circumstances under which a repairman and warehouseman may sell articles not claimed by their owners within certain time limits to cover his charges.

• If the bailee performs only a part of the work because of reasons of his own, he is entitled to be paid on a *quantum meruit* basis if the work is of some value to the bailor. Nothing is payable for part work if a complete job was specified, or is obviously necessary. If it is the bailor who instructs the bailee to cease work, he must pay for all the satisfactory work so far done, at the least.

• The goods that the bailor entrusts to the bailee must not be "noxious"; that is, liable to explode or give off fumes when worked upon, or otherwise to endanger health, safety or comfort.

The bailee's responsibilities are:

• He must take "reasonable" care of the goods in his care. This responsibility is increased to absolute liability for their safety if he puts the goods to his own use; for example, if a jeweller wears a ring that was left with him for repairs and loses a stone out of it.

• He must do the work within the specified time, or at least within a reasonable time. Thus, if a repairman keeps putting his customer off with excuses, the customer has the right to get his goods back. Whether he will have to pay for any labour or parts already put into the goods will be decided on the *quantum meruit* principles discussed above.

• The repairman is not entitled to charge for any unauthorized extra work he did on the article; in fact, he is not even allowed to remove any parts or materials he used on this unauthorized work. As everyone knows, it is therefore very dangerous practice to give unknown repairmen a blanket authority to do "whatever repairs they consider necessary" to your car, watch, T.V., etc.

• If a man claims the ability to repair particular items, he must actually possess and exercise such ability, and he is not entitled to payment if he lacks this ability. In fact, he may be liable for damages if he causes damage to the article, even if he did the work gratuitously.

STORAGE OR WAREHOUSING

Various examples of stored articles are furniture in depositories, commodities in elevators or warehouses, cars and boats in garages or marinas, precious articles in safety deposit boxes.

The bailor's responsibilities are:

• To pay the agreed-upon, or customary, or reasonable rental. In Ontario and some other provinces, the warehouseman has a statutory lien on stored goods on which the rental has not been paid. In the other provinces, a standard contract term gives the warehouseman this right. It is sufficient if the warehouseman displays a notice to this effect in his office where the customer can see it, or if the notice is clearly printed on the receipt the customer gets.

• Not to store noxious goods. As before, the goods must not be harmful, but they must also be properly packed. Thus, if goods are packed in wooden cases, the cases must be so strong that they will not collapse when other customers' cases are stacked upon them; or, if liquids are stored in casks, the casks must not spill or leak so as to damage goods stored adjacently.

The bailee's responsibilities are:

• He must exercise reasonable care over the stored goods. Again, if he uses the goods, he becomes completely responsible for their safety. However, the riding of a horse by a livery stable operator, to the extent of giving the horse its necessary exercise, has been considered normal procedure.

• If the bailee accepts goods that require special storage conditions (e.g., the proper temperature and humidity for meat, fruit, furs, etc.), he must provide storage space that is fit for the known purpose.

• The bailee, subject to his above right of lien, must on request return the goods to the depositor, who must then surrender his receipt. Warehouse receipts are frequently the subject of assignment between businessmen; consequently it is quite proper for the bailee to hand the goods to the person whose name is shown on the receipt as the assignee of the goods. If the warehouseman cannot or will not return the stored goods, he can be compelled to make good only their value; he is not responsible for any consequential losses that his failure to return them entailed.

• A restaurant owner is also liable as a warehouseman for the safety of his guests' belongings that were "placed in his charge." This can take place by providing a check room (free or for a charge), or by the cashier's offering to look after a guest's packages. The restaurateur is not responsible for those belongings of the guest over which the guest chooses to retain control—for example, by placing them on the adjoining seat, or by hanging them on the hook adjacent to his table. If the guests are asked to hang their coats in specially designated places, the restaurateur is technically taking charge of them and is therefore assuming responsibility for them. He is, however, allowed to escape this responsibility by placing clear signs on these special places, disclaiming his liability. Even then he remains liable to the guest for his or his employees' negligence or dishonesty. Thus, he would not be liable if some other guest walked off with a patron's coat, but he would be liable if his waiter spilled soup over it.

PLEDGES OF SECURITIES AND VALUABLES

To secure a loan, a bank or other creditor will require the borrower to lodge bonds, a life insurance policy, etc., as *collateral*. Similarly, if a person is buying stocks "on margin," the stockbroker will require such stocks to be "pledged" with him. (When promising to make a gift to charity, a person "pledges his word" to the charity.) Precious articles left as security are called *pawns* and are said to be "left in pawn" ("in hock") with a pawnbroker (see Usury in Chapter 9), usually identified by the sign of the three Brass Balls (originally the sign of the goldsmith).

Again, the bailee is responsible for reasonable care of the goods in his charge, provided he does not put the goods to his own use. He must return the goods to their owner (or to the holder of the pawn ticket) on full payment of the debt and all accumulated lawful interest. In a transaction of this nature the bailee need not call on any right of lien, since the right to retain possession of the goods is obviously an inherent part of the contract.

In due course, the unpaid creditor may "realize his security" by selling it—on the best possible terms, of course. If a definite time limit had been set for repayment of the loan, the security may be sold immediately after default, without any notice having to be given to the debtor. If the repayment date was indefinite, the creditor should first make a written demand for payment from the debtor and give him ample notice of the intended sale. Pawnbrokers customarily wait for a year from the last interest payment before selling "unredeemed pledges."

After the sale, and after the creditor's claims to the principal amount, interest, and expenses have been satisfied, the pledgor is entitled to any surplus left over from the selling price. Conversely, he is liable for any deficit if the sale of the security has not fully satisfied all the claims of the creditor.

Note: In the above four types of bailments, we have heard that the bailee is normally responsible if the goods in his charge are lost or damaged through his negligence. While generally in negligence cases the onus of proving negligence lies on the plaintiff, in bailment cases this onus is, for obvious reasons, usually reversed. How, after all, is the owner of a table that originally had four legs to prove that a missing leg came off through the warehouseman's negligence, when the owner was not there to see what happened? The bailee cannot get away with saying (as the English maidservant) that "it just come to pieces in me 'ands"; the rule that applies is *"res ipsa loquitur"*—"the thing speaks for itself." The sensible thing to do, then, when leaving one's goods with someone else, is to make sure that the goods are covered by insurance—either the bailee's (most repairmen and warehousemen carry insurance to cover all their customers' goods), or one's own blanket or floater policy.

CARRIAGE OF GOODS

When a person transports some goods as a favour for a friend, he is called a *gratuitous carrier*. Persons transporting goods for payment just once in a while as a sideline, or carriers specializing in the transport of particular goods (e.g., furniture, sheet glass, gasoline), are called *private carriers for reward or value*. Both these types of carriers are subject to the same general rules covering bailees we have discussed earlier. However, there is yet another type of carrier, the *common carrier*, to whom a completely different set of rules applies.

The common carrier is one who offers, at certain maximum rates set by various authorities, to accept anything for transport for which he has the facilities. Examples of common carriers are the railroads, steamship lines, truck and air lines. When a person goes into the business of carrying cargo, he virtually becomes a public utility; he must provide service for all who demand it, and he has no freedom of selection of his customers. (There are other such slaves to duty: hotels—discussed next—and doctors, who must be prepared to answer calls at all hours of the night.) Fixed rates of charges are set by the government, and anyone working in a firm's traffic department will be familiar with the railroads' voluminous schedule of rates. Periodic applications to the government for leave to increase freight rates are a complicated and lengthy proceeding.

Responsibilities of the bailor, who in contracts of carriage is called the shipper or the consignor (the bailee being the carrier), are:

• He must pay the statutory schedule rates; usually they must be prepaid, but goods can also be sent "freight collect." The contract with the carriers (i.e., the bill of lading) will always reserve a right of lien to them for nonpayment.

• The goods must be described correctly on the bill of lading; that is, they must not be falsely described as goods to which a cheaper carriage rate applies.

• The goods must not be noxious (see Storage above). A "clean" bill of lading will declare the goods to have been received by the carrier in "apparent good order and condition." If a record is made of, say, a broken slat in one of the crates, the bill of lading is said to be "marked." (Merchants buying goods sight unseen, by having order bills of lading endorsed over to them, are reluctant to take such "marked bills.")[1]

For historical reasons, the common carrier is liable not only for his negligence; but he undertakes to make safe delivery of the goods at destination, come what may (with but very few exceptions). In other words, the charges he makes the customer include not only carriage, but also, in effect, an insurance premium to cover almost all accidents. That is why the carriage charges for a ton of steel are much less than those for a ton of gold: while the cost of carrying the goods is about the

---

[1] Goods shipped under an order bill of lading (which is a combined receipt, contract, and document of title) are delivered only to the person named in it as consignee, or to the person to whom it was endorsed by the consignee; the order bill of lading must then be surrendered to the carrier.

Goods shipped under a straight bill of lading cannot be assigned by its endorsement; they are delivered without formality to the person named on it as consignee. A straight bill of lading, then, is a combined receipt and contract, but not a document of title.

same for both, the replacement cost of the latter, in case of loss, is obviously much higher.

Numerous statutes permit carriers to enter contracts in which, for the sake of quoting more competitive rates to their customers, they are allowed certain reductions of their absolute liability. For example, the standard contract provides for maximum compensation of $100 per carried horse. The same maximum amount is paid in Canada to a railroad passenger with a regular ticket for each *checked* trunk (or other package) of *personal* belongings that has been lost or damaged. If the shipper wants more coverage, he can obtain it by paying a higher rate; if the traveller wants more protection, he can buy cheap extra insurance at all station baggage counters.

Common carriers were saddled with this almost unlimited liability for the safety of the carried goods because they were in complete, unsupervised charge of them during transit. This is not the case with passengers; carriers also operating a passenger service are liable only if their negligence caused injury to a passenger. Also, by statute, passenger carriers are allowed to reduce their liability to passengers by inserting a clause to that effect in special "cheap excursion tickets."

Exceptions to the absolute liability of common carriers. The important exceptions are:

• Damage caused by acts of God, or *force majeure*; that is, violent upheavals of nature such as storms, lightning, floods, and earthquakes. Under this heading there may not be included any other unusual causes of accidents; thus, a cow wandering onto the tracks and derailing a train is not an act of God.

• Damage caused by violent action of the Queen's enemies during times of war or rioting.

• Inherent vice or defect in the goods. Included in this category would be goods which were improperly packed; or perished foodstuffs which contained the germs of spoilage in them when shipped; or shipped cattle or horses that "acted up" and injured themselves or each other.

• If goods were shipped under an improper classification, the carrier is liable not for their true value but only for the lower value stated by the shipper on the bill of lading.

Even in the above exceptional circumstances, the carrier is responsible for any negligence of which he may have been guilty. For example, after a train has been wrecked by an act of God during a heavy rainstorm, the carrier will be liable for water damage to delicate goods if he could have conveniently taken them to shelter but failed to do so.

Generally, the absolute liability of a carrier ceases and is converted to the liability of a warehouseman for stored goods, once the consignee has been given notice of the arrival of the goods plus a reasonable time (usually 48 hours) in which to come to pick them up. After this time, the consignee can be charged storage fees, called *demurrage*.

HOTELS

An innkeeper, as the law still prefers to call him, is also virtually in the public service. He inherited this obligation from the Middle Ages when he was in an easy position to pilfer his guests' purses as they slept on the rush mats of the one communal chamber of which houses then consisted; and since he practically enjoyed a monopoly, it was felt that he should not be in a position to unmercifully fleece the travelling public.

The innkeeper, as well as the common carrier, has the liability of an insurer for his guests' belongings. He is fully liable even if the loss is not his fault. He is not liable, of course, if the goods are lost, etc., by the guest's own negligence; for instance, by entertaining and not properly supervising unsavoury visitors he has invited to his room. Failure by the guest to lock his room may or may not be regarded as negligence, depending entirely on the circumstances. There is even no exemption from liability for the innkeeper for acts of God, etc., except for statutory protection afforded him in some jurisdictions.

Most provinces have a statute similar to the Ontario Innkeepers Act. According to the Act, the innkeeper is allowed to limit his liability to $40 if he posts the relevant section of the Act in the bedrooms, the office, and the public rooms. Even then, he is still fully liable for his guests' goods if:

1. They are lost or damaged through the dishonesty or negligence of the innkeeper or any of his servants; or

2. They were offered to him or to his proper representative (the desk clerk, or cashier) for safekeeping; whether the innkeeper actually so accepted them, or not; or

3. The article was the guest's horse or car left in the stable, garage, or lot operated by the hotel; for these the innkeeper still retains full responsibility.

Regarding the guest's person, the innkeeper is responsible only for taking reasonable care of him. In the following cases the hotel was *not* held guilty of negligence:

• Where a guest, reading in a chair in the Waldorf lobby in New York, was injured by a heavy floor lamp that fell against him when a fellow guest knocked the lamp over by leaning back in his chair.

• Where a guest, on returning to her hotel at 3 a.m., fell on the slippery floor of the lobby and injured herself. She had seen that the "bucket brigade" was soaping and washing the floor, and proceeded across it without first asking for assistance.

• Where a guest, shy of asking directions for the washroom, stepped into a dark room in the hotel's service quarters and fell down a laundry chute.

• Where a guest, deciding to use the more convenient *service* elevator himself, opened the door and fell into its shaft.

In the following cases, however, the hotels were held liable for injuries to their guests:

• Where a guest was injured by falling down the shaft of an unguarded *passenger* elevator.

• Where a guest drove a needle into her foot while walking barefoot on the bedroom rug.

• Where a bed collapsed, injuring the occupants. (On appeal, the onus was held to be on the hotel to prove lack of negligence; "res ipsa loquitur"—or, beds should not normally collapse).

• Where guests were injured by plaster falling from the ceiling or scalding hot water issuing from the shower.

• Where guests, in the presence and approval of the innkeeper, injured a fellow guest by pinning paper on his coat tails and setting fire to it.

Common law definition of "innkeeper." To differentiate the innkeeper from others with lesser obligations, (e.g., rooming and boarding house operators, and apartment landlords), we should note his common law definition as:

(1) A person who offers to, and in fact, must

215

  (2) at set rates
  (3) accept at all hours
  (4) any "fit and orderly"
  (5) transient
  (6) with ability to pay
  (7) plus all his baggage
  (8) if he has a vacancy
  (9) and furnish him with food, drink, entertainment, and
 (10) safe shelter.

Let us now examine the implications of each of these requirements:

1. An aggrieved person who has been denied accommodation in an establishment can sue it successfully if he can prove that he complied with all the above requirements and if the court concludes that the establishment was, in fact, being conducted as an inn.

2. An innkeeper is not allowed to charge "what the traffic will bear." In Ontario, the Hotel Registration of Guests Act requires the innkeeper to post in each bedroom the maximum he will charge for that room; he must not exceed that maximum. Since these rates are the ones that are advertised, good business sense will prevent the innkeeper from posting exorbitant prices.[2]

3. The innkeeper must be ready to receive guests at all hours of the day or night, including holidays. (The Ontario One Day's Rest in Seven Act entitles nonexecutive hotel personnel to one day a week off.)

4. Nobody is unfit or disorderly merely on account of his race, religion, nationality, or tender age. However, hotels like the Martha Washington in New York can restrict their guests to the female sex.

The following have been held *not* to be "fit and orderly": people who are drunk, or disorderly, or filthy, or profane; common brawlers, or people who enter the hotel with intent to make a fight or an affray; a thief, an ex-convict, a person known to be a card-sharp, a bawdy-house keeper, a denizen of the underworld, or any other notorious public character (e.g., a usurer preying on young officers in a Scapa Flow hotel in war time); anyone guilty of offensive conduct or

---

2 The Hotel Registration of Guests Act also requires innkeepers to keep a register of guests and to make guests use it. The Act also requires all guests to register their correct names in it. In England it is no offense to register under a false name, provided this is not done with the intent to defraud someone.

unpleasant habits, or suffering from a contagious disease; or anyone so insane, or conducting himself so irrationally, that it disturbs the peace and quiet of the house.

If a person who was originally fit and orderly afterwards becomes unacceptable, he may be asked to leave the hotel; and if he does not do so peaceably, he may be ejected—with not the slightest bit more force than absolutely necessary, of course. As a matter of prudence, the house officer (hotel detective) should always have a witness present when ejecting a guest or when entering a guest's room (which right the innkeeper or his representative has under the proper circumstances), to protect himself and his employer against trumped-up assault and slander actions. On the other hand, they should be most circumspect before accusing a guest of improper conduct.

The innkeeper is within his rights, however, to set reasonable house rules; for example, for guests to turn down radios, etc., at midnight, and for guests "not to entertain visitors of the opposite sex behind closed doors" beyond a specified hour. While a guest is thus entitled to receive visitors in his room at reasonable hours, they must not sleep in his room overnight without paying an additional charge. A hotel is not a public place whose amenities any one is entitled to enjoy. The lobby, for example, technically is for the use only of the hotel guests and of people visiting or having business with such guests. This provision entitles a hotel to demand the departure of unwelcome trespassers from its premises. (In Ontario, where there are few public lavatories, any member of the public is usually permitted to have the free use of hotel and service station washrooms.) However, since a hotel is designed for the well-being of travellers, an innkeeper may not grant a monopoly to any one transportation company to solicit business from the guests in his hotel. And while the hotel may operate a restaurant, laundry, beauty shop, etc., there is nothing to prevent a guest from sending out for his meals or other services to be brought in to him in the hotel.

5. A person is "transient" (literally, going through) until his business in the region is finished. This may extend from the time it takes him to eat a meal in a hotel restaurant while breaking his journey, to the six months it might take him to be cured while staying in a hotel at a health resort. The transient never binds himself to stay for any fixed length of time. He "checks out" when he feels like it; of course,

if he leaves this beyond a specified hour, he will have to pay for an extra day.

6. A person who pays in advance is, obviously, able to pay. It used to be considered very rude to ask guests to pay in advance, but this is now common practice in motels. Good luggage that the guest brings with him is also evidence of ability to pay; for the innkeeper has the right of *lien* on practically all goods the guest brings to the hotel, even if they have not been paid for—nay, even if they have been stolen. He may even retain a blind man's seeing-eye dog.[3] Exceptions are articles which the guest rents locally with the hotel's knowledge; for example, a typewriter, a car, or a piano. Also excepted is a defaulting postman's bag with mail, as being government property. Naturally, a guest, or members of his family, may not be personally detained—that would constitute an assault and false imprisonment. Nor may clothing or goods be taken off a guest's person—for that might lead to pneumonia or indecency.

The innkeeper's lien extends to all the guest's goods for *all* hotel charges. Thus a guest's luggage can be retained if he did not pay for his gas in the hotel garage; and his car can be retained in the hotel garage if he did not pay his bill in the hotel gift shop.

The right of lien (though not as wide as the innkeeper's) also extends to operators of rooming and boarding houses; but not to apartment landlords, who, however, have the right of *distress* (see Leases, Chapter 29). All such operators have the right to pick and choose their customers; to demand special rates; and to make long-term contracts; but they are responsible only for taking reasonable care of their guests' belongings. Large establishments may operate in several capacities at once; for example, hotels may also have permanent guests.

7. An inn must accept not only the traveller, but everything he requires on his travels. This includes a salesman's samples; of course, an extra sample display room must be paid for. Noxious goods need not be accepted; nor need animals—not even seeing-eye dogs—unless the hotel has special provision for animals. Formerly, accommodation had to be provided for the traveller's means of transport—his horse, car-

---

3 The reason why an innkeeper is given this generous right of lien is probably to compensate him partly for the rigid controls he is otherwise subject to.

riage, or car; this no longer appears to be a requirement.

8. Vacancy means a vacancy in a regular bedroom, not elsewhere. A guest cannot demand to sleep in a room that is designed as a sitting room; on a divan in the lobby; in a bathtub; or on a billiard table (all actual cases). However, he must put up with poor accommodation if that is what the innkeeper decides to allot to him, even if better quality quarters are standing vacant.

9. The old requirement for food and drink is also going by the board. Motels are being considered as inns, even though only a minority of them provides meals. Some provide free "continental breakfasts," and almost all of them have soft-drink machines and ice cubes. The selling of liquor is governed in most provinces by laws which constitute a science all to themselves.

"Entertainment" does not necessarily mean a T.V. set; it means the normal amenities such as water to wash in, linen, coat hangers, illumination, and the ever-present bottle opener.

10. The safe shelter for the guest's person and belongings, the most important feature of all, has already been discussed.

LIEN

We have already made frequent mention of this right to retain goods as security for payment. The following persons have a *specific lien* on individual articles: the unpaid seller; the repairman; the auctioneer; the warehouseman; the carrier; the innkeeper; the boarding and rooming house operator; the insurance broker on the policy for the unpaid premium.

The following have a *general lien* on *any* goods, documents, or securities of the debtor's that they happen to have in their possession: the banker, the lawyer, the stockbroker, and the agent.

A lien is the right to retain, *not to take*, possession of the debtor's goods until paid. Once possession of the goods is given up *voluntarily* (not through trickery or stealth), the right of lien is lost and is not re-establishable even if the goods happen to get into the creditor's power at some later date.

In some cases the right of lien is granted by common law; in some, by provincial statute; and in others, by contract. It is designed to embarrass the debtor by depriving him of the use of his goods. The creditor is allowed to sell the article only with the permission of some statute or contract. Thus, the Ontario Mechanic's Lien Act permits the unpaid repairman to sell the repaired article at auction after three months if he has given the debtor notice and advertised the auction one week before. And the Ontario Innkeeper's Act allows such a sale under similar conditions, but in the case of a horse and car after just two weeks; it costs money to feed a horse.

Trained animals that have been retained may be exhibited (and the admission fees used to reduce the debt), but otherwise the creditor may not use retained articles. Any surplus realized by the auction sale (after expenses) must be made available to the debtor, if he should come to the creditor to demand it.

The lien comes to an end once payment has been made, even by cheque. But if the cheque "bounces" and the creditor still possesses the goods, the lien revives.

QUESTIONS

1. Ward stored his furniture with the Price Warehouse Company. The warehouse was not weathertight, and the furniture was damaged. Has Ward a legal claim against the warehouse company? Explain.
2. Stuart, an overnight guest at Tudor's home, was allowed to put his car in Tudor's garage. The garage and its contents were destroyed by fire in the night. Has Stuart a legal claim against Tudor? Explain.
3. Stringer rented his imported power scoop to Twining for three months for $1,500. A month before the end of the term, Stringer is offered $1,000 for a week's use of the scoop by someone who urgently needs it. If Twining refuses to return the scoop to its owner, Stringer, how can he be compelled to do so?
4. Evelyn stored Lillian's coat without charge. Evelyn wore the coat to a banquet on one occasion and checked it in the restaurant's check room. Armed bandits held up the check room and made off with all its contents.
   (a) Can Lillian hold Evelyn legally responsible? Explain.
   (b) Is the restaurant liable for the loss of the coat? Explain.
5. Grant took his watch to a jeweller with instructions to replace the crystal and the strap; for these the jeweller agreed to charge $5. When Grant came to pick up the watch, the jeweller charged $10,

explaining that the watch works were dirty and had needed cleaning. Explain how much Grant can legally be made to pay.

6. Carpenter sent a load of new furniture by railroad freight to a distant town. Explain what Carpenter's rights are against the railroad company if the railroad cars containing the furniture were completely destroyed by fire under the following circumstances:

(a) The fire was set by an arsonist.

(b) While the cars were sitting overnight on a siding, lightning struck an adjacent building from which the fire slowly spread to the cars while the railroad company's night watchman was asleep.

7. (a) Under what circumstances is an innkeeper completely responsible for the safety of his guests' belongings?

(b) When is the innkeeper absolved from all such liability?

(c) Under what circumstances is the innkeeper only partly so liable?

8. Carter took his truck and his car to a garage for repairs. After the work was completed, Carter drove away the truck, stating he would pay later. Later, he called for the car, tendering the contracted price of $3 for the brake adjustment on it, and promising to pay the bill for the repairs on the truck ($180) "in a week or two." Discuss whether the garage is entitled to retain the car until it is paid $183 (and tax, if any).

CHAPTER TWENTY

Insurance

HISTORY OF INSURANCE

Insurance is quite an ancient institution, whereby members of a community try to protect themselves against financial disaster consequent on some catastrophe which singled them out as the victim. This they achieved in ancient times by having all participating members of the community assume a proportional share of all disasters that struck any other participating member. Thus, while participation in the scheme cost each member the regular payment of a relatively small amount, he was assured against the possibility of a crippling loss. Many Anglo-Saxon communities operated this scheme as protection against losses by fire, water, robbery, etc. The Romans operated commercial fire insurance on a modern basis and maintained fire-fighting departments to boot, for the protection of their clients. Marine insurance existed in Europe in the twelfth century and was operating on a commercial scale by 1400. Fire insurance became widespread after the Great Fire of London in 1666, and in 1688 Edward Lloyd's London coffee house was on its way to becoming the centre of insurance operations. By 1774 these operations had attained such proportions that they were moved into the Royal Exchange. At this time, also, insurance law was clearly formulated in England. The first London life insurance company was founded in 1696 and is still in operation.

Insurance can be defined as a contract (contained in a policy) by which one party (the *insurer* or the *underwriter(s)*) for a consideration (called the *premium*) undertakes to compensate the other (the *insured* or other designated *beneficiary*) for loss on a specified thing (in which he has an *insurable interest*) from specified causes (the *risk*).

Thus a person can achieve great security for small premiums.

INSURABLE INTEREST

Anything can be insured in which one has a genuine insurable interest. As was mentioned under Illegality, Chapter 9, one normally stands to lose nothing if a flipped coin comes down "heads," and any so-called contract insuring against this eventuality is void. However, a person may properly insure against anything happening that will cause him loss. The large insurance companies often specialize in just one type of insurance; for example, life, fire and automobile, etc. However, groups of individual underwriters who are members of Lloyd's will, at carefully calculated premiums, issue policies against all kinds of off-beat risks; for example, against bad weather ruining the success of an outdoor event; against Betty Grable's famous dancing legs becoming disfigured; or against a picture of poker-face comedian Ned Sparks being published showing him with a smile on his face.

One cannot insure, however, against anything that will tend to make one careless (e.g., against one's own business failure); or anything that is difficult to prove (e.g., against an unhappy marriage); or anything illegal, or its consequences (e.g., against having to pay libel damages, against imprisonment, against death by legal execution or during the commission of a crime); nor will an arsonist or murderer be able to collect insurance on what he destroyed. By a recent amendment of the Ontario Insurance Act, however, a life insurance company may, under certain circumstances, be compelled to pay the beneficiaries of a deliberate suicide.

Insurance against damage to property can be taken out not only by its owner, but also by anyone else who stands to lose by its destruction or damage: thus, a manufacturer may insure the plant he leases; or a mortgagee may insure the property which serves as his security; or a long-term employee may insure the business, or the ship, in which he works since his employment depends on its continued existence.

COMMON INSURABLE RISKS

Apart from life, fire, automobile, and carriage of goods insurance that are discussed in greater detail further on, the following are some risks that are commonly insured against:

• Personal accident, sickness, and disfigurement; to cover medical bills and loss of earnings.

• Theft; a "floater" policy will cover anything belonging to the insured and his family, whether at home or while travelling.

• Crop failure and death of livestock.

• "Casualty" insurance; for example, breakage of plate glass, boiler explosion, a plane or car smashing into one's property, and other accidents.

• Damage by the elements: fire, smoke, and water; flood, storms, rain, hail.

• Marine insurance for ships and for their cargoes.

• Liability insurance for people injured on one's property, by one's car, or by one's employees.

• Business interruption through all sorts of reasons: for example, fire, or municipal construction preventing the access of customers to a store.

• Fidelity guarantee (bonding) against a servant's dishonesty.

• Products insurance against goods being harmful to a customer's safety or health.

• Malpractice insurance protecting a professional man (doctor, lawyer, architect, etc.) against the consequences of his negligence.

• Bailee's insurance for the safety of customers' goods that are being repaired, cleaned, stored, etc.

• Golfers' combined policy against theft of or damage to equipment, injury to self, liability to others injured by his golf ball or golf club, and even for his bar bill after scoring a hole-in-one (but not for lost balls).

• Dealers in babies' furnishings often supply full insurance against twins.

• The government supervises many insurance schemes, compulsory or voluntary: for example, health (Saskatchewan's Medicare and Ontario's hospital insurance); government annuities; unemployment; old age; workmen's compensation; Motor Vehicle Accident Claims Funds (or Unsatisfied Judgments Funds); and the insurance to exporters of overseas customers' credit. (The last is rather an expensive proposition for the exporter who must pay a premium on goods shipped not only to the poor risks but also on those shipped to well-established, reliable customers.)

FIRE INSURANCE

Fire insurance protects one against the direct consequences of a "hostile" fire—one that got started where it had no business to; for example, as the result of lightning, defective wiring, etc. A "friendly" fire is one that had its proper purpose to begin with but then got out of hand; for example, an ember falling from the fireplace onto the rug; the fire in the kitchen range setting the curtains alight; the smoker's cigarette setting fire to his bedclothes. The standard fire policy also protects against water and smoke damage and also against deliberate destruction of one's property to prevent the spread of a large-scale conflagration. For extra premiums, additional *riders* can be attached to the policy to protect against friendly fires, business interruption, and fires caused by the enemy or rioters.

A standard fire insurance policy (whose contents are strictly controlled by statute) imposes a number of logical duties on the buyer: He must not store more than a maximum amount of combustibles or explosives (gasolines, rifle shells) in his premises without advising the insurers. He must give them notice of any added risks (e.g., attaching a garage to the insured house). He must not leave the premises vacant or unsupervised over thirty days without permission. He must keep chimneys, fireplaces, and other heating equipment in a safe condition.

AUTOMOBILE AND BOAT INSURANCE

Automobiles and boats are not usually included in an insurance of household goods but are the subject of separate policies. The owner of a car is subject to risks under three main headings and he may take out insurance against any or all of them:

1. Theft, fire, and other *casualty*. The premium for this category is relatively small.

2. *Collision*—with anything; for example, hitting another car, being hit by another car, or running into a fixed object. Full coverage is quite expensive; to reduce the cost of the premium, it is common to insert a "deductible" clause whereby the insured agrees to bear the first $25, $50, or $100 of any loss. An insurance company which has compensated its

insured for loss caused by someone else's negligence is *subrogated* to the injured party's claim against the negligent party; that is, the company acquires the victim's right to sue for negligence.

3. The most important insurance for the owner or driver of a car to carry is *liability* insurance to cover people or property injured by his car, when driven by himself or by anyone else with the owner's consent. The minimum amount of insurance in Ontario is for $35,000; but much larger coverage is very desirable, since the extra premiums are relatively quite low.

No benefits (except liability insurance up to $35,000) will be paid by the insurer for the results of an accident that was incurred while the driver was impaired by alcohol or drugs; or while he was unlicenced to drive; or while he was improperly engaged in racing another vehicle; or if he was driving for an illegal purpose such as smuggling, or even illicitly carrying passengers for hire.

Premiums for auto insurance vary according to the purposes and extent for which the vehicle is used and the class of driver(s) operating it.

CARRIAGE OF GOODS

In view of the virtually unlimited liability of the common carrier for the safety of the carried goods, it may seem unnecessary, at first sight, to take out insurance for them. However, carriage of goods insurance is quite necessary for the following reasons:

1. To obtain protection against the "excepted risks." One example of an excepted risk is damage by the *Queen's enemies*. An illustration is *war risks*. The premium for war risks is very low in peacetime and protects ships against mines left over from a previous war; against being accidentally shelled in a local war or insurrection; and against pirates and rioters. At the height of the German submarine attacks during the last war, however, the premium for war risks insurance climbed to 105% of the invoice value of the cargo. (This is not absurd, in view of the much higher resale value of the goods.) One of the most common types of excepted risk insurance is insurance against *acts of God*: Protection must be bought against damage by the elements (e.g., for goods on a train derailed by a landslide.) The complicated standard marine insurance policy (still couched in archaic terminology) affords

226

protection against only the most basic of these risks, and there are many different kinds of common risks for which separate protection must be bought for additional premiums. Finally, protection is also required against *inherent defect*; namely, against goods being damaged because their packing proves to be too weak to withstand normally rough handling. To be sure of having full protection against all possible risks, a shipper should take out a *comprehensive* policy to cover all his shipments.

2. It will be remembered that several statutes permit the carriers to limit their liability to specified amounts. Consequently the shipper will have to carry insurance to protect him completely. The owner of carried goods should also take out insurance against the loss of his normal profit on their resale.

3. Even though the carrier may be fully liable legally, he may be insolvent. Bad disasters have in the past bankrupted large carriage concerns.

4. Claims against a carrier are hedged in with all kinds of formality. The claim must be proved up to the hilt, and it must be lodged on specified forms and within short time limits. There is thus a good chance of losing one's claim on a technicality. In fact, the standard letter of a carrier in response to a claim begins: "Your claim is denied because of ..."

LIFE INSURANCE

This is insurance not against death itself, of course, but against our untimely demise; while death is certain, its date is not.

Most frequently, a person insures his own life. The coverage can range from *term insurance* (which offers pure protection for the term of the policy only), to an *endowment* policy (which is a combination of protection and a heavy investment). Insurance can be carried for the protection of one's dependent survivors, as in a *whole life* policy, or for one's old age; for example, by purchasing an *annuity*, or by taking out an endowment policy which becomes payable to the insured at a specified age (let us say 65), or to the person named by him as his beneficiary should he die before attaining that age.

It is also quite in order to insure the life of anyone else who consents thereto, or the life of anyone in whose continued life one has a genuine insurable interest. One automatically has an insurable interest in the life of oneself (to an unlimited amount, if one is prepared to pay the high premium and the insurer accepts the risk) ; of one's spouse, and of one's children under 25 years of age. However the insurance on their lives must not be of a completely unreasonable amount; in fact, the maximum for babies under five in Ontario is $1,000.

Also insured can be the life of anyone whose death would prove a detriment to one; for example, a debtor, a sponsor, or a valuable employee. A firm will take out "shock insurance" on the lives of key executives to compensate for the temporary disrupting or halting of business proceedings that would be consequent on the executive's death. The members of a partnership will insure the lives of each other for the cash amount of his share in the partnership to be paid to his estate on his death; otherwise the surviving partner(s) may have to liquidate, usually at a loss, the dead partner's share of the assets in order to meet the payment to the estate.

Curiously enough, the insurable interest in the life of the insured person need exist only at the time of taking out the policy. If I take out a one-year policy for $1,000 on the life of a debtor to whom I lent that amount; and if he has repaid me $500 by the time he dies six months later, I am entitled to the full $1,000 from the insurance company.

The insured may instruct the insurer to make payment of the policy to any of the following *beneficiaries*: himself; or his estate after his death (which will be distributed according to the terms of his will or under the rules of intestacy) ; or any other beneficiary—most commonly members of his immediate family. (A wife loses her rights under the policy after a divorce, even though she was not specifically eliminated from the policy.) The insured may remove beneficiaries from his policy and replace them at will (always notifying the insurer, of course), except such whom he designates to the insurer as being appointed irrevocably—such a one cannot be removed except with his written consent. Consequently, a creditor in whose favour a policy is being taken out, should make sure that the insurer has been notified that he is an irrevocable appointee. This step was not necessary before 1962, since such a "beneficiary for value" would automatically have enjoyed

228

this protection; those appointed before then, still do. In a similar category were the *preferred beneficiaries*; namely, the insured's spouse, direct descendants, parents and grandparents (but not siblings—i.e., brothers or sisters). Prior to 1962, they could not be removed without their consent, unless they were replaced by other members of the same category.

The proceeds of a policy that is payable to a beneficiary other than the insured or his estate are not available to the insolvent insured's creditors, since the proceeds are not considered a part of the insured's estate. However, a policy may be surrendered to the insurer for a cash refund, unless the beneficiary is irrevocable, or was a beneficiary for value, or was of the preferred category. The insured may also borrow money from the insurer against the security of the cash surrender value of his policy, except if the beneficiary is irrevocable, or was a beneficiary for value.

The following are some standard policy clauses:

• No benefits will be paid if the insured kills himself within two years from taking out the policy.

• If a policy is taken out in wartime and the insured is killed in military service, only 25% of the insured amount is to be paid.

• The insured shall have thirty days of grace in which to pay premiums.

• If the insured has allowed the policy to lapse, he shall have two years in which to reinstate it, on payment of all back premiums.

• If any innocent misrepresentation is made in the contract, it can only be avoided by the other party within two years. If the insured misrepresented his age (older persons have to pay higher premiums), the premium will be increased, or payments will be reduced, correspondingly. If the lie about the age is material (i.e., if the insurer refuses to accept insurance from people over a certain age), the contract is voidable within five years.

INSURANCE CONTRACTS IN GENERAL

It has already been stated that the policy holder must have a genuine insurable interest in the insured thing or life. While in life insurance it is sufficient for that interest to have existed at the time of taking out the insurance, in other contracts the insurable interest must exist at the time the policy is paid out. For example, if I insure my employer's or debtor's premises against fire and they burn after I have left my employer (or have been repaid by my debtor), I am not entitled to receive any payment from the insurer (except a refund, perhaps, of that portion of the premiums from which I received no benefit).

Thus it is no use to over-insure property. If I insure my house and contents valued at $25,000 for $100,000 and they are destroyed completely, the insurer will have to compensate me only for my actual loss. There are a few exceptions: as has been mentioned earlier, one can insure one's own life for an almost unlimited amount; and the same holds true for ships, since the loss of a ship is accompanied by so many intangible losses—lost cargo, liability to injured crew and passengers, lost contracts of carriage, etc.

"Under-insurance" has different consequences in various fields of insurance. If I insure my $1 million ship for $600,000, I shall be allowed to collect only 60% of any loss suffered up to $1 million—in effect, I expressed a willingness to be my own insurer for the other 40%. (Many large operators with spread risks—e.g., operators of trucking fleets—do not carry collision insurance, but are "self-insured." They figure that their losses due to accidents are smaller than the premiums they would have to pay. The $25-$100 deductible clause in car insurance is also a form of partial self-insurance.)

On the other hand, if I insure my $25,000 house against fire for $15,000, I shall be able to collect the full amount of any damage up to $15,000; but I shall have to suffer the balance of the loss if it is any larger. (However, if I have undertaken by a *co-insurance clause* in the policy—whose existence must be stamped clearly in red on the face of the policy—to insure for a stated minimum percentage of the house's value, say for 80% or $20,000, and I fail to do so, then I am self-insured for the balance. Thus if I insure for only $18,000, I shall be able to collect only eighteen-twentieths of any loss suffered up to $18,000.)

In discussing "genuine intention" in Chapter 10, we stated that a contract of insurance is one of the *utmost good faith* and that the insured must volunteer, unasked, any material information to the insurer; that is any information that might influence his decision to issue insurance coverage. Such statements in insurance applications are called *warranties*, but they have the effect of conditions in that they entitle the insurer to cancel the policy if they are incorrect. (However, a boarding house operator was entitled to collect fire insurance even though in his application he had stated, "This house is not operated as a boarding house." His statement was true at the time, but he converted the private house to a boarding house immediately after having the policy issued to him. The court felt that the insurer was careless in not framing the clause more carefully in words such as: "This house is not, *and will not be*, operated as a boarding house." Nor was operating the house as a boarding house considered an added risk, notice of which must, of course, be given to the insurer.)

While insurance policies have to be in writing, it is common practice for coverage to be extended to clients over the telephone in the form of a verbal "binder"; this is followed by an informal "cover note" until the policy itself is issued. No reputable insurance broker would violate such an oral undertaking: nor would a stockbroker who also executes many telephonic orders; nor a bookmaker, where bookmaking is legal (e.g., the English "turf commission agent"). While the broker acts as the agent for the insurer for the issue of the policy, he is, curiously enough, the principal as far as the payment of premiums is concerned. If the insured does not pay them, it is the broker who has the right to enforce payment of them; for example, by exercising his right of lien over any policy he happens to have in his possession.

Generally the insured is entitled to payment even if the injury to his person or goods is the result of his own negligence. Excepted, of course, is any damage that he caused deliberately, or in violation of certain contract provisions (e.g., racing a car, or storing combustibles in a house).

The insurer can sell (assign) the contract to someone else. This happens when a firm "re-insures" parts of a large risk it has undertaken with other firms (like a bookmaker "laying off" bets. The author begs forgiveness for his many references to bookmakers, but the whole field of insurance is not unrelated to betting. For example, in fire insurance, the insured is virtually betting the insurer, against long odds, that his house will burn down; if the house does burn, he wins and is entitled to payment). Since such re-insurance amounts to the assignment of a liability, the insured, if unsatisfied by the assignee, can still hold the original insurer responsible for payment.

The insured can assign any insurance he holds to others as security for a debt. If he sells property, he may assign the covering insurance to the buyer, provided the consent of the insurer is obtained.

Insurers must be notified promptly of any claims arising against them. In turn, they must make settlement of undisputed life insurance claims within thirty days; of other claims, in sixty days.

In Canada, as in most other countries, insurance companies are governed by the most stringent regulations and are the subject of most careful government inspection and supervision regarding the investment of the huge funds they hold in trust for their clients; so there is little financial risk in dealing with any of them. The main difference between companies is their degree of reluctance in making payment of claims; which is what differentiates the "good" companies from the "bad" ones.

QUESTIONS

1. Under what circumstances will a ship owner be able to collect insurance on a ship, on which he had taken out insurance *after* it had already sunk? (Refer to "common mistake" in Chapter 10.)
2. Tom went to his friend Jim (an important employee in a large firm) and told him that he had a hunch that his (Tom's) $20,000 house would burn to the ground within the next year. Jim bet Tom that his house would not burn down, and he gave Tom odds of $20,000 to $50. Tom deposited his $50 stake with Jim's firm and received a written document as a receipt for his payment. If Tom's house is burnt by accident within the ensuing year, will he be entitled to collect his bet? Explain.
3. List the risks against which insurance should be taken out by:
   (a) A prudent house owner.
   (b) The prudent head of a family.
   (c) A prudent businessman.
   (d) A prudent automobile owner.
4. Summarize a shipper's reasons for insuring his goods during transit.
5. Under what circumstances will a person be able to collect insurance on the death of someone else, on whose life he has taken out insurance?

6. What are the restrictions on a person who has insured his life in favour of an irrevocable beneficiary?
7. Within what length of time must claims against insurance companies generally be lodged? (See Chapter 13.)
8. You are planning to take out life insurance. Company A's rates are lower than those of Company B. Company B requires you to submit to a physical examination by its doctor, while Company A relies on you to complete a questionnaire about your medical history. With which company will you place the insurance? Give your reasons.
9. Archer owns a $100,000 house and a $100,000 boat. He insures each for $80,000. In a fire each suffers a $50,000 loss. How much insurance will Archer be entitled to collect?

Guarantee or Suretyship

THE NATURE OF A GUARANTEE

Guarantees were discussed briefly, when dealing with the Statute of Frauds, as being one of the few transactions that require writing in order to be enforceable. Guarantees are often given by wives for the overdraft of their husbands' bank accounts; by bonding companies issuing *fidelity bonds* for the honesty of employees, and *performance bonds* for the completion of buildings according to contract; and by parents in co-signing the contracts of their under-age children. Guarantees are also given to friends by "backing their paper" (see Accommodation Endorsements in the next chapter); and anyone endorsing a cheque or other negotiable instrument to someone else is thereby virtually guaranteeing that "the paper is good." The value of an NSF (not sufficient funds) cheque[1] will be "charged back" to a bank depositor who paid it into his account. The bank credited his account with the value of the cheque in the first place, because of its trust in his endorsement. Orillia, Ontario, demanded (but did not receive) a $200,000 guarantee that the Mariposa folk music festival to be held there in 1964 would not result in a repetition of the previous year's disturbances.

A guarantee is a promise by the guarantor (or, surety), made directly to the creditor to be responsible for the primary debtor's liability, on condition the latter defaults. In other words, the guarantor assumes a secondary or "contingent" liability that the person primarily responsible will fulfil his obligation, such as paying a debt, or fulfilling a contract, or making good any damage he causes. A guarantee can be given

---

[1] An NSF cheque is popularly called a "rubber cheque"; therefore it is said to "bounce."

for credit to be granted to a debtor in the future, or for payment of a debt that is already in existence.

Consequently, a person assuming direct, or primary, responsibility for another's indebtedness is not a guarantor (or surety, related to a hostage), and the contract need not be in writing. Nor, as we have heard, need a *del credere* agency be in writing. The writing requirement is possibly due to the fact that the guarantor is, on the face of it, not getting much in return for his "going out on a limb" for someone else, and the law wants to be sure that he undertook such a liability with his eyes open. Consideration must be present, however; while the surety may not be getting much, the creditor is giving something in exchange—namely, credit to the debtor. A wife, it will be remembered, can escape liability for guaranteeing her husband's debts if she can prove undue influence by him; which she will not be able to do if she first obtained independent legal advice.

RIGHTS OF THE CREDITOR

Unless the contract with him provides otherwise, the creditor may make the guarantor responsible as soon as the debtor defaults on his obligation; it is not necessary first to sue the debtor, although demand for payment should first be made of him.

If there are several guarantors, the creditor may pick on any one of them to fulfil the total obligation; but such paying "victim" afterwards has the *right of contribution* from his co-sureties of their proportionate liabilities.

The creditor's rights against a guarantor continue, even after the primary debtor has received his discharge in bankruptcy (see Chapter 25).

RIGHTS OF THE SURETY

Under his own contract with the debtor, the surety may sue the debtor to pay the creditor as soon as the obligation becomes due.

The surety may ask the creditor to sue the debtor rather than himself, on lodging an adequate indemnity for court costs and legal expenses.

If a surety is sued by the creditor, he may set up any defense or counter-claim that is available, not only to him, but also to the debtor.

235

Once the surety has paid to the creditor the debt that the debtor should have paid but didn't, the surety, by the right of *subrogation,* virtually steps into the creditor's shoes. He inherits from the creditor any right to sue that the creditor had, and he is entitled to have transferred to him for his use any security that the debtor had given to the creditor.

The surety is discharged from any further obligation if:

• The creditor's claims have been met in full.

• The surety or the debtor have been otherwise released from obligation by the creditor.

• The rights of the surety are not fully protected; e.g., if the creditor fails to properly register a conditional sale.

• If the creditor allows the security to become impaired (thus weakening the surety's position when he takes over the security under his right of subrogation).

• If there was an unauthorized change in the terms of payment between the creditor and the debtor; e.g., if the debtor was granted an extension of time; the surety might then never become rid of his contingent liability.

• If an employer, at the request of the bonding company, does not discharge a bonded employee who has been proven dishonest.

• If the guarantee was obtained by fraud.

QUESTIONS

1. Mr. Smelter enters a jewellery store, where he is a valued customer, and finds his sister, Dana, in tears because she has forgotten her wallet and cannot pay for a lovely bracelet which is on special sale for $39.95. At Mr. Smelter's request, the jeweller lets Dana have the bracelet and charges it to the account that Mr. Smelter has with the jewellers.

   In the store Mr. Smelter also meets Eddy, a trusted young employee of his, who is vainly trying to persuade the jeweller to let him have a $39.75 wrist watch on credit. Mr. Smelter assures the jeweller that Eddy is to be trusted and, in fact, he vouches for his reliability. Thereupon the jeweller lets Eddy have the watch.

   If Mr. Smelter becomes bankrupt, which of the above obligations will his trustee have to honour? Explain.

236

2. What is meant by:
   (a) Fidelity insurance.
   (b) Performance bonds.
   (c) Co-signatures.
   (d) *Del credere* agencies.
3. Explain what is meant by a surety's right of:
   (a) Contribution.
   (b) Subrogation.

Negotiable Instruments

NATURE OF NEGOTIABLE INSTRUMENTS

Negotiable instruments (according to the federal Bills of Exchange Act) consist of promissory notes (e.g., bank notes) and bills of exchange or drafts (e.g., cheques). They are virtually the same as money, and, in view of their widespread use, it is important to know the requirements for a valid negotiable instrument; the methods for making use of them; and the rights and duties of the parties becoming involved with them.

In many respects a negotiable instrument is not very different from other contracts. The important difference lies in the fact that the creditor's rights under this particular contract are freely assignable, or, *negotiable,* without notice thereof having to be sent to the debtor. As was mentioned in Chapter 12 under Assignments, the Bank of Canada does not have to be notified every time you spend a dollar bill—and spending it is, in effect, the assigning of a promissory note issued to you by the Bank of Canada. Also, in most circumstances, the assignee of a negotiable instrument is no longer subject to any defenses that the debtor might have had against his original creditor; which, as will be remembered, is the contrary case with assignees of other contracts.

DEFINITION

A **promissory note** *is a written, signed promise that is unconditional, to pay a certain sum of money on demand, or at a future time that is fixed or determinable, to the bearer, or to a specified person(s) or his order.*

The meaning of each term of the above definition is set forth below:

WRITTEN: The writing may be by hand, printed, or

typed, etc. It need not necessarily be in ink; but if it is in easily erasable pencil, special rules apply. It need not be on paper—documents written on egg shells, barn doors, and melon rinds have been held valid (these, of course, being used only in emergency or for stunts).

SIGNED: The note must be signed by the debtor, who is called the *maker* of the note, or by any one else properly authorized by him. Signing with an "X" or other mark is acceptable, provided the mark can be identified; for example, by the person who signed as a witness.

The signature need not necessarily be placed in the traditional bottom right-hand corner of the note; the following way of signing would be quite proper: "I, John Jones, promise to pay . . . ," if in John Jones's own handwriting.

The signature is usually hand-written, but it need not be. A person is not obliged to sign his own name; for example, if so authorized, he may sign his firm's name. If a bank is to be involved in making payment, the signature must be strictly in accordance with the specimen signature that has been lodged with the bank.

PROMISE: This promise must be unequivocal. That is, it should read: "I promise to pay," or "I will pay." It must not read, "I hope to pay." An IOU can be construed as a promise to pay, provided it includes a date of payment.

UNCONDITIONAL: Since the promise must be unconditional, a document stating, "I promise to pay if the goods are satisfactory," while an enforceable contract and assignable, is not a negotiable instrument— not even if the goods turn out to be completely satisfactory.

A CERTAIN SUM: A promise to pay "my week's wages" would be too uncertain, in view of possible deductions for lost hours, increased withholding taxes, etc. However the following have been held to be "sums certain": "$1,000 and exchange" (or "free of exchange" or "F.O.E." or "at par.") ; $1,000 with interest at 6% p.a."; also a promise to pay in specified instalments.

MONEY: "Money" means money in Canadian currency. It is permissible to make out the note in a foreign currency provided the rate of exchange is fixed or determinable and if actual payment is to take place in Canadian legal tender. Thus a promissory note made out for U.S. $1,000 will be a valid note (in 1965) for about $1,080 in Canadian money.

The following would not be "money": "$1,000 worth of grain, jewellery, gold dust, etc." Nor would the following qualify: "I promise to pay $1,000 in cash or in merchandise." The following would qualify: "I promise to pay $1,000; the payee having the choice of taking it in cash or in merchandise."

A FUTURE TIME THAT IS FIXED:

Examples of a fixed future time would be: "I promise to pay on June 30, 1966"; "I promise to pay 30 (or 60) days from date" (i.e., from the date which the note bears); "I promise to pay in one (or three) months," which means on the day with the same number in the future month as the date which the note bears, *provided there is such a day*. If there is no such day, the note is due on the last day of that future month. Thus, a note payable one month from either May 30 or May 31, falls due on June 30; and a note payable two months from December 28, 29, 30 or 31, 1965, falls due on February 28, 1966.

In Canada, three days of grace still have to be tacked on to the above expiry dates; unless they are expressly eliminated in the body of the note to conform with the revised laws in the U.K. and the U.S.A. The final day on which payment must be made is called the *maturity date*. If the maturity date falls on a "non-juridical day" (i.e., a non-business day such as a Sunday, a holiday, nowadays generally a Saturday, or a Monday following a Christmas, New Year's, or Dominion Day which happens to fall on a Sunday), then the time for payment is extended until the next following business day. However, interest, if any is payable, must be paid until the date payment of the note is actually made.

DETERMINABLE: "I promise to pay when I marry"; or "when the building is erected"; or "when I pass my exams" are not determinable times because these events may never take place. However, a promise to pay on, or x days after, Y's death refers to a determinable time since Y must die sooner or later.

Anticipating, a draft that is payable "at sight" (i.e., on acceptance) or "x days after sight" is also an instrument payable at a determinable future time. Unless specifically excluded, three days of grace apply also.

ON DEMAND: A person promising to pay "on demand" must be prepared to do just that, provided:

- The note is presented to him for payment by the payee (creditor) or other proper holder of the note (see later)—
- At the place specified for payment; and if none is specified, then at his place of business during business hours or at his residence at "reasonable hours" (e.g., not in the middle of the night).

If the note mentions no time of payment, it is deemed to be payable on demand; for example, cheques which bear no date of payment are payable on demand. There are no days of grace on demand notes.

BEARER: The bearer is anyone who is in possession of the note. Notes are considered to be made out "to Bearer" if they read as follows: "I promise to pay Bearer"; or "J. Smith or Bearer." Also considered as bearer notes are notes where the name of the payee has been left blank; or notes that say "I promise to pay you" if the name of the payee does not appear elsewhere in the note; or where the name of the payee is intentionally fictitious (e.g., Mickey Mouse or Humpty Dumpty). Again anticipating cheques, orders to "pay cash" or to "pay payroll" are also bearer cheques.

SPECIFIED PERSON OR PERSONS: He, or they, need not be named. For example, the following are specified persons: "The Receiver General of Canada"; "the members of the graduating class of '65"; "the Jones brothers." However, a promise to pay "any of the Jones brothers" would not refer to a clearly specified person.

ORDER: The promise to make payment may be made "to X"; or "to X or his order"; or "to the order of X." The significance of this will be discussed presently.

Bill of exchange. The definition of a bill of exchange (or draft) is the same as of a promissory note, with the exception that we must substitute for the "promise" an *order* by the drawer of the document to the drawee to make payment to the payee. The drawer will issue this order, or command, only if the drawee is under some obligation to obey it, usually because he owes the drawer some money. The order must again be unequivocal; it must not say, "you may pay"; or "you are hereby authorized to pay." It must say "Pay——!" To say "Please pay——" is still regarded as an order, even though a polite one.

A draft can (and most frequently does, nowadays) order the drawee to make payment to the drawer himself, or to his bank.

A cheque is merely a special kind of draft. It is drawn by a person on the bank in which he has an account, and payment must be made on demand. (Cheques can be post-dated, but are not negotiable until the stipulated date arrives.)

REQUIREMENTS OF NEGOTIABLE INSTRUMENTS

It must be repeated that a document which does not strictly comply with the above requirements may still be a readily assignable and perfectly valid contract, even though it is not a negotiable instrument. Warehouse receipts and order bills of lading involve goods instead of money; conditional sales contracts are not unconditional and therefore, although all these are consistently traded, they are not negotiable instruments. A truly negotiable instrument must be visualized as something the corner druggist will have no hesitation in accepting as payment from a customer; for example, a bank note, or the customer's pay cheque.

The negotiable instrument obtains validity as soon as it is *issued*; that is, as soon as its maker (or drawer, respectively) makes physical delivery of the complete instrument to the payee.[1]

NEGOTIATION

The payee may, if he wishes, hold on to the instrument until its maturity and then collect payment for it from the debtor. But one of the features that has made this form of payment so popular is the possibility of transferring it to others, with the minimum of formality, by *negotiation*. Thus an appliance store can negotiate its customer's long-term promissory note to the finance company; and the wholesaler can "discount" his customer's long-term accepted draft (see later) at the bank. Both are then in a position to grant their customers credit without having to use their own money to pay the manufacturer. Similarly, when you pay a cheque, made out to you, into your bank

---

[1] Thus the following are *not* properly issued:

(a) A cheque that I make out to someone, and which I place in my desk with the intention of giving it to him at a later date, and which is unauthizedly taken by him from my desk.

(b) A cheque that I have delivered to someone omitting some vital particular—such as the amount. However, proper issue would take place if I had given him authority to fill in the blank space.

account, you actually assign your claims against the cheque's issuer to your bank to compensate them for immediately crediting your account with the amount of the cheque.

NEGOTIATION BY DELIVERY

All that is technically necessary to negotiate a bearer instrument is to make physical delivery of it; for example, by paying someone with a bank note. In practice, when accepting some other bearer instruments in payment, the payee should insist that the transferor write his name on the back of the paper for identification, in case anything goes wrong (e.g., to assist in tracing a forgery. In England, storekeepers customarily require their customers to write their names on large bank notes with which they make payment.).

An instrument that was originally made out "to Bearer" always remains a bearer instrument and can never be restricted. Obviously, my notation on a dollar bill to "pay John Smith only" would be quite ineffective.

NEGOTIATION BY ENDORSEMENT

To negotiate an order instrument, it must, before delivery, first be *endorsed* by the payee; that is, he must sign his correct name[2], preferably on the back of the instrument. (U.S. money orders are "endorsed" on the front, although etymologically the word "endorsement" means "something on the back.") There are many methods of endorsing a cheque or other negotiable instrument, and some of the more common endorsements are as follows. Let us assume that D. Debtor has made out his $100 cheque on the B. Bank in favour of C. Creditor.

Endorsement in blank. C. Creditor may simply write his name on the back of the cheque and nothing else. This manner of endorsement is generally employed by a depositor at the bank counter just before he cashes a cheque or pays it into his account. The effect of this endorsement is that the cheque has become a bearer instrument; the corner druggist who cashes the cheque as a favour for C. Creditor can pay it

---

[2] Even when it was misspelled; in this case the common practice is for the endorser to sign both names, first the incorrect one and then the right one: e.g., H. Himenez
José Jiménez

into his own bank account without further endorsement being technically required and, through the clearing process, the B. Bank will pay the druggist's bank in due course. The danger of endorsing in blank is that, if the instrument is lost or stolen, the innocent drawee (the B. Bank in this case) would be safe in paying the finder or the thief and would not have to pay the true owner again.

Alternatively, it is open to any holder to reconvert the bearer cheque into an order instrument by writing after C. Creditor's endorsement in blank: "Pay to W. Wholesaler, P. Pillpusher."

A special endorsement is effected by the payee's naming the assignee and signing his name; for example: "Pay F. Friend"; or "Pay F. Friend or his Order"; or "Pay to the order of F. Friend," followed in each case by C. Creditor's signature. The effect of this endorsement is that the cheque remains an order instrument and can be negotiated further by F. Friend; either by endorsement in blank, a special endorsement, or any of the others which follow. (Theoretically this chain of endorsements can go on almost indefinitely; the size of the paper is no handicap since, if it proves too short, an extension, or "allonge," can be fastened to it.)

An accommodation or anomalous endorsement is placed on the back of an instrument by a person who is prepared to guarantee payment of it; he is said to be "backing" it, even if he writes nothing on the bill or note except his bare signature, "G. Guarantor."

By the above three types of endorsement, each endorser guarantees payment of the instrument to *all* future transferees. Thus, if C. Creditor on trying to cash the cheque found it to be dishonoured (i.e., not paid), he could only sue D. Debtor. If C. Creditor had obtained G. Guarantor's guarantee and negotiated the cheque to F. Friend, the latter could sue either D. Debtor or C. Creditor or finally G. Guarantor. And if F. Friend had negotiated it still further, F. Friend could also be sued. It will thus be seen that a negotiable instrument gains in value to the eventual holder by having been negotiated often.

A restrictive endorsement stops further negotiation of the order instrument, except to the transferee's own bank. C. Creditor might endorse the cheque: "Pay J. Jones Only, C. Creditor," if he does not want his signature to get into unlimited hands. If C. Creditor sends a messenger to his bank with a cheque he wants to deposit in his account, or with a promissory note he has received, he will endorse them respectively as follows: "Pay the B. Bank for deposit only in my account, C. Creditor"; or "Pay the B. Bank for collection only, C. Creditor," as a safety measure.

An identification endorsement may have to be obtained by C. Creditor if he wants to cash a cheque in a strange place. If the endorsement reads, "C. Creditor is hereby identified, F. Friend," F. Friend incurs no liability if the payee really is C. Creditor. F. Friend should, of course, be careful to use the above or similar words; if he signs his name and nothing else, he becomes a guarantor.

Qualified endorsement. An instrument can also bear a qualified endorsement. By endorsing the cheque "Pay F. Friend without recourse, C. Creditor," C. Creditor is assigning his claim on D. Debtor to F. Friend without incurring personal responsibility. F. Friend might not be very happy about accepting an instrument bearing such an endorsement. But it has its place if F. Friend is a collection agency who has bought for a cheap price C. Creditor's claim on D. Debtor outright; or if C. Creditor is F. Friend's agent, and customer D. Debtor has made out his cheque to C. Creditor personally instead of to his principal, F. Friend, in the first place.

A partial endorsement is entered on the back of a promissory note by its holder, as a form of receipt for partial payments of the note made by the debtor.

We have said that in many respects a negotiable instrument is not much different from other contracts. One difference is that consideration is presumed to exist; in other words, the onus is on the debtor to prove the total lack of it by his creditor. A negotiable instrument is valid even if given in settlement of outlawed debts or of debts which are unenforceable for lack of writing under the Statute of Frauds.

Another difference is that the holder of the instrument can sue "on the instrument." All he has to prove is that, as its proper holder, he has not been paid on the due date; whereas the creditor under an ordinary contract must substantiate his claim by furnishing the court with full particulars of the contract. Therefore, by getting a debtor to give you his promissory note or to "accept" your draft (see Acceptance of Drafts, below), you have evidence of his indebtedness in clear-cut terms and time limits; and, if he dishonours his "paper," his credit rating suffers far more severely than if he had just been exasperatingly slow in paying the invoice on which you had extended him open credit.

RIGHTS OF THE HOLDER IN DUE COURSE

Personal defenses. If a debtor has a defense available to him against a creditor under an open contract (e.g., that the contract is illegal, or that there was no genuine intent, or that the debtor was legally incompetent, or that the creditor had committed a breach of contract), he retains such *personal defenses* against his creditor, even if the debtor has signed a negotiable instrument. He even retains these personal defenses against someone to whom the creditor negotiated the instrument, if that assignee has a full knowledge of the debtor's claim. However, the situation is different if the instrument passes into the hands of an innocent *holder in due course*. Him the debtor will have to pay on the due date; all he will be able to do after that is to sue his original creditor.

The holder in due course is a party
1. *to whom there was duly transferred* (by delivery and probably endorsement)
2. *for value*—that is to say that the holder paid an actual consideration for the negotiable instrument.
3. *in good faith*—that is, not dishonestly. In other words, he knew of no defense with which the issuer might defeat the claim of the original creditor; even though he may have been somewhat negligent in failing to learn of this.
4. *without notice of any defect*—that is, he was unaware that the transferor had come by it dishonestly; and in this connection the transferee must not wilfully close his eyes to shady circumstances.
5. *an instrument that was complete and regular on the face of it*—that is, there were no improper omissions, contradictions, or alterations in it.
6. *and that was not overdue or dishonoured.*

Real defenses. Thus we can say that a holder in due course takes paper free from any personal defenses. However, *real defenses* can be used by the debtor not only against his original creditor but even against holders in due course. Real defenses are such as make a nullity of a so-called negotiable instrument; for example, the instrument is null if it was issued by an infant,[3] or if it was forged. Forgery can be committed of a signature, or of the amount (when it is said to be "raised"), or of the date or place of payment, or of the payee's name. Tantamount to forgery is the "non-delivery of an incomplete instrument"; for example, where a person takes from another's desk a half-completed cheque *and* fills in some particulars, such as the amount and/ or the name of the payee. (The unauthorized filling in of a delivered, incomplete instrument or the unauthorized taking of a non-delivered, completed instrument are personal defenses valid only against the "immediate party" but not against a "remote" holder in due course.) An innocent holder in due course of a bearer instrument is entitled to payment, however, even if the instrument was stolen at some time between issue and its getting into his hands. However, any endorser is liable to all future transferees even on such invalid paper: he, after all, guaranteed by his signature that the future transferee would be paid. Thus, the person who ultimately has to bear the loss is he who took it from the forger; this includes a bank making payment on a forged cheque. **Notice of forgery.** Before an endorser of an invalid negotiable instrument can be made liable, he is entitled to receive immediate notice of the forgery or other invalidity as soon as it is discovered. If the discoverer fails to give such immediate notice, he himself will have to suffer the loss. This is in order that the endorser may, in order to safeguard himself, take immediate steps to have the forger apprehended. An endorser who has received such notice should similarly notify all who endorsed the instrument previously to him. It must not be forgotten that the holder can ask *any one of the endorsers* to make good his loss, regardless of the order in which they made their endorsements (with the exception that an accommodation endorser must be left to the last). Similarly, the endorser who has been called upon to make good, can demand pay-

---

[3] While an infant is not bound by a negotiable instrument issued or endorsed by him, he can still be sued by his immediate creditor on the contract which gave rise to it; for example, if it involves delivered necessaries. However, a bank is justified in making payment out of an infant's account against a cheque properly issued by him.

ment, in any order, from anyone who made an endorsement *previous* to his.

ACCEPTANCE OF DRAFTS

The maker of a promissory note, by signing it, thereby undertakes an obligation to pay it. However, the drawee of a draft (the person on whom the draft is drawn) obviously comes under no obligation to the payee to pay it by the mere fact that the drawer named him as the drawee in the draft. If I make out a cheque to you for a million dollars on a bank in which I have no account, the bank is under no obligation to pay you. But if I order my debtor (by drawing a draft on him) to pay my bank $1,000 in thirty days and he expresses his willingness to do so by "accepting the draft," he makes himself liable to the same extent as if he had made out his promissory note for that amount on those terms.

Method of acceptance. Until quite recently, the drawee made acceptance by signing his name diagonally across the face of the draft. This method was messy, and now the printed draft forms reserve a space for the drawee's signature of acceptance in the top left corner of the draft. The drawer's signature has the same guaranteeing value as an endorser's; by sending the draft to the payee, the drawer is impliedly giving an undertaking that it will, in due course, be paid by the drawee. The drawer's signature is traditionally in the right bottom; the draft is addressed to the drawee in the left bottom; while the payee's name is shown in the body of the draft.

The acceptor's signature is the really essential feature of the acceptance. Adding the date of acceptance is important, for it determines the date of payment if the draft is drawn "payable at sight" (i.e., at acceptance) or "*x* days after sight." The acceptor may, at his option, add a place of payment (e.g., at his local bank); but writing the word "accepted," while customary, is unnecessary.

Presentment for acceptance. There are a number of technicalities regarding the time within, and the manner in which, a draft must be presented to a drawee for his acceptance. Suffice it to say that a draft payable by a certain date must be presented for acceptance before it is overdue; a draft payable at sight or *x* days after sight must be presented for acceptance within a reasonable time (alternatively, it may be negotiated within a reasonable time; in which case the new holder must present it for acceptance within a reasonable time or negotiate it still further as above). While a draft payable on demand need not be presented for acceptance at all, its holder would be wise to get the drawee's acceptance to assure himself of the drawee's intentions.[4] If the holder of the draft does not present it for acceptance as required, he releases the drawer and any endorsers from their obligation as guarantors. If the drawee has not accepted the draft unconditionally within two business days after it was presented to him, he is said to have "dishonoured it for non-acceptance." Such a dishonour is not necessarily a black mark against the drawee's credit rating—that is, not if the drawer was not entitled to draw on him in the first place.

PRESENTMENT FOR PAYMENT

The holder's requirements to present a negotiable instrument for payment to its payer (maker of note or drawee of draft, respectively) may be summarized as follows:

Demand paper. If the negotiable instrument is payable on demand, it must be presented for payment at reasonable hours at the place specified in the instrument or at the payer's place of business or residence. It must also be presented within a reasonable time after issue. In the case of promissory notes that are given as security for a long-term loan, quite a long time would still be reasonable; demand drafts should be presented at a time that is customary in the parties' particular trade—very often simultaneously with the time at which the goods covered by the draft are due to arrive at the buyer's destination; and cheques should be presented by the next business day. The consequence of making late presentment (whether for payment or for acceptance) is that any endorsers, including the drawer of a draft, are released from their obligation to make good the primary debtor's failure to pay.

Time paper. In the case of negotiable instruments that are payable not on demand but at a specified time, the rules are different depending on whether a place for payment was specified or not. If the place is specified, the holder must present for payment at that place, as above, on the

---

[4] A good illustration of a demand draft is a cheque, which is presented to a bank for payment, but not for acceptance. However, getting a cheque "certified" is virtually an acceptance by the bank. By "marking" a cheque, a U.S.A. bank actually does accept it.

due date, within business or reasonable hours, and to the proper person. Failure to present as required above renders the instrument unnegotiable; the debtor naturally still remains under a contractual obligation to pay his debt.

If no place is specified, technically the debtor should make payment to the holder unasked. But even in this case it is wise for the holder to make presentment: first, because, on account of intervening negotiation(s), his identity might be unknown to the debtor; and second, because failure to make presentment would absolve all endorsers from any liability.

Procedure after payment. Having made payment, the payer should not be satisfied with merely getting a separate receipt. The payee should endorse the paper itself and surrender it to the payer; or the payer should assure himself that the paper is completely destroyed (we are familiar with the mortgage-burning ceremonies of churches, etc., that have finally paid off their indebtedness). If only an instalment has been paid, the payer should make sure that the payment is properly recorded by the payee on the note itself. The danger in not getting back the paid instrument itself is that the person who was paid might negotiate it further (e.g., if it was a demand paper, or if it was paid before maturity and thus was not overdue), and any innocent holder in due course would then be within his rights in demanding payment all over again.

DISHONOUR AND PROTEST

We have heard that a drawee who fails to accept a draft drawn on him within two days, or one who makes a qualified acceptance (e.g., "accepted, if ..."), has "dishonoured the draft for non-acceptance." If payment is refused by the principal debtor on the due date, he has "dishonoured the paper for non-payment"; whereupon the holder can make the parties with secondary liability (i.e., the endorsers and the drawer of a draft) liable in any sequence he chooses— except that the accommodation endorser(s) come(s) last.

Notice of dishonour. But, as in the case of a forgery, the endorser(s) can only be held liable if the holder tells them of, or sends to them, notice of any dishonour by the next business day. If the paper is then presented to an endorser for payment, and he also dishonours it, the holder must give similar notice of this second dishonour to all the other endorsers.[5]

Protest is required of foreign paper and always in Quebec. It is also useful because it furnishes prime proof of dishonour in court and because it raises the debt to a higher category in case the debtor goes bankrupt. Protest is effected as follows:

1. A notary public (or a justice of the peace) on the same day presents the dishonoured paper to the debtor all over again.

2. He then gives the required notices of dishonour.

3. He writes a formal declaration of his activities onto the dishonoured paper.

If a holder receives no satisfaction from any of the endorsers either, he can sue all or any of them along with the primary debtor. If the paper he holds does not qualify as a genuine negotiable instrument, he will be able to sue only the immediate party who endorsed the document over to him, for breach of any contract which existed between them.

Interest. As mentioned earlier, no interest is payable on negotiable instruments until the date of maturity, unless this was expressly agreed upon. However, interest is always payable on overdue paper by way of damages; if no rate of interest is specified, this will be at the "legal rate" of 5%. If a rate of interest is specified, say at 6%, it is changed to 5% after maturity, even if the document requires 6% "until paid." To remain at 6%, the words "6% both before and after maturity" must be used.

Lost instruments. If the holder loses, or claims to have lost, the instrument before it is overdue, he may demand a duplicate from its issuer provided the loser gives indemnity (lodges security) against the original's showing up in other hands and being cashed. While the owner of an instrument that was accidentally destroyed may give evidence of its contents, it is not clearly established whether he is entitled to a duplicate.

---

[5] Notice of dishonour need *not* be given to persons who waived this right by adding to their endorsement: "Notice of dishonour waived." Similarly an endorser can also waive the requirement that the payer must be presented with the paper for payment. The waiver might read: "Presentment, notice of dishonour, and protest waived." An endorser will waive these rights in order not to have to bear the additional cost of these formalities when called upon to pay.

SPECIAL FEATURES OF DRAFTS, PROMISSORY NOTES, AND CHEQUES

All the foregoing remarks (except Acceptance of Drafts) apply equally to drafts and to promissory notes. The following features, however, are particular to the individual instruments.

DRAFTS

Drafts are usually handed to one's bank for collection. The bank, through its many agents (branch banks in Canada and correspondent banks abroad), for a small charge arranges to present the draft for acceptance and for payment, and to take the necessary steps on dishonour. To save subsequent time-wasting enquiries, the draft is usually given to the bank along with full instructions. Some typical instructions would be:

• To waive demand for payment from the debtor of any small interest charges about which he feels strongly.

• What steps to take in case of dishonour.

• The manner in which progress on the collection is to be reported and the proceeds transmitted—viz., by inexpensive (but slow) mail, or by fast (but expensive) cable.

• Giving the bank the name of a "referee in case of need"—that is, a business friend at the distant place with the power to make emergency decisions on matters such as the disposition of unaccepted goods (whether to sell them elsewhere, to return them, or to destroy them).[6]

As already mentioned, a draft attached to an order bill of lading is called a *documentary draft*. By it, the bank is authorized to endorse the bill of lading over to the consignee of the goods as soon as the consignee honours the attached draft by paying it, or by making acceptance of it according to the terms of the sales contract.

A commercial *letter of credit* is a convenient way of facilitating payment for goods between a distant buyer and seller who have not yet learned to trust each other. It is a conditional (and therefore, non-negotiable)draft, drawn by the buyer on his bank, and payable to the seller

---

6 The instruction HAG (Hold for Arrival of Goods) means that a draft payable at sight is not to be presented to a distant customer for payment until the ship carrying his goods has arrived at his port.

through a bank in the seller's country as soon as the seller makes proper shipment of the contracted-for goods. A seller should make sure that such a letter of credit is "irrevocable"; and, in the case of a foreign letter of credit, that it is "confirmed" by a local bank he trusts.

PROMISSORY NOTES

The most common examples of promissory notes are the bank notes issued by the Bank of Canada, by which the bank promises to pay to the bearer on demand. Bonds, and the interest coupons attached to them, are also examples of promissory notes under seal.

Instalment notes. We have earlier referred to a note which is payable in stated instalments. This note is called an *instalment note*, and it should be considered as a group of separate notes (each with its own days of grace) for each instalment. Frequently such a note will contain an acceleration clause, making the entire amount of the note payable the moment default is made in the payment of one instalment. It bears repeating that the debtor should insist on having a partial endorsement of his part-payment recorded on the note itself and that he should not be satisfied with a separate receipt. For his protection against the operation of the Statute of Limitations, the creditor under a long-term note should, every few years, get the debtor to write on the note "acknowledged" along with the date and the debtor's signature or initials.

A promissory note incorporating full details of a conditional sale probably contains too many conditions in it to make it freely negotiable; however, it can still be assigned by the creditor. On the other hand, a *lien note*— a promissory note which contains a statement to the effect that the goods it covers are still in the ownership of the seller—has been held to be negotiable.

Joint notes. If several persons issue one promissory note, it will have to be determined from the wording of the note whether they are liable *jointly* (as an indivisible group) or *severally* (i.e., individually). If the note reads, "We promise to pay," it is a *joint note*; with the consequence that action can be brought on it only once, against any or all of the joint makers, and the creditor should be careful to name every one of the joint makers as defendants if he sues on the note. If he gets his judgment, he will be able to collect from whichever one of them he chooses. But if he should omit one of the co-makers from his suit, and the others are impecunious, the creditor will not be able to take subsequent action against the omitted one.

Several notes. A several note would read as follows: "I, John Smith, and I, Peter Jones, each promise to pay $500 . . ." In this case, John Smith could be sued for $500, and Peter Jones could be sued for $500; but neither one could be sued for $1,000, which is the value of the note.

Joint and several notes. The note is said to be a *joint and several* one if it reads, "I promise to pay," and is signed by all the co-workers; or if it reads, "We promise to pay jointly and severally," again followed by all the signatures. In this case the creditor does not lose his right to sue subsequently any co-signer whom he omitted to include in the suit originally. (But he will, of course, have to bear a second set of court costs.) Incidentally, members of a legally established partnership who sign a note that begins, "We promise to pay," are liable severally as well as jointly.[7]

CHEQUES

Except in the case of a certified cheque (which virtually bears a bank's acceptance), it is a curious fact that the holder of a cheque has no legal means of enforcing payment from the bank on which it is drawn. The bank is, of course, under an obligation to the drawer of the cheque, as his agent, to honour cheques drawn by him as long as the following circumstances prevail:

• The cheque is in a proper form; that is, it is dated, signed, and the amounts in words and in numbers do not conflict.

• The drawer has sufficient funds in his account to cover the amount of the cheque. If not, the cheque will be returned to the payee or his bank marked NSF, meaning Not Sufficient Funds. (In England, the notation RD is used, meaning Refer to Drawer; that is, get him to explain why the cheque was not honoured. Today, the term "not arranged" is often used.)

• If the bank is unaware of the drawer's death, or bankruptcy, or of a court order "attaching" (i.e., freezing) the account. If the bank has

---

[7] For the sake of completeness, mention should be made of notes given in payment of patent rights. These are void in the hands of all transferees except of an innocent holder in due course; and no holder of one can be deemed "innocent," since the fact that it is a *patent right note* must, by statute, be clearly stamped on it.

been informed of one of these circumstances, it must honour no cheques until the account in question is granted an official *release* by the competent authorities.

• The holder of the cheque is not a person prohibited from holding it by a restrictive endorsement on the cheque.

• A post-dated cheque is not presented before the date appearing on it.

• The cheque is presented within six months from its date; this rule is one of the regulations that banks are permitted to draw up and to enforce for their own protection and for that of their customers (the reader will easily find many good reasons for this requirement).

• Payment of the cheque has not been countermanded; that is, the cheque has not been "stopped." To protect themselves against accusations by a customer that they improperly withheld payment of a cheque issued by him, banks require such countermands to be issued very clearly, and in writing—usually in a book reserved for that purpose. An obliging bank manager will, however, "stall" a person demanding payment until the customer can hasten to his bank to issue the written instructions. Cheques can properly be stopped only for good reasons; for example, if the drawer finds out that he has been cheated, or if a bearer cheque has been stolen or has become lost.

When paying by cheque, a person is safe in foregoing a receipt; the cancelled cheques (called "vouchers" in the U.S.A.) serve as receipts. A person who feels that he has been overcharged can mark his cheque "in full of account, if cashed." By cashing such a cheque, the payee of the cheque gives up any further claim on the drawer to that date (unless the payee simultaneously notifies the drawer that he is only applying this amount to the account and claims the balance).

By *certifying* a cheque, a bank vouches for sufficient coverage of that cheque. A certified cheque is still not quite as good as cash since (admittedly, only under the most unusual circumstances) even it can be "stopped," if it was certified at the request of the drawer. If it is certified at the request of the holder, however, it becomes a direct obligation by the bank to pay—in effect, the bank becomes the holder's banker, and after such certification the drawer and all endorsers are discharged from liability. The holder may ask for certification for a variety of reasons; for example, if he does not want to carry cash on his person; if he wants to negotiate the cheque to someone else; or if he has received the cheque as a deposit.

A *banker's cheque* (called a *cashier's check* in the U.S.A.) is a cheque issued by a bank and drawn on itself. It is almost the same as the bank notes that commercial banks formerly issued, except that those were only issued in round figures.

A *bank money order* is also a cheque issued by a bank, but it will be honoured by any branch of that bank.

A *bank draft* is a cheque issued by a bank but drawn on another branch, or on a totally different bank if it is to be sent to a place where no branch is accessible.

A *traveller's cheque* may be issued by a bank, an express company (e.g., American Express), or a travel agency. Arrangements for its cashing all over the world have been made by the issuer, provided the owner signs in the presence of the payer identically to the specimen signature he wrote on the cheque when he bought it. No exchange[8] need be paid for cashing this cheque.

The above order documents are safe and quite inexpensive means of sending or carrying money, since a thief cannot utilize them.[9]

Incidentally, the holder of a cheque is only entitled to "cash it" at the particular branch of the bank on which the cheque was drawn. If your own branch bank gives you money in exchange for a cheque that you endorse over to it, it is not technically cashing it; it is advancing you the money until (through the clearing process) it cashes the cheque at the bank on which it was drawn. (Many first-time visitors to Toronto are surprised when they cannot cash in a Toronto branch of their home-town bank a cheque drawn on that bank. In practice, the visitor is not left destitute: a friend will vouch for the cheque; a telegram or phone call from the Toronto bank to the local bank will clear up matters; or a friendly Toronto branch manager will authorize the advance of a

---

8 Exchange is a fee one has to pay on an ordinary cheque if it is cashed in a town other than that of the issuing bank.

9 A *crossed cheque* is one that bears two lines diagonally across its face. This "crossing" does not cancel the cheque but is used in England as a restrictive endorsement: The payee cannot negotiate a crossed cheque further; he cannot even cash it. All he can do with it is to pay it into his bank account. Crossed cheques safeguard the payee who, in England (in contrast to Canada and the U.S.A.), enjoys no protection if the bank makes payment of the cheque to someone who forged the payee's endorsement.

small amount, pending clearing of the cheque.)

BANKS

Functions and services. The main function of banks is to provide a safe place for deposits of money and, as the depositor's debtor, to pay him interest on his savings account. The other principal function is to lend to sound debtors, at a profit of course, the moneys of the depositors and the moneys invested in the bank by its shareholders. Granting a depositor an overdraft is a variation of this.

Additional services offered by banks are:

• To furnish, at a rental fee, safety deposit boxes and to take documents and valuables into safe keeping in their vaults.

• To honour their customers' cheques, promissory notes, and acceptances (of drafts) by making payment to the holders of these according to the customer's instructions. In this regard, the bank acts as its customer's paying agent.

• The bank also acts as a collection agent for the customer who lodges with it cheques and promissory notes made out to him, or drafts on others drawn by him. Alternatively, the bank will discount such notes and drafts for the customer; that is, the bank will immediately credit the customer's account with their present value, and it will keep for itself the somewhat larger amount it will collect at the future maturity date.

• While all banks used to issue currency, only the Bank of Canada does so now. In addition to issuing the various cheques (described above), banks further facilitate the transmission of funds by issuing not only the commercial letters of credit (described under Drafts) but also *circular letters of credit* for the convenience of travellers who can, up to a maximum amount named in the letter of credit, make withdrawals against it at correspondent banks all over the world. Circular letters of credit are less expensive and bulky than traveller's cheques but they cannot be utilized on holidays or after banking hours.

• Banks also buy and sell foreign currencies; they furnish credit information; they buy and sell government bonds; they execute standing orders (e.g., to pay insurance premiums regularly); and for favoured customers they will perform many other little services (e.g., an English bank can be used as a mailing address).

257

Rights and duties. A bank has a general lien for its customer's overdue debts on all documents and moneys of his that it has in its possession; but not on goods that have been left with it in trust or in escrow, or on the goods in the customer's safety deposit box. The bank has a lien on this box, to the extent of not allowing the customer access to it, if its rent is unpaid.

Banks have a duty to obey attachment orders issued by the court, forbidding the customer access to his account and/or to his box; they have the same duty when they learn of the customer's death or bankruptcy.

Banks also have a duty of secrecy. Without the customer's consent they may only give NSF information to the holder of a dishonoured cheque—not the amount that the customer actually has in his account. No holder of a cheque is entitled to be told the amount in the drawer's account; though the bank is allowed to tell him if there are sufficient funds to cover the cheque.

A bank can be held liable by its customer for negligence if it is careless or disobeys instructions. Not knowing a customer's signature well enough would constitute negligence; thus, if a bank were to pay money out of a customer's account against a forged cheque, the customer could make the bank refund this amount into his account. Of course, the bank would not be liable if the forgery were made possible through the customer's own negligence; for example, if the customer had written out the cheque in easily erasable pencil. Another example of a bank's negligence would be to wrongly tell a holder of a customer's cheque that the customer's account has NSF—this might amount to a libel.

An example of disobedience would be for the bank to ignore a written order from their customer to stop a cheque, and to pay it regardless.

In discussing Agency it was noted that it is common practice for the owner of a bank account to authorize others to draw on his account, either to a limited or to an unlimited amount. The bank must be furnished with specimen signatures of such authorized persons and with a power of attorney signed by the account owner. Also, two or more people may own an account jointly; either with each one of them having the right to make withdrawals from the account independently (this is generally the case with joint accounts of a husband and wife); or with all owners being required to sign the cheques. The important feature of a joint account is that, at the death of one owner, the contents of the account automatically become the property of the survivor(s), regardless of any will the deceased may have left.

Opening a joint account is not an easy way of avoiding death duties, by the way; these still have to be paid on that portion of the funds that the deceased contributed toward the joint account. For example, in Ontario, in the case of a husband and wife's joint account that is solely "fed" by the husband, no death duties regarding the joint account will have to be paid on the death of the wife; but the whole account would be taxable if the husband died. Another point to bear in mind is that, on the death of one of the joint owners of the account, the bank account is "frozen" like any other. It may therefore be wise for joint account owners also to maintain small separate bank accounts, so as not to be left without ready cash if the other joint account owner dies.

While banks are now permitted to lend money on land mortgages, they still may not engage in business or trade, or deal in merchandise, company shares or realty. They are, however, allowed to own the buildings in which their premises are housed and to have a trustee conduct a business, pending its liquidation, of which the banks came to be owners in the due course of realizing their security for a loan they had granted.

QUESTIONS

1. Distinguish a negotiable instrument from other contracts with regard to:
   (a) Consideration
   (b) Assignability
   (c) Personal defenses by the debtor against: (i) the original creditor; (ii) assignees.
2. List the advantages to a seller of receiving the signature of a credit customer on a promissory note rather than on an ordinary contract.
3. You have given your promissory note to a creditor. To what extent does your position become weaker when he negotiates the note to someone else?

4. How many days of grace are allowed in Canada on a draft payable
    (a) On demand?
    (b) At sight?
5. When are the following promissory notes due?
    (a) Five days from Tuesday, February 20, 1968.
    (b) Two days from February 20, 1968.
    (c) Thirty days from January 31, 1968.
    (d) One month from January 31, 1968.
6. Are the following hand-written notes negotiable or not? Explain.
    (a) (No date or place.) "I promise to pay bearer $1000. (One Hundred Dollars). A. Bell"
    (b) "Toronto, May 31, 1965. Sixty days after my arrival in Hamilton I promise to pay to the order of C. Dee $100. E. Fish"
    (c) "Sudbury, June 1, 1966. On demand, I promise to deliver to Dr. G. Howse, dentist, or order, two fine ounces of 100% pure platinum in exact settlement of my debt to him of $300. I. Jakes"
    (d) "London, June 2, 1967. On demand, I promise to pay to the order of K. Linton $300 with interest at the rate of 5% per annum on the return to me of this instrument. M. Nobbs"
    (e) "Windsor, June 3, 1968. Sixty days from date O. Perkins promises to pay Q. Rush $100."
    (f) "Kitchener, June 4, 1969. I will pay S. Timms $500 on July 5, 1969. If this note is not paid on that date, this instrument is to be null and void. U. Vance"
7. (a) Give a complete definition of a holder in due course.
    (b) What defenses are available against him by a debtor?
8. Cass sent his son a cheque which read "Pay Jack Cass or bearer $100."The son had his school principal cash it for him. The principal, without having Jack endorse it, included the cheque in his next bank deposit. However, the bank refused the cheque since it lacked Jack's endorsement. Was the bank correct? Explain.
9. What legal steps should be taken when a negotiable instrument has been dishonoured?
10. Under what circumstances should a bank teller refuse to honour a cheque?

CHAPTER TWENTY-THREE

Partnerships

SINGLE PROPRIETORSHIPS

Before going into the details of partnership law, a few points should be mentioned concerning the person who goes into business independently. One thing he should be very clear about is the fact that he cannot limit his liability in any way. If his business fails, his creditors, in satisfaction of judgments they have obtained against him, are entitled to have just about all his possessions "sold up" including even those which he put under the name of his wife or other trusted persons just previous to judgment. (See Chapter 25, Bankruptcy.)

Next he must make sure that he has obtained any licences that may be necessary; and has complied with any other requirements of the federal, provincial, or local authorities; for example, the payment of a "business tax."

The last point concerns the name he may use for his business. He may always make *bona fide* use of his own name (even if it happens to be the same as that of a famous competitor), provided he does not deliberately use it in a manner that will deceive the public. (E.g., along the U.S.A. highways there are now several restaurants bearing a striking similarity of name and appearance to the well-known Howard Johnson chain.)

A person may also use a name in his business that is other than his own. Thus, Simon Smith may call himself "Jack Jones," "Simple Simon," "Smith & Co.," or "Smith & Sons" even if he has no children; however he is not allowed to end this name with "Ltd." or "Limited." If, however, he uses such a made-up name, and he is in the business of trading, manufacturing or mining, he must register full particulars of himself and his business at a Registry kept for that purpose in his district. A competitor can stop the use of this assumed name if he can show that

1. He had already registered this name; or
2. This name is the same as his own, and the use of it by someone else is harming his business. (More will be said about registration further on.)

FORMATION OF A PARTNERSHIP RELATION

Instead of operating a business by himself, a person may wish to team up with one or more associates and thus form a partnership. The purpose in doing this is to pool finances, equipment, and different abilities and skills in order to cut down overhead and to eliminate competition. The two main points to remember in connection with partnerships that do not incorporate as limited companies (see next chapter) are that:

• An unincorporated partnership is not a separate entity but is an association of individuals. Thus, the partnership does not make out an income tax return; the share of the partnership's profit that a partner receives is shown as part of his income on his individual tax return.

• Each general partner (even the most junior of them) is fully liable with all his resources (business or personal) for the full satisfaction of all obligations incurred by the partnership in contract or in tort. If a creditor chooses to pick just one of several partners to satisfy his claim, it is his privilege to do so; but the victim may subsequently exercise his right of contribution from his partners.

Therefore a person with an established business should be most careful about taking in untried fresh blood; the newcomer may wreck the business. Similarly, a person with money should not be tempted to accept a partnership in a business that he has not thoroughly investigated; his money may have to be used to meet the demands of the partnership's creditors.

The formation of partnerships in Canada comes under statutory regulations. In Ontario, a partnership can be formed by an unlimited number of persons who must, however, be legally competent. Partnerships can be created in the following ways:

262

BY EXPRESS AGREEMENT

While an express agreement may be verbal, it is wise for partnership agreements to be drawn up in writing. Many friendships, and even families, have been broken up through a failure to have an experienced lawyer draw up a contract—even where the partners were such good friends that they thought they would not need anything in writing.

Of course, the contract must be in writing if some statute requires it; for example, the Statute of Frauds requires a written contract if the partnership is to be carried on for more than a year from the date of the contract. Each province has Partnership Acts which lay down the law regarding points which the contract omitted to cover; an example is the standard regulation that partnerships last for life, unless the contract otherwise specifies.

BY IMPLICATION

It may sometimes be to someone's (e.g., a creditor's) interest to have one person declared as another's partner. Even if there was no partnership contract between them (not even a verbal one), the court will declare them to be partners if it finds that they had the *intention* to be partners. If they dispute that they are partners, the court will regard the following features as evidence of a partnership intention:

• That they carried on a business in common. Just being joint owners of income-bearing property is not, in itself, the same as operating a business.

• That they planned to make a profit from the business venture. Participating in an enterprise that amounts to a public service or a charity does not serve to stamp the participants as partners.

• That they were prepared to participate in any losses the business might incur.[1]

• That they participated in management; not necessarily equally, since a junior partner often defers to the judgment of a more experienced associate.

• It will also be considered evidence of the existence of a partnership if the parties contributed capital towards it, equally or otherwise; al-

---

1 Even the Romans refused to consider as partners two persons of whom one could only stand to profit and not to lose; they called this a "Leonine association."

though, as we shall hear, this feature is not a legal requirement at all.

BY CONDUCT

If a person "holds himself out as" (pretends to be) a partner in an organization to a third party who afterwards acquires a claim against that organization, then the third party will also have a good claim against that person. Similarly, if a person or a firm holds someone else out to a third party as their partner, the third party has a claim against the firm for any obligations incurred with it by the "held out" partner.

Similarly, a retired partner (like a retired agent) can continue by his actions to obligate the firm he has left; for he still has apparent authority to bind the firm with people who have received no notice of his retirement.

CLASSES OF PARTNERS

GENERAL PARTNERS

All general partners have a full liability with all their possessions for all the firm's obligations as explained above. General partners can be:

Active partners—this is normally the case.

Silent, dormant, or sleeping partners. Some of these have secret interests in the partnership, while others take no active part in it; yet they can all be held as liable as the active partners. (It must be borne in mind that a person who is declared to be a partner in an express contract need not necessarily take part in management.)

Ostensible partners who have no real interest in a partnership. An ostensible partner is virtually a guarantor; by voluntarily allowing his name to be used as one of the firm's partners, he enhances its credit rating. He, too, incurs full liability.

LIMITED (OR SPECIAL) PARTNERS

In provinces that permit limited partnerships (e.g., Ontario), a person may invest money in an unincorporated firm and limit his liability to no more than the amount of money that he has put into the business. He enjoys this protection provided *all* the following requirements have been observed:

1. His contribution must consist of actual cash. He may not have this

cash returned to him during the life of the partnership.

2. He does not join in the conduct of the business. However, he has the right to inspect its books, and he may give his advice, particularly when it is sought .

3. His name is not mentioned as a partner at all. Alternatively, letterheads and other literature may expressly designate him as a limited partner. Thus, many stockbroker firms have pamphlets which bear a list, first of their active partners, and then a second section listing the limited partners.

4. He is registered as a limited partner in accordance with the provinces' Limited Partnership Acts.

If he fails to comply with any of the above requirements, he can be made to share the unlimited liability of the general partners. While there can be any number of limited partners in a partnership, the partnership must contain at least one general partner with unlimited liability.

REGISTRATION OF PARTNERSHIPS

Just as an independent person conducting a business under a name other than his own must register, so must any partnership that is engaged in trading, manufacturing or mining, even if it uses no made-up name. Thus, partnerships of professional people (doctors, lawyers, etc.) are excused from having to register.

If registration with full particulars does not take place within sixty days of the formation of the firm (changes in the constitution of the firm must be similarly registered), neither the firm nor any of the partners can go to court to enforce a contract made by the partnership in the partnership name. Each partner also renders himself liable to a summary $10 - $100 fine. The Ontario Partnership Registration Act has an exception, however, to the rule that "ignorance of the law is no excuse"; that is, a judge has the power to forgive any registration that is late due to such ignorance. It only costs $3 to register, and 10c to 25c for any interested person to search the register.

RIGHTS AND DUTIES OF PARTNERS TO ONE ANOTHER

Since every partner is automatically an agent for the firm of which he is a partner, the same rules of equity that we discussed under Agency also apply to partners. In other words, a partnership is a contract of the utmost good faith, with the result that no partner must make a secret profit, and each must immediately make full disclosure to his partner(s) of any interests he has which might conflict with the interests of his partner(s). For example, a partner must not make purchases for the partnership from a firm in which he has a financial interest; or from a firm that gives him a "kickback"; at least not without reporting these circumstances to his partner(s).

As the partnership's agent, each partner is entitled to sign the firm name to orders and other contracts, and to make the firm liable for all acts done within his authority, whether actual or merely apparent authority. It is therefore even more important than with ordinary agents to notify the outside world of a partner's retirement:

1. To protect a partnership from being bound to contracts by a retired partner continuing to exercise his apparent authority; and

2. To protect a retired partner from being saddled with contract debts which the firm incurs after his retirement—after all, creditors who do not know of a partner's retirement are entitled to continue to regard him as a partner. However, even without notification, a retired partner is not liable for any torts which the firm commits after his retirement.

How this notice of retirement is to be given has been discussed previously; suffice it to repeat that a written notice of a partner's retirement should be sent to everybody with whom the partnership has had any business dealings; and constructive notice should be given to everybody else by an advertisement in the provincial Gazette.

If the partnership is registered, a partner's retirement must also be registered.

The liability of partners for contracts entered into by the partnership is a joint one. However, in the case of a written contract that is signed by more than one of the partners, each of the signing partners is also liable severally; with the consequence that if a signing partner was not named as a defendant originally, another suit can be entered against him subsequently. The question of the joint and several liability of partners is more or less of a dead issue in those provinces (e.g., Ontario) where the defendant partners need not be named individually in the writ but where the partnership may be sued in the firm name.

Where the partnership (or any of its employees in the course of employment) has committed a tort, each partner is also liable severally. Before suing anybody for anything, it is not a bad idea to search the register of partnerships to see if the person you intend to sue has any partner(s) whom it might be worth while to join in the action.

The following are some provisions of the various Partnership Acts which are to take effect if the partners, in their express partnership contract, have not made provisions to the contrary:

• A partner, newly entering an already existing partnership, is not liable for its earlier obligations. An agreement to the contrary can be inferred if the new partner pays a lump sum for his share in the firm which is based on the firm's balance sheet. For example, suppose that the firm of A and B has assets worth $30,000 and liabilities amounting to $3,000; if C buys a one-third interest in this firm for $9,000, he obviously assumes responsibility for $1,000 of the existing liabilities.

• A retired partner is not liable for subsequent debts incurred by the partnership. He can, however, be held liable by any creditor who was not properly notified of the partner's retirement; in which case, the retired partner is entitled to reimbursement from the other partners.

• A partner remains liable, after retirement, for his share of the still outstanding debts that were incurred while he was still a partner. However, an agreement between the partners will normally provide for his being released from this liability when calculating the financial settlement connected with his retirement. To spare him subsequent complications, the creditors concerned should be persuaded to join in a novation agreement wherein they release the retired partner and restrict their claims to the surviving partners.

• Unless other arrangements have been made in the contract, a partner is not to receive any extra payment for any special services (e.g., for working overtime) that he performs for the partnership; nor is a partner to be docked any pay for being lazy. In the latter case, the remedy is to end the partnership. A partner is, of course, entitled to reimbursement for any outlays he properly undertook on behalf of the partnership.

• While the partners have to be unanimous in deciding issues of major importance (such as changing the scope or the location of the partnership business), a majority opinion rules on less important decisions.

267

• If a partner (to raise personal funds) is forced to pledge, or even to sell, his interest in the partnership, the transferee does not become a new partner in the business. In fact, he is not entitled to join in the conduct of the business in the slightest, or even to see its books. He is entitled only to receive the assigning partner's share of the profits, as determined by the partners.

CAPITAL AND PROFITS

It was briefly mentioned previously that it is not necessary for partners to make equal contributions to the capital of the partnership. They may contribute capital in any proportion that is agreed upon. Capital can consist of tangible items such as money (or its equivalent), land, buildings, machinery, equipment, or goods; or of a person's labour, skill, experience, business connections, or reputation; or of a patent or well-established business name that he has to contribute.

If there is no express agreement making other provisions, all profits that the firm makes and losses that the firm suffers are shared among the partners—it should be well noted—*equally*; and not, as is generally thought, in proportion to the partners' contributions to the capital. This latter arrangement is, however, frequently provided for expressly in the partnership contract. In fact, even the tangible capital contributions will be divided equally among the partners on the dissolution of the business, unless the partnership contract was induced by fraud or the contract safeguarded the interests of those contributing the larger shares by arranging for, not an equal, but for a rateable distribution.

If the contract provides for an unequal distribution of the profits among the partners but omits to state how losses are to be shared, then any losses are to be borne in the same ratio that the profits would have been shared.

DISSOLUTION OF PARTNERSHIP

A partnership comes to an end under any one of the following circumstances:

• On the expiry of the term fixed for the duration of the partnership in the partnership agreement, or on the achievement of the determined object for which the partnership was formed.

• By the death of any one of the partners. This provision of the Partnership Acts may, however, be freely amended by contract, so as to preserve a continuity of operations and to prevent a disruption of business on a partner's death.

• By the bankruptcy of any one of the partners; or if any one partner's share in the partnership assets is attached (frozen) by a court order; or if a partner pledges or sells such share.

• By any of the partners' giving the amount of notice required in the partnership agreement of his intention to retire from the firm; or by the addition of a new partner to the firm. In the case of any such reconstitution of the firm, a new agreement should be drawn up which will come into existence at the same instant that the old firm expires; in fact, provision for such changes should have been made in the original contract.

• If the business becomes illegal; or if it is subsequently discovered that the business was formed for an illegal purpose to begin with.

• Since the expulsion of a partner from the firm is a matter of major importance, it cannot be decided upon by a majority of the other partners (unless the contract expressly permits this). To achieve expulsion, an application has to be made to the court on any of the following grounds:

That the partner suffers from an incapacity, such as insanity or serious illness.

That the partner has been guilty of misconduct such as drinking, dishonesty, or acquiring a criminal record.

That the partner is guilty of persistently breaking the terms of the partnership agreement.

The granting of such an application will also result in a dissolution of the partnership, unless it is immediately re-formed by a contract among the surviving partners.

• On application by any of the partners, the court will also order the dissolution of a partnership on the grounds of its inability to make a profit or *for any other just reason.*

DISTRIBUTION OF PARTNERSHIP ASSETS

When a partnership is dissolved, all its assets must be realized (converted into cash) and distributed as follows:

1. The claims of all business creditors must be met first. To satisfy them, the funds to be used first are:

(a) Those standing to the credit of the firm's profits account.

(b) If these are insufficient, inroads must be made into the firm's capital.

(c) If this, too, is insufficient, the partners will be called upon to make good the losses out of their personal fortunes, in the ratio provided for in the contract.

It should be noted, however, that before a partner's personal fortune is used for the satisfaction of the partnership's creditors, it must first be available to satisfy the claims of his personal creditors. (Conversely, a partner's personal creditors have no claims against his interest in the partnership until this has served to satisfy the claims of the creditors of the partnership.)[2]

If even the combined personal assets of the partners are insufficient to meet the demands of the creditors in full, the creditors will have to take bankruptcy proceedings and suffer their losses in the ratio that the Bankruptcy Court decides.

2. Once the claims of the business creditors have been met in full, loans will be repaid that have been made to the firm by any of its general or limited partners. If these cannot be repaid in full, each partner-creditor is to receive a proportionate share. If any funds are available after a full repayment of these loans, interest at 5% per annum is payable on them.

3. Any further available funds are to be used to repay their capital investments to the partners. The contributed capital will be divided equally among all the partners, as previously mentioned; but the contract will usually entitle them to a refund of their original contributions. Again, if the funds are not sufficient to meet these claims in full, they will be divided rateably.

4. Anything left over after a full refund of the capital investments represents a profit and will be divided among the partners in the ratio that profits are to be divided.

---

2 If one partner is unable to contribute his required share of the losses, the other partners will have to bear it. According to the decision in the English case of Garner v. Murray, where the defaulting partner went bankrupt, his partners had to suffer this deficiency not in the ratio provided for losses in the contract, but in the ratio of their capitals at dissolution.

Death or retirement of partners. To prevent disputes on the death or retirement of a partner, a good partnership agreement will make provision for the surviving partners to buy out a deceased or retiring partner's share at a predetermined rate and to carry insurance for the death of the partners. However, if no such arrangements have been made and the surviving partners wish to continue the business, it might be very uneconomical to have to raise the funds quickly to pay off his share to the retired partner (or to the estate of a deceased partner). Pending a final settlement, a retired partner (or the estate of a deceased partner) is entitled either to an equitable share in the firm's profits or, at his option, to interest at five per cent per annum of his investment in the partnership.

In conclusion, it is again strongly recommended that persons entering into a partnership have an experienced lawyer draw up *articles of co-partnership* that will fairly and adequately cover at least the following most important points:

Date of the agreement.

Names and addresses of the partners.

Name, address and purpose of the firm.

Term of the partnership (e.g., that it is to last for one year; but that it is to renew itself automatically for another one-year period subject to each partner's right to give written notice of dissolution to the other(s), three months before any such renewal date).

Amount of capital investment; and any interest it is to bear.

Opening of a bank account; the signing of cheques.

Keeping books of account; annual audit.

Drawing privileges.

Distribution of profit or loss.

Loans to firm by partners; or by firm to partners.

Limiting partners' rights to individual action (e.g., not to enter alone any obligations over $500).

Giving of guarantees.

Hiring and dismissing of employees.

Duties of partners (e.g., to devote an eight-hour day to business exclusively.)

Division of responsibilities.

Division of assets (or liabilities) on dissolution of the partnership.

Buying-out partner's share on death, retirement or expulsion.
Establishing value of goodwill.
Carrying of insurance on life of partners for benefit of partners,
and/or of deceased partner's estate.
Arbitration clause to govern disputes among partners.

QUESTIONS

1. (a) Tom Eaton plans to operate a retail store by himself. Explain
   whether or not he may call it: (i) Eaton's; (ii) Tom Eaton
   and Co.; (iii) The T. Eaton Co.; (iv) Eaton's Ltd.; (v)
   Smith & Jones.
   (b) Which of the above names must be registered? Why?
2. You are earning a salary of $450 a month when your two employers
   propose giving you an equal partnership in their business, which
   has been averaging a net profit of $25,000 a year. What basic consid-
   erations might deter you from accepting this favourable offer?
3. (a) List the circumstances existing between business associates from
   which the court may assume the existence of an implied partnership.
   (b) Why may it be of importance to determine whether the relationship between persons is that of partners?
4. List the requirements which a limited partner must fulfil to avoid
   being regarded as a general partner.
5. Algernon, Basil and Clarence enter into partnership; Algernon puts
   up $5,000 capital, Basil puts up $4,000, and Clarence contributes his
   charm and personality. On dissolution of the partnership, how will
   its capital be divided among the partners?
6. (a) Tutti and Frutti were partners in the ice cream business. Tutti
   wanted to stock up with a particularly large assortment of
   flavours, but Frutti was afraid of the risk. Thereupon Tutti
   agreed with Frutti in writing, to bear three quarters of any
   loss that might be suffered. A cool summer made it impossible
   for the partners to pay the wholesaler on time, and the wholesaler thereupon obtained a judgment against both partners.
   What share of the debt could he make Frutti pay? Explain.
   (b) Using the facts in the above case as an illustration, explain a
   partner's right of contribution.

7. Shirker and Striver were partners. Shirker left unexpectedly on a long holiday and let Striver do all the work. During this time Striver allotted himself a reasonable salary for his extra work and drew one half of the remaining profit. When Shirker returned, he claimed that Striver was not entitled to do this. Was Shirker right? Explain.

8. Your partners, on a business trip, happen upon some property which they feel the partnership should buy for a substantial price. Unknown to them, the property's owner turns out to be your married sister. How should you act when your partners ask you to concur in its purchase?

Commercial Corporations

NATURE OF A CORPORATION

Once or twice during the discussion of partners, reference was made to unincorporated partnerships; that is, associations of individuals carrying on business together for profit, and each being fully liable with all his personal goods for any loss incurred by the partnership. The risk of full liability can be avoided by the partners if they *incorporate*; that is, if they form a company wherein the liability of each partner is limited to the amount that he invested in the company.

The Dominion Companies Act, and each of the provincial Corporations Acts, authorizes the formation of such bodies. In law, such a company is almost the equivalent of an individual person: it has a name; it has an office; it has its own capital; and it sues (and gets sued) in its own name. Of course, it can only act through human agents, and it signs documents by an agent affixing the company's *common seal* thereto. In some respects, it enjoys advantages over humans; for example, while its life can be ended forcefully or voluntarily, it need never die a natural death, as we shall see. If it commits a crime, it can only be punished by fining since "you cannot kick its back-side or hang its common seal"; this will not preclude any accomplice, such as a fraudulent company director, from being punished more drastically, however.

While municipalities and utilities are corporations, and while social, religious, literary, athletic associations, etc., can also become incorporated (for a $20 fee in Ontario), this chapter will be concerned only with business companies. Railroads, banks, utilities, insurance and loan companies are often created by special acts of the Dominion or provincial government, but business firms must make application for a charter of incorporation to the Dominion and to half of the provincial governments (in the other provinces, an *agreement is registered*—a slightly different procedure). Incidentally, firms of professional people (e.g., doctors or lawyers) are not allowed by their professional associations to incorporate. While co-operatives and credit unions are also incorporated, the rules governing them are somewhat different and will not be discussed here either.

OBTAINING A CHARTER

The procedure for obtaining a charter in Ontario is as follows:

1. Three adult *promoters* must agree to incorporate and to take shares in the new company. For convenience, these will often consist of the lawyer who is making the application and two members of his staff, each applying for one share.

2. An application form is secured from the office of the Provincial Secretary and is completed with the following information:

(a) The name, address, and occupation of each applicant.

(b) The proposed name and the address of the new company.

(c) The objects of the new company. It will be remembered that a company, in order not to be guilty of acting *ultra vires*, must not engage in activities that were not authorized in the charter. The objects clause should therefore be worded widely enough to permit the company to expand the scope of its activities without first having to apply for an expensive amendment to its charter.

(d) Particulars about the capitalization of the company (see later).

(e) If the company is to be *public* or *private*. If private, it will be allowed to have a maximum of fifty shareholders, and the company will not be allowed to solicit capital from the general public. A shareholder in a private company is not allowed to sell his shares indiscriminately, and the application must specify how his freedom will be restricted (e.g., by first having to obtain the approval of the majority of the directors).

(f) The names of the persons who will be the company's first directors.

(g) The number of shares to be taken by each applicant.

(h) The signatures of the applicants and the witnesses.

3. The application is then sent to the Provincial Secretary, accompanied by:

(a) Affidavits of the witnesses attesting the signatures.

(b) An affidavit by one of the applicants regarding the *bona fides* of the new company.

(c) The incorporation fee based on the amount of the authorized capital (see later). This can range from $100 for a capital of $40,000 to $735 for $2,000,000, and 20¢ for each $1,000 after that.

4. The application is then checked by officials in the Provincial Secretary's department who may demand changes in the company's objects or name; for a company will not be allowed to use the name of an already existing company or registered business unless the use of this name is not likely to deceive the public (e.g., a firm manufacturing underwear could call itself Hercules without harming an explosives manufacturing company already bearing that name). Such a name may also be used with the consent of its earlier user if he is in the process of going out of business. Nor must the name of the company imply any connection with the Crown (e.g., Royal, Imperial) except with proper authority. The name of every trading company must terminate with "Limited" or "Ltd."; and it must generally be displayed at the door of its head office.[1]

5. After approval of the application by the Provincial Secretary, the charter is issued to the company by *letters patent*, which is a very formal document bearing the province's seal in red wax; and it contains the name and place of the company, the names of the original shareholders and directors, the company's authorized capital, and its objects. As mentioned when discussing legal incapacity (Chapter 8), the Corporations Acts extend many auxiliary powers to companies (e.g., a company that is formed to "buy, sell and trade in goods, wares and merchandise" may also hire and dismiss personnel; lease, buy or sell business premises, etc.).[2] The issue of the letters patent is then advertised in the provincial Gazette.

6. If the company wishes the general public to invest money in it, it

---

[1] Some foreign counterparts for Ltd. are as follows. U.S.A.: Incorporated or Inc.; French and Spanish: SA; German: GMBH.

[2] However, unnecessary land may not be owned or leased by a company without a *licence in mortmain* first being obtained from the province; any land held that turns out to be unnecessary, must be disposed of within seven years. Any company that plans to own land must incorporate in the province where that land lies, or obtain a licence in mortmain from that province.

must first file a *prospectus*[3] with the Securities Commission. A prospectus contains full particulars about the organization and the activities of the company, and it must be scrupulously accurate. Once it is approved by the Securities Commission, it can be advertised or sent to prospective investors.

FINANCING

A person may decide to incorporate his own business for various reasons—the principal ones being to escape unlimited liability and to enjoy income tax benefits. There are numerous such "one-man companies"—for practical purposes, the two other persons required for incorporation are frequently figureheads and can be ignored. A person incorporating for the sake of limiting his liabilities will, of course, find it more difficult to obtain generous credit unless he personally guarantees the credit granted to his company. With the present (1965) tax structure, it is to a person's advantage to incorporate his business if it makes him a net profit of $10,000 to $35,000 per year, or over $90,000 per year (i.e., after he has received from the company his salary as its general manager, and interest on any loan he may have made to the company).

Another important reason for incorporating is that a limited company possesses machinery for obtaining its capital (limited only by the amount of public confidence placed in it) from many people, in large or small amounts. The amount of capital must not exceed the amount that is specified as its *authorized capital* in the company's charter; but this can be set at virtually any amount. To illustrate the financial structure of a newly formed company, let us imagine it to have an authorized capital of $250,000, consisting of *common shares* to a value of $150,000 and of 6% *cumulative participating preference shares* (preferred as to dividends and as to assets) to a value of $100,000.

COMMON SHARES

If this company needs $100,000 to start operations, it may invite the public to buy 2,000 shares having a stated *par value* of $50 each.[4] Appli-

---

3 See Contracts of the Utmost Good Faith under Lack of Genuine Intention. (Chapter 10)

4 Alternatively, the shares might bear *no par value*, but be offered for sale at the same price of $50 each. The advantage of no par value shares is that they may be offered for sale at any price, while shares with a stated par value must not be sold by the company to the public at a discount, unless they are mining shares.

cants for shares are frequently asked to make a deposit, with the balance to be paid soon after the company has allotted the requested share(s) to the applicant. If more than 2,000 shares are applied for in this illustration, the company will allot the available 2,000 shares to the applicants in its discretion; these applicants then become the shareholders of the company. (If the company goes "broke," no shareholder can lose more than the money he has paid for his shares—or has promised to pay for them, if not yet fully paid.)

These shareholders are then entitled to divide among themselves, in proportion to the number of shares each holds, the dividend that has been declared by the company's directors. The dividend is the amount of surplus profit that is not required to "be put back into the business" for its improvement, development, or expansion. Each common shareholder also has one vote at meetings (see later) for each share that he holds—each share virtually entitling him to ownership of one two-thousandths of the business.

Since the charter authorized the issue of $150,000 worth of common stock and only $100,000 has actually been issued, it may at any time issue a further $50,000. It is customary to give existing shareholders the first opportunity of buying these additional shares by issuing to them *rights* or *warrants*.

PREFERRED SHARES

Preferred shares are issued in the same manner as common shares, but they always have a stated par value. Their holder is entitled to a fixed rate of interest, which is payable out of the declared dividend before the common shareholders are entitled to any dividends. Thus, if a company declares only a small dividend (e.g., 8%), the preferred shareholders (getting 6%) will be better off than the holders of the common shares (who will get only 2%). However, if a very large amount of profits is available for distribution in the way of dividends (e.g., 20%), the preferred shareholders will continue to get only 6%, while the common shareholders will get 14%.

If the preferred shares are *participating*, their holders will be entitled, in addition to the 6% they get, to participate in any profits that are left over after the common shareholders have been paid a specified amount (let us say 10%). Thus, in the last illustration, the preferred shareholders will get 6%, the common shareholders will get 10%, and the preferred and the common shareholders will divide the remaining 4%.

If preferred shares are *cumulative*, a preferred shareholder who did not get his full dividend in any one financial period will be entitled to payment of the deficiency out of future profits, before the common shareholders are entitled to any dividends.

Holders of shares that are preferred also as to assets have a claim (for what it is worth) on the assets of the company, on its dissolution, that ranks before that of the common shareholders. Preferred shareholders do not generally have the voting rights enjoyed by the common shareholders. For income tax purposes, preferred shares also benefit from the 20% exemption from double taxation and depletion allowance as common shares do.

BONDS

In addition to issuing shares, a company may borrow money by issuing bonds (in North America, these usually offer as additional security a mortgage on the company's fixed assets) or debentures (which are usually supported by a similar mortgage in England). The bondholders are entitled to a fixed rate of interest and to repayment of the full face value of the bond at its stated maturity date. If the bonds are stated to be *non-redeemable*, the company does not have the right to pay them off before maturity; otherwise, they are like an "open mortgage" (see Mortgages, Chapter 28) and may be paid off earlier. *Convertible* bonds give the holder the privilege of exchanging his bonds for a stated number of the company's shares. A company's entire bond issue is usually bought by one or a group of *investment dealers* at a discount and then usually distributed by them at face value to the general public.

Bond interest is entitled to no direct income tax benefits; however, bonds bearing a low rate of interest can often be bought in the open market for considerably less than their face value; and the profit realized on them when redeemed at their full face value at maturity represents nontaxable *capital gains* (provided the tax payer is not in the business of buying and selling bonds).

After their issue, the various shares and bonds can be bought and sold at their market value through brokers. Common shares will rise and fall in relation to the growth and profits of the company; preferred shares and bonds will, instead, fluctuate in relation to the current rates of interest obtainable.

THE ORGANIZATION OF A COMPANY

The organization of a company is a highly technical matter that must be left to specialists and will only be summarized here. Once the charter has been granted, the persons who were provisionally named in it as the company's original directors will ratify the acts done for it by its promoters (the terms of the contract with the promoters must be disclosed fully in the prospectus, incidentally). The directors then draft some provisional *by-laws*. For example:

• What meetings are to be held.
• The length of notice of meetings to be given to shareholders and directors.
• The number of persons to constitute a *quorum* (the Companies Act requires a minimum of two-fifths of the directors to be present at directors' meetings).
• What officers the company is to have.
• The form of the company seal and the signing powers of the officers.
• The rules governing the recording of share transfers.
• The powers of the directors to borrow money for the company by the issue of bonds.

The company's bank is then issued with a copy of the by-laws and with the specimen signatures of the authorized signing officers.

After the issue of the required amount of shares to the original incorporators and the government approval of the prospectus, company shares will be issued to the public as described earlier, and the first general meeting of the shareholders will be called. This must be held within eighteen months of incorporation at the latest; and others, at least once a year after that. At this first general meeting of the shareholders, the actions and draft by-laws of the provisional directors will be ratified or amended; the transfer back to the company of the shares issued to the original incorporators will be accepted, and the shareholders will elect new directors. These can quite well be the provisional directors, but they must all own at least one share. The directors, in a meeting of their own, then make appointments to the previously designated offices (e.g., president, vice-president, secretary, treasurer, etc.), and decide what salaries to pay them.

This right of electing directors and voting on other company matters is one of the most important rights a common shareholder has in the management of the company in which he has a part—whether a large part or an insignificant one. He has one vote for every share he owns, and he can delegate this by means of a written *proxy* to any substitute. He is usually sent a blank *proxy* form by one of the company's directors along with the notice of the next meeting and a copy of the company's *annual report* which he is entitled to have mailed to him regularly in good time. The annual report contains a condensed balance sheet and trading statement, verified by the report of an independent auditor who is also appointed by the majority vote of the shareholders. At the annual meeting, the company president reads his *statement of affairs*, and the shareholders then have full rights to question and to criticize the company's officers.

Except for his right to vote at meetings, a shareholder has no voice in the management of the company. He has no right to inspect the *books of account* (which must be kept in a form specifically designated in the Companies Act); but he, as well as any of the company's creditors, has the right to examine the *documents of record* a company must keep, which include:

• Minute books, containing the minutes of all shareholders' meetings.

• A copy of the company's charter and any supplementary letters patent.

• A copy of the company's by-laws.

• A share register, listing all the company's shareholders and their holdings for the last ten years.

• A register of share transfers.

• A register of the company's directors, past and present.

Another record that a company must keep is the minute book which contains the minutes of all directors' meetings. It, however, is not open to the general inspection of all shareholders; the directors alone have the right to inspect it.

Several provinces require specific publication to be made of all trading by directors in the shares of their own company. The independent auditor has full access to the company's books of account at any time; he has the right to demand information and explanations from the directors; and he can attend and speak at all meetings.

If a shareholder feels that the company is not being properly run, he, by his vote, can refuse to confirm the decisions made by the directors since the last meeting, and he can refuse to re-elect them. Even if the company has made a substantial profit, the shareholder is not entitled to a share of it unless the directors have decided to distribute it by declaring a dividend. If a shareholder feels disgruntled and if he can get together shareholders owning between them one-tenth of the company's shares, he can force the directors to call a special shareholders' meeting within sixty days. If he feels that he has been harmed by the company, he can sue it.

DIRECTORS

Frequent mention has been made above of the company's directors. There must be at least three of them who are over twenty-one years of age, are shareholders in the company, and are not bankrupt; they are the persons who manage the business as trustees and agents for the company. They have the power to make all decisions for the company (some in the form of motions or resolutions, others in the form of by-laws), and these are completely binding until the next shareholders' meeting—either the annual meeting or a special meeting, summoned either by the directors or by the shareholders. If the majority of the shareholders does not approve of the directors' actions, it has been explained that their remedy is to vote them out of office.

Some of the important powers of directors are the following:

To allot shares to applicants.

To declare dividends.

To borrow money by issuing bonds.

To buy land and other property for the company and to pay for it by the issue of shares.

To sell shares at a premium, or at a discount where this is not prohibited.

To fix the issue price of no par value shares.

To fix their own remuneration.

To change the address of the company.

On the other hand, a director also has responsibilities, and he can be held liable in any of the following situations:

• If he has an interest that conflicts with the interests of the company, and he does not make a full disclosure of this conflicting interest. In this regard, he is in the same position as an agent or a partner; in addition, even after having made full disclosure, he must not vote on any such issue.

• If he assists in having untrue entries made in the company's books or minutes, or mis-statements made in the prospectus.

• If a dividend is declared either when the company is insolvent, or out of capital rather than out of profits, and a loss results to the company.

• If the directors consent to the sale of not fully paid-for shares by their holder to an insolvent person.

• In the case of the company's insolvency the directors are personally liable for up to one-half year's back wages of its workers.

• If they improperly sell shares at a discount or (what amounts to the same thing) issue "bonus" shares; or if they loan company funds to a shareholder or to a director for the purpose of buying the company's shares.

• If the company fails to comply with any of a number of requirements imposed on it by law (e.g., if it fails to use "Limited" after its name; if it does not make the required *annual return*—i.e., an information return to the government; if it does not insert advertisements in the Gazette when this is required; if it fails to send out notices of meetings in the required manner; etc.).

DISSOLUTION OF THE COMPANY

A company is dissolved when its charter is revoked by the government for failing to comply with some legal requirement (e.g., for failing to file annual reports; for allowing the number of shareholders to fall below three; for not beginning operations within two years of the granting of the charter).

It can also be "wound up" at the request of the shareholders to the Provincial Secretary. This request will be granted as soon as all the company's debts have been paid and everything else is found to be in order. The proceeds from the remaining assets of the company will be divided among the shareholders by the liquidator according to the company's by-laws, and its charter will be surrendered. Any property that is accidentally "left over" is forfeited to the Crown.

A company can be compulsorily wound up for its insolvency. This will be discussed in the next chapter which deals with bankruptcy. A winding-up order can be issued by the court for any other just reason.

After a winding-up order has been issued, a company ceases to exist and it can no longer sue or be sued. Any transfer of its shares is then void without the court's consent. Its dissolution must be advertised in the Gazette within fourteen days. In Ontario, any unsatisfied creditors of the company preserve their claims for one year against the proceeds of the dissolution in the hands of shareholders who shared in its distribution.

ADVANTAGES AND DISADVANTAGES OF INCORPORATION

Except for stockbroking firms, there are not many large unincorporated partnerships left, and it might be interesting to conclude this topic by summarizing the chief advantages and disadvantages of incorporation:

• The psychological prestige to a small firm that the bearing of the title of "Limited Company" brings.

• The liability of shareholders in a company is limited; this, however, might result in less generous credit being extended to a company.

• Machinery for obtaining capital is simple; yet the people who put up the money have no right to interfere with the running of the business (except by voting). On the other hand, lawsuits against the company do not involve the shareholders personally.

• Investors can realize their investments readily, simply by selling their shares without anyone's consent (provided the shares are fully paid for and the company is not a private one).

• The death or bankruptcy of one or several of the shareholders does not affect the existence of the company. The shares go to the defunct shareholder's successor, and the company continues indefinitely.

• Many irritating and expensive formalities are required of a company at its formation, annually, and in connection with the keeping of its records; but its operation is always under the watchful eyes of the government, the shareholders, and their auditor.

• Companies cannot make major decisions as quickly as partners; a directors' meeting must first be called, and any decision arrived at by its vote is only good until the next shareholders' meeting. This decision must not be anything that is *ultra vires* or contravening any of the many statutory requirements.

• Finally, a large corporation sometimes lacks the personal contact of a private enterprise with its customers and employees, and it provides more opportunities to unscrupulous persons for malpractices and unethical manipulations.

QUESTIONS

1. Describe the necessary steps for incorporating a trading company in your province.
2. List the ways in which a company may be capitalized.
3. Under what circumstances can the directors of a company be held personally responsible?
4. What are the rights of the shareholders in meeting?
5. What are the functions and the rights of a company's auditor?
6. Set up a three-part tabulation, listing the comparative advantages and disadvantages of operating a business:
   (a) As an independent operator.
   (b) In partnership.
   (c) As a corporation.

Bankruptcy

INITIATION OF BANKRUPTCY PROCEEDINGS

In Chapter 5 the debtor's voluntary composition with creditors was described, which is workable if every one of the creditors agrees with the debtor's proposal for the arrangement of his affairs. If not, the Dominion Bankruptcy Act of 1950 and the Winding-up of Companies Act ensure that there is a just distribution of the debtor's remaining assets among all his creditors. These Acts also try to prevent a dissipation of such assets; they provide uniformity of proceedings across Canada with a minimum of expense; and they arrange for blameless bankrupts to obtain a discharge and to be allowed to make a fresh, unsaddled start in business life.[1] This legislation is presently the object of review, to prevent abuses of it by unscrupulous persons who get rich on "profitable bankruptcies."

VOLUNTARY BANKRUPTCY

When a person becomes insolvent—that is, when his debts exceed his assets—he can make a *voluntary assignment* of his assets to the bankruptcy official in his district, the Official Receiver, or to a licenced trustee; his case will then be treated in the same manner as that of a person who was compulsorily bankrupted (see below). Incidentally, a farmer or professional fisherman cannot be compulsorily bankrupted, nor can a person whose income of not more than $2,500 is derived from wages and commission payments. The best remedy of a creditor against such a person is to get a court order for the garnishment of his wages;

---

1 The derivation of the word "bankrupt" is interesting. It comes from the Italian word for a broken bench; the unfortunate trader had his place of business, which often was a bench on the street, broken up by his disgruntled creditors.

286

that is, his employer will be ordered to pay a portion of his wages into court. This order is not available against employees of the Dominion government, or against judges or pensioners, or against receivers of alimony, or owners of post-office savings accounts. Other wage earners are entitled to an exemption from garnishment of up to 70% of their wages, unless the debt is for board and lodging, or if the debtor has no dependants whatsoever.

COMPULSORY BANKRUPTCY

The provisions of the Bankruptcy Act for compulsory bankruptcy follow. (The provisions of the Winding-up Act are very similar; they will be invoked when a large corporation fails. The chief distinction is that the company's liquidator has less freedom of action and is more subject to control by the court than the trustee in bankruptcy.)

If the debtor has debts of $1,000 or more (to one or more creditors), such creditor(s) can present a *bankruptcy petition* to the province's Supreme Court. The court will hear the case and will grant a *receiving order* (i.e., adjudge the debtor bankrupt) if it is satisfied that he owes at least $1,000, and that within the last six months he has committed an *act of bankruptcy*, namely:

That he is insolvent; that is, unable to meet his obligations as they fall due; or

That he has attempted fraud; for example, by making an improper bulk sale, bill of sale, or chattel mortgage; or by secreting assets; or

That he has given undue preference to a creditor (see later); or

That he has absconded from Canada or gone into hiding; or

That he has an unsatisfied writ of execution against him.

After granting the receiving order, the court (or the *official receiver*, in the case of a voluntary assignment) will appoint a licenced and bonded trustee in bankruptcy to take charge of the debtor's affairs. His first step is to advertise for creditors in the Canada Gazette and in the local newspapers, and to call a meeting with them. Each creditor has a number of votes proportionate to his unsecured claim against the debtor; for example, a claim of $25-$200 has one vote, a claim of $500-$1,000 has three votes, and any additional claim of $1,000 has one further vote. The creditors then either confirm in his office the trustee appointed by the court, or they appoint another one in his place; they also elect one to five *inspectors* to assist the trustee. A trustee is well paid for his endeavours; the inspectors receive a small honorarium.

The trustee then becomes the legal owner of everything the debtor has or that he is entitled to, with the exception of certain exempted goods and of items that the debtor holds in *bona fide* trust for others. The trustee can either continue operating the business (if that is regarded as being in the best interests of the creditors), or he can proceed to liquidate its assets.

He is empowered to compel the attendance for interrogation of anybody who may help in this process or who may have information regarding assets or claims of the debtor. One of the bankrupt debtor's many duties (violation of many of which is a punishable offense) is to assist the trustee to the best of his ability and to make full disclosure of all facts that might make the trustee's task easier.

The trustee hears all the creditors' claims and either approves them in whole or in part, or disapproves them. A creditor whose claim has been disallowed may appeal to the bankruptcy court within thirty days. A creditor who deliberately makes a false claim commits a punishable offense.

The trustee checks to see if the debtor has made any sales, gifts, or other transfers of property, without full consideration recently. If any have occurred within the last year, they will be declared void, and the property will revert back into the bankrupt's estate, held by the trustee. It is open to any party, however, to prove the *bona fides* of the transaction, if he can. If there were other such transactions within the last five years, the trustee can have them annulled if he can prove that the debtor would then have been insolvent without that property.

The trustee can also assume to be fraudulent, and have declared void, any payments that the debtor made within the last three months to a creditor which amounted to an *undue preference* in favour of that creditor; after all, one of the chief purposes of bankruptcy legislation is to give all creditors rateable distribution—that is, an "even break." With regard to a payment made by the debtor to a creditor earlier, the trustee must prove that there was a deliberate intention to make an undue preference before it is declared void.

After all the above matters have been attended to, the trustee proceeds to the division of the debtor's assets among the creditors who have

288

proved their claims—generally in cash, but also in kind, if this meets with everybody's approval. The trustee will declare interim dividends (make instalment payments) as the assets are realized until he declares a final dividend. The final dividend is coupled with strict formalities since creditors retain no claims after that point (unless any additional property happens to come into the trustee's hands later). The trustee must follow a certain order in paying off the creditors, of whom some might have higher ranking claims than others; if the top-ranking creditors exhaust all the available funds, the ones at the bottom of the list will be out of luck. The creditors must be paid as described below:

I. SECURED CREDITORS.   Secured creditors are holders of mortgages, bonds, liens, and pledges and persons who have registered a general assignment of book debts to them (see Assignments); and landlords who have exercised their right of distress (see Leases) over their tenants' belongings for three months' back rent. If the trustee does not exercise his option of redeeming (buying) these securities, the creditors may realize (sell) them. If the sale realizes more than the amount of the debt, the excess must go to the trustee; if less, the secured creditors rank with the general creditors, described in (3) below, for the balance of their claims.

2. CREDITORS WITH PREFERRED CLAIMS. Preferred claims are:

(a) The legal and funeral expenses connected with a deceased bankrupt's death.

(b) The bankruptcy expenses and legal fees.

(c) Three months' back pay to employees (but excluding company directors and officers) to a maximum of $500 each.

(d) Two years' arrears of municipal taxes.

(e) Three months' back rent to a landlord without a right to distress.

(f) The legal costs incurred by the creditor who initiated bankruptcy proceedings.

(g) Unpaid contributions to workmen's compensation, unemployment insurance, and income tax withheld from employees' pay cheques and not forwarded to the Receiver General of Canada.

(h) Insurance settlements forwarded by insurance companies to the bankrupt employer on behalf of injured workers.

(i) Any other Crown claims.

3. ALL CREDITORS WITH GENERAL CLAIMS ON AN EVEN FOOTING.
These include creditors with proven claims in contract, and plaintiffs who have had tort damages awarded to them in a court action. If there is not enough to pay them all, they share what is available rateably.

4. CREDITORS WITH RESTRICTED CLAIMS. Restricted claims are:
(a) Loans and wages due to a bankrupt woman's husband.
(b) Wages due to a bankrupt's wife.
(c) More than three months' wages due to relatives and to silent partners of a bankrupt, and to directors of a bankrupt company.

5. SURPLUS.
Any surplus belongs to the debtor. In the case of a wound-up company, the surplus will be divided among the shareholders rateably, with the preferred shareholders ranking first.

DISCHARGE

Within three to twelve months after the bankruptcy and after the administration is completed, the trustee applies to the court for a hearing which is to decide whether the bankrupt is to receive his discharge or not. The trustee must file a detailed report on the progress of the liquidation, and he must give the creditors notice so that they may raise objections if they so desire.

The bankrupt will usually receive his discharge if:

• The creditors have been paid at least 50¢ on the dollar (or even less in deserving cases).

• The bankrupt acted in a *bona fide* manner throughout (in other words, if the bankruptcy was not his fault but his misfortune), and he was not guilty of recklessness.

• This is his first bankruptcy.

• He has committed no fraud, nor any of various specified bankruptcy offenses (e.g., obtaining a loan over $500 or engaging in business without disclosing his condition).

A discharge gives the debtor a "clean sheet" legally. He is no longer liable for the balance of any old debts, except for: unpaid court fines; alimony payments; debts incurred for the purchase of necessaries; and property obtained by fraud. Fortunately, there are many cases of debtors subsequently voluntarily paying off their moral obligations (in New York State a written promise to this effect is binding).

A discharge does not release the bankrupt's partners or sureties (guarantors) from any liabilities they may have had. And, on proper grounds, the bankruptcy court may annul a discharge it has granted.

QUESTIONS

1. What classes of persons cannot be compulsorily bankrupted?
2. How may a creditor start bankruptcy proceedings?
3. From what obligations does a discharge not release a bankrupt?
4. List the various purposes of the provincial "Gazette."
5. (a) What is a fraudulent conveyance? (See Chapter 2.)
   (b) What is undue preference?

TWENTY-SIX

Real Property

HISTORICAL SIGNIFICANCE

The law of *real property*—that is, land and anything attached to it such as structures and trees, also called *immoveable property, real estate,* or *realty*—is very complicated. Although of infrequent application to most individuals, it is still a highly important subject since it usually involves large sums of money and is beset by many pitfalls. It is, of course, of prime importance to builders, real estate brokers (realtors), and investors in real property as owners, tenants, or mortgagees.

The reason that this branch of law is so different from the law dealing with personal property (or chattels or moveable property) is that land cannot be moved and is always there. Things can be done to it, with it, on it, and under it perpetually; but ownership or possession of it cannot be passed by physical delivery of it. The formal deed, sealed and witnessed, which is required to transfer any of the many various interests in land that we shall hear about, is just one of the topics connected with land (the most important form of wealth in bygone years) for which the early law makers made provision in great detail; much of this detail is followed today with but little change. One great change has taken place in the method of transferring interests in land, and that is by the important system of *registration*. To safeguard any interest he has acquired in land, a person should immediately register it in the local registry office. Registered should be purchases, mortgages, long leases, mechanics' liens, appliances and other fixtures bought on credit and affixed to the land in permanent form, and any restrictions which are to govern the use of the premises; all of these will be discussed in detail presently.

TYPES OF HOLDINGS

Before we discuss the manner of transferring interests in land, let us examine what these various interests are. **Tenancy in fee simple of freehold property** is the highest form of "estates" in land and virtually amounts to full ownership of the land. Technically, however, for historical considerations originating with the feudal system, no one except the Crown (i.e., the province) can have outright ownership of land. The so-called owner has a grant from the Crown—either directly to him or, more usually, to a previous "owner" of the land. That the person, generally considered as its owner, does not have out-and-out control of the land is evidenced by the following circumstances:

• The Crown, acting through the province or its delegate such as a municipality or a utilities corporation, by its right of *eminent domain*, still has the power by way of *condemnation* proceedings to expropriate land when this is necessary for the benefit of the public (e.g., for the building or widening of highways). Proper compensation is usually paid to the bereft owner, the amount sometimes being settled by arbitration.

• Land, and other property, *escheats* (reverts) to the Crown if its owner dies without heirs and without leaving a will.

• In some provinces (e.g., Ontario, Quebec, Alberta), the mineral and oil rights do not automatically go with the surface, but form the subject of a separate grant.

• The municipalities have the right to establish zoning regulations, regarding the use to which "property"[1] may be put in the area. The municipalities may also have short- and long-range town-planning schemes to which property owners must conform, and they have the right to lay sidewalks and to install sewers, cables, etc., on one's land.

Tenancy in fee simple is granted by the *grantor* (the Crown, or a subsequent vendor) to the *grantee* (usually a purchaser) by the use in the deed of the archaic words, "to have and to hold to the use of X and his heirs." The more modern words, "to X in fee simple" or "to X absolutely," can also be used. In fact, if title is conveyed just "to X," he will get a fee simple today.

---

1 This is a loose expression, popularly used to denote real property.

Fee tail, or an entailed estate. This type of holding is included here only for reasons of curiosity. It is still employed sometimes in England, to ensure that the holder of a title of nobility also gets to hold the land long associated with it. A *fee tail* holding is granted by the words, "to X and the heirs of his body" (or perhaps "to the heirs male of his body"), which means that the grantee cannot dispose of the land as he wishes. After the grantee's death, the property descends according to the rules laid down by the person who created the entail, often corresponding to the rules of intestate succession. This restriction cannot be imposed in perpetuity because it would violate the principles of *mortmain*, according to which the restrictions regarding the transfer of land must not be too rigid. An entail can be imposed only for the length of "a life in being" and twenty-one years beyond that. If a subsequent holder of the land then wishes to continue this tradition, he can impose a fresh entail on the land for a similar length of time—usually in his will. On the other hand, such an entail can be "broken" very easily by the heirs of the land-holder concurring with him in a sale or other disposition of the land he wishes to make. Fees tail can no longer be created in Ontario.

Life estates are quite common; the principal reason for establishing them is to avoid two (or more) sets of death duties. For example, a husband may leave (usually by will) his land and other property to a trustee for the use and benefit of his wife for as long as she lives, with the "remainder" (i.e., the fee simple, subject to this life estate) to go to a child or other named person(s). A life estate may also be granted by deed to someone (e.g., to a parent) for his lifetime with the "reversion" of the property to go back to the grantor. A life estate may also be granted for the length of someone else's life (e.g., to my nephew N during the life of my son S; but after the death of S, to his son, my grandson, G).

The holder of a life estate may sell or otherwise dispose of as much of an interest in the land as he himself has (i.e., its purchaser will have to give up the land on the death of the life tenant to the "remainder-man" or to the "reversioner"). The life tenant must not "commit waste"; that is, tear down a building, or cut more timber than is required for heating or repairs. He must also preserve "heirlooms," such as pictures of ancestors, coats of mail, armour, etc.

Dower is the right a widow still enjoys in some provinces (e.g., Ontario) to a life estate in one-third of her deceased husband's fully owned, improved real estate. After her husband's death, she may occupy one-third of the premises; or she is entitled to one-third of the income that the property brings in, or would bring in, if rented; or to a lump sum settlement. Therefore a buyer or mortgagee of land should always get the seller's wife to add her signature to the deed, thereby "barring her inchoate right of dower." Otherwise, the buyer of a $30,000 house might find himself having to pay the interest on $10,000 for the rest of her life to the widow of the seller after the seller's death—occurring perhaps years after the sale!

Curtesy is the right that a widower in some provinces still has to a life estate in all of his deceased wife's real estate, provided she gave birth to a live child at some time during the marriage. This right is of little concern to a buyer of the land, since a wife extinguishes it by the act of selling the land over her own signature, or by willing it away from the husband.

Trusts. While the trustee of land (and of personal property) is its full legal owner, he is under an equitable obligation to administer it on behalf of the beneficiary who is called its *owner in equity*. Trusts are created when the beneficiaries are to be minors, unprotected widows, charities, or where life interests are created. Trusts are created by will, or by a deed proclaiming someone (even oneself) as trustee.

Leaseholds are technically not estates, but merely interests in land (they originated as personal property, carved out of the real property, to provide a source of income for a testator's younger children—the eldest customarily getting the entire land); but they are of great importance and will be discussed separately in detail.

MULTIPLE OWNERSHIP

Any of the above "tenancies" can be held:

In severalty; that is, by one individual.

By "tenants in common." This method of holding a tenancy is the same as that of partners owning the partnership property. Each owns a proportion of the undivided whole. On one tenant's death, his share of the property goes to his own estate, or he can sell (or otherwise dispose of) his share during his lifetime; the assignee becoming a tenant in common with the other(s). If property is sold to two or more persons, they get to own it as tenants in common, unless the deed makes a different provision. On selling or otherwise disposing of the property, all the tenants must join in the sale. To make sure of getting full title, the buyer's lawyer should be certain to get all their signatures, or to get a court order granting the buyer full title, despite a missing signature.

By "joint tenants." Joint tenants of land, as of a bank account discussed earlier, enjoy the right of *survivorship*. On the death of one, the other automatically becomes the owner of the other's share. To create a joint tenancy, the tenants must expressly be designated as *joint* in the deed of grant. As in tenancies in common, all joint tenants must join in a sale or any other transaction regarding it. If a joint owner disposes of his share of the property, the assignee becomes a Tenant in Common with the other owner(s). But if there originally were three or more joint tenants, the non-assigning owners remain joint tenants among themselves.

RIGHTS OF THE LANDOWNER

At common law, the landowner (as we shall henceforth call him, realistically) enjoys full control over his property within its lateral boundaries and from its nadir to its zenith; that is, he can build to Heaven and dig half-way to Australia (beyond that he would be encroaching on the rights of his opposite number in Australia!). This unlimited freedom is subject, of course, to municipal zoning regulations limiting the type and height of buildings; to mineral rights under his land enjoyed by others; to building restrictions to which he submitted himself voluntarily—for example, by entering into covenants with the seller, or by knowingly assuming previously existing ones "running with the land" (e.g., in land development areas). He does not have to tolerate trespassers on his land, and he can prevent the commission of *nuisances*. Thus, he may remove encroachments; but, as we have learned in the chapter on torts, he must submit to the reasonable crossing of his air space by planes and radio waves. As a matter of fact, the nations are considering a plan for the limitation of private air-space based on the pattern that is used to declare the high seas international waterways beyond certain limits (e.g., three or twelve miles). If a person's land adjoins navigable waters, he must grant reasonable use of its banks to navigators.

Right to support. An owner of land has the right to have his land supported by his neighbour's land. In other words, a landowner must not dig his land so as to cause a settlement of his neighbour's land. This right does not extend to the support of a building that an owner has placed close to his boundaries, unless the neighbouring land is owned by the person who sold him the building (or unless he has acquired the right to have his building supported by *prescription*, discussed below).

Rights to water. A person, through whose land water runs, has the right to receive an *even flow* of *unpolluted* water.

Pollution consists of contaminating the water in any way, even of hardening it or changing its temperature (this might change the habits of the fish inhabiting it). The aggrieved landowner may sue the person responsible for the pollution for an injunction, or for damages for nuisance without having to prove any actual damage.

While a landowner may use the water flowing across his land for all "natural purposes" (e.g., to water his cattle, irrigate his land, operate his water-wheel), he must not otherwise change its even flow—

1. By cutting it off altogether. In this case, any affected landowner may sue without having to prove any damage.

2. By reducing its flow; therefore, if water is used for an abnormal purpose, such as industry, any diverted water must be returned within the user's boundaries. Any landowner who actually suffers loss by a reduction of the flow may sue for an injunction or damages.

3. By a lower owner damming the water or otherwise causing it to back up. If the upper owner suffers loss, he may sue as above.

Right to game. By law, the landowner (including his guests) is the only one entitled to take game from his land and waters. Even then, he must observe the game laws regarding the size of his catch or bag, and the open and closed seasons. In the wide expanses of Canada such hunting and fishing rights are frequently granted by implication to the public in reason.

EASEMENTS

Easements limit any of the above rights of ownership. For example, the owner of the *dominant tenement* (land which benefits from the easement) may have acquired an easement to interfere with the water of the *servient tenement* (land subject to the easement); he may have the right to encroach on his neighbour's land with overhanging balconies, etc.; or by having placed a structure on it, such as a fence or a shed; he may have a right of way over it—either a general one, or one limited as to its use; he may have a right to take things off the servient land—e.g., hay, wood, gravel, or minerals (these taken things are called *profits à prendre*); he may have the right to have not only his land but even his buildings supported by the servient land; or he may have acquired the right not to have the light coming in his windows obstructed. (In England, *ancient lights*—i.e., windows that have been unobstructed for twenty years—automatically enjoy this privilege.)

Such easements come into being:

By express contract (which must be in writing since it involves an interest in land). The easement might be granted as a favour, for money, or for counter services. Any restrictive covenant (undertaking) that a landowner submits to "runs with the land" and will become binding on any future owner of the land, provided it was registered. If a subsequent owner of the land can prove that due to a change in circumstances (such as a change in the character of the neighbourhood) the restriction has become unwarranted, he may apply to the court to be released from it. If in a land development (e.g., a building scheme) a seller imposes equal restrictions on all his purchasers for their mutual benefit, a violator (or his assignee) can be sued not only by the seller but also by any of his neighbours.

By prescription: that is, by twenty years of open, uninterrupted, undisputed, adverse use, without the owner's express or implied permission, a legal right to any of the above easements is acquired by the user. It is to prevent such a legal right from arising that landowners, who voluntarily grant privileges of this nature to their neighbours, periodically withdraw these rights with a fair amount of publicity; for example, by drawing a heavy chain over a voluntary right of way for one day, once a year.

By implication. One example already mentioned of an easement by implication is the seller's duty to support with his land a building that he has sold to a neighbour.

298

Another one is a right of way of necessity, illustrated in the following situation: if the owner of estate *A* sells a lot *B* in its centre, then the owner of *B* acquires an automatic right of way over *A*'s land to the outside world (e.g., to a road or waterway). *A* may, however, pick out any route for *B* that he chooses, as long as it is not an inconvenient one. *B* similarly acquires a right over *A*'s land where both buy their lots from a common seller, *C*.

The remedies for the violation of any of the above landowners' rights are an injunction and/or damages. It should be noted that if a building has been erected improperly, no order will be issued to tear it down; damages are the only remedy available to the injured party.

QUESTIONS

1. (a) What is the highest form of interest that a Canadian can have in land?
    (b) To what extent does this interest fall short of amounting to full ownership?
2. In connection with life estates, what is meant by:
    (a) Remainder.
    (b) Reversion.
    (c) Waste.
3. Why is it important for a purchaser of land to know about the seller's marital status?
4. What is the fundamental distinction between owning land jointly and owning it in common with someone else?
5. Make a list of easements which can be enjoyed over another's land.
6. By means of illustrations, show two situations in which rights of way of necessity can come into existence.
7. What is meant by a landowner's "right to support"?

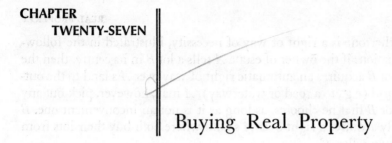

Buying Real Property

WAYS OF ACQUIRING REAL PROPERTY

Before discussing in detail the purchase of land, let us briefly list the other ways in which ownership can change hands:

By inheritance; by will or on intestacy. (See Chapter 30, Succession to Property.)

By prescription—varying in length of time in the different provinces. In Ontario, a person acquires land by prescription after ten years of open, uninterrupted, adverse, undisputed use without any sort of permission. As mentioned under Limitations (Chapter 13), ungranted Crown land cannot be acquired by prescription; but a "squatter" gets such rights after twenty years if during that time he fences and cultivates land granted to someone else who fails to utilize it .

By "foreclosing" mortgaged land. Details will be discussed in Chapter 28, Mortgages.

By forfeiture. While a felon's land is no longer forfeited to the Crown, forfeiture of land from an incorporated company is still possible if it violates the Mortmain Acts. Unnecessary land held by a company having perpetual life would otherwise be forever unavailable to anybody else.

SOME HINTS FOR HOUSE BUYERS

This chapter will be regarded principally through the eyes of a person buying a house, and since many of this book's readers are on the threshold of buying their first one, some general words of advice outside of law should not be out of order.

• Shop carefully. Acquaint yourself with materials, construction, and values as carefully as a girl buying her first fur coat, or a boy his first car.

- If in doubt, don't! You will possibly live in the house of your choice for the rest of your life. A house is not as easy to "trade" as an unsatisfactory car; in fact, often this is financially impossible after one has made mortgage arrangements, paid the lawyer, and invested in necessary repairs and alterations to the house.
- Consider getting other than a brand-new house. True, a larger down payment will probably be required, but a house that has been standing for a few years is well "driven in," and defects in construction will have had a chance to show up.
- Consider also a larger house than is immediately necessary, with a view to future family; any surplus accommodation can be rented meanwhile.

Realtors. Your shopping will be done with the aid of helpful agents, or *realtors*. Never forget, however, that realtors are legally the representatives of the *vendor*, and that a considerable amount of "puffing" by the vendor, short of actual misrepresentations, is the accepted rule. Subject to protection against such misrepresentations and to the vendor's duty to reveal any serious latent (hidden) defects he knows of, the rule of *caveat emptor* applies (in spades!). It is the buyer's responsibility to spot (with the aid of a knowledgeable friend, perhaps) rot or termites in the rafters or basement, settlements and cracks in the walls, damp in the cellar, cracked plaster "accidentally" camouflaged by pictures or furniture.

Before signing the fateful "offer," again check the price with the following factors in mind:

- The location. Is it desirable, or near slums?
- Zoning. Will it allow you to conduct a business? Or will industry be allowed next door to your retreat?
- Are the municipal taxes relatively moderate or disproportionately high—perhaps because the land is a corner lot?
- Is the construction of solid brick or veneer?
- Are the heating system and furnace of good design and quality, and in good repair?
- Are the roof, chimney, and eavestroughs in good repair?
- Is there a garage or parking facility?

301

WRITTEN OFFER TO PURCHASE

After you have decided in favour of a house, the agent will suggest that you sign an offer to buy it. This offer is called an *offer to purchase* and, if accepted, an *agreement of purchase and sale*. It must be borne in mind that "making an offer" is not a bargaining step; once accepted by the vendor, it is an irretrievable, binding obligation to go through with the terms of the offer as made, subject to breach of contract damages if violated—even if the offer was not accompanied by any deposit payment. In view of the importance of this step (often represented to the buyer as a trifling preliminary matter), the buyer should never allow himself to be panicked into signing the offer, without first showing it to his lawyer for approval. The lawyer usually makes no extra charge for this service if he handles the subsequent purchase; and if the changes he suggests in the offer for your protection are not accepted by the vendor, the small charge he might make you will have been a profitable investment.

If the lawyer approves the offer, the buyer signs it and initials any changes made in it. A deposit will have to accompany the offer; 10% of the purchase price is customarily asked; equally customarily, 5% (the usual agent's commission) is counter-offered and accepted. The deposit is usually in the form of a cheque made out to the agent, who pays it into a special *customers' deposits account*. The offer need be signed by one of the purchasing spouses only; if the other is to become a joint owner, it will be mentioned in the subsequent *deed of conveyance*. The lawyer will have seen to it that the offer is to stay irrevocable for only a short length of time (e.g., one to three days). Otherwise, the buyer would remain obligated for a long time, while the seller still had an opportunity to shop for more advantageous offers. It is principally for this reason that offers are generally under seal; if they were not, they could be revoked by the offeror at any time before acceptance.

CONTENTS OF THE OFFER

It must be remembered that no promises made by the vendor are binding unless incorporated in the contract in writing; therefore, the agreement should repeat any promises that the vendor made to paint, repair, or otherwise improve the house. Also, it should list all debatable items that are to go with the house, such as broadloom, room air-conditioners, etc. If this is not done and a dispute arises, then fixtures (i.e., items that are part of the land or have been permanently attached to it) will have to go with the house; while non-fixtures may be removed by the seller. Whether an item is a fixture or not is frequently the subject of heated argument (this is sometimes a matter of local custom; for example, in some areas a sump pump, embedded in the basement to drain off water, is not regarded as a fixture).

Even if the lawyer has checked the vendor's receipts for recent repairs and additions to the house (e.g., roof or furnace), he will insert in the agreement an undertaking by the vendor to pay off all outstanding debts in this connection; also an undertaking to give absolutely vacant possession of the premises—otherwise, it might be burdensome for the buyer to have to evict any undesirable or undesired tenants. A survey, to check if the house stands on its own land and that it has not violated any planning code, should be required of the vendor; and if he cannot furnish one, it is a sound investment for the buyer to have one prepared.

Terms of payment. The most important feature of the offer is the terms of payment. In the case of a $20,000 house, let us assume a down payment of $5,000 (of which $1,000 has already been paid by way of deposit), with a mortgage for the balance. The terms of the mortgage must be specified in the agreement most accurately, for they will be in effect until the mortgage is finally repaid. If the vendor already has a mortgage that will be taken over by the purchaser, the existing mortgage must be described in full: how much is still outstanding, when it falls due, what rate of interest must be paid on it, and in what instalments the principal is to be repaid.

If the vendor is financing the purchase by taking back a $15,000 mortgage from the purchaser for the balance of the purchase price, these details are the subject of bargaining; for example, to establish the rate of interest to be paid. If the mortgage is to be repaid after, say, five years, the purchaser should try to get an option for a further five-year period in which to repay. He should also try to get an "open" mortgage; that is, he should try to get the privilege to prepay the mortgage before its maturity date without becoming liable for any further interest payments. This will release him if he should "strike it rich" by way of a leg-

303

acy or fortunate speculation. In Ontario, any mortgage may be repaid after five years, on paying three months' additional interest.

Once the buyer has signed an offer which has been accepted, he can get out of it only if he can prove misrepresentation of a material fact, or that the vendor has lied about or secreted a latent defect that he knew to be vital, or if the vendor is unable to deliver what he agreed to.

CLOSING THE CONTRACT

The contract is completed when the offer is accepted in writing by the vendor. Acceptance should not take place on a Sunday, as discussed earlier. The signature of the vendor's wife should also be obtained, to bar her right of dower. Since the acceptance customarily contains an undertaking by the vendor to pay the agent his commission, one of the copies of the signed agreement will go to the agent. For his protection in case the deal falls through due to no fault of his own, the vendor should stipulate that he need not pay the agent until the completion of the sale, and unless one takes place.

Search. The agreement will have made provision for a certain length of time (ten days is rather short; thirty days is ample) during which the buyer's lawyer is to have an opportunity of checking the seller's title to the property. At the local registry office he will peruse the *abstract of title*. An abstract of title is a summary of the land's legal history, going back as far as possible; for example, it might list the following documents: an original Crown grant of land to A; a probate of A's will, leaving the land to B; a sale by B to C; a sale by C to D; a mortgage by D to E and a foreclosure by E; and the letters of administration (see Chapter 30) granted to F on E's intestate death.

The buyer's lawyer (or at least his conveyancing clerk) then "searches" the documents listed in the abstract to check if the vendor has a good title to the land for the last forty years. The lawyer will make sure, for example, that all claims to dower rights have been signed away, and that all co-owners of joint tenancies and of tenancies in common have signed, where necessary. A search covering a period longer than forty years is not strictly necessary by statute. The buyer's lawyer will also check if there are registered against the land any mortgages, leases, easements, restrictive covenants, unpaid fixtures, mechanics' liens, etc.; and he will check at the competent places if any judgments or executions have been filed against the vendor or his predecessor in title, and if he is up to date in the payment of his municipal taxes, water rates, etc. The reason for this careful *search* (as this process is called) is that the property serves as security for these unpaid items; in other words, if unsatisfied by the vendor, they would be a charge against the buyer's property.

Requisitions. If the buyer's lawyer comes across anything in his investigations that looks questionable or unclear, he will address a *requisition* to the vendor's lawyer to clear up the point. If the vendor is unable or unwilling to satisfy any valid objection to the title, the standard form of agreement allows him to rescind the contract.

Lawyer's responsibility. The buyer's lawyer is professionally responsible for ensuring that his client gets a good and clear title. If he has overlooked some flaw or some encumbrance, he has to make good; that is why (in the County of York, Ontario) he is allowed to charge the rather substantial fee of $1\frac{1}{4}\%$ of the purchase price (the vendor's lawyer is entitled to three-quarters of this amount as his fee). For their own protection, most lawyers carry malpractice insurance. In some American states, the lawyer is not thus responsible; his fees are much lower consequently, and there are title insurance companies which render this service for a commensurate premium.

Completion. If the buyer's lawyer is satisfied with the title, *completion* will take place on the date specified in the contract (this should not be on a non-business day). Until then, the contract makes the vendor a trustee of the property for the purchaser; he must treat it considerately, and the contract usually makes him cover it fully with insurance until completion (or "closing"). An apportionment of all income and expenses, prepaid or due, is prepared and incorporated in an *adjustment statement.* Included will be such items as rent from tenants, heating oil remaining in the tanks, municipal taxes, insurance premium, water rates, and mortgage interest. The gas, hydro-electric, and telephone companies will have been instructed to disconnect their services on closing day and to send their statements as of that date to the vendor (the purchaser should remember to sign contracts with these institutions for new service to him).

At the moment of completion, legal ownership in the property, with the accompanying risk, passes to the buyer. Completion consists

305

of the vendor's lawyer delivering to the purchaser's lawyer a *deed of conveyance* previously signed and sealed by the vendor and witnessed; and of the purchaser's lawyer delivering to the vendor's lawyer his cheque for the exact amount worked out on the adjustment statement and a mortgage previously signed and sealed by the purchaser and witnessed.[1]

Steps after completion. The first step each lawyer should take after completion is to register promptly the documents received by him; his client's title and priority are dependent on this. In some parts of Canada (e.g., northern Ontario and western Canada), the *Torrens system of land titles* is in effect, whereby the land titles office not only registers the documents but virtually guarantees the titles. In such cases, no deed is required; instead a *transfer of title* is used.

After looking after multitudinous routine matters (e.g., notifying the insurance company of the seller's change of status from owner to mortgagee), the seller's lawyer sends his cheque to his client for the balance remaining after having paid the rest of the agent's commission and having retained his own fee.

MECHANICS' LIENS

When discussing bailments and liens (Chapter 19), we learned that most provinces have statutes (e.g., the Ontario Mechanics' Lien Act) which permit a repairman who has not been paid his repair bill to sell the repaired article after complying with certain requirements, such as waiting for three months, advertising the proposed sale for one week, and then selling the article in question at public auction. This provision of the statutes gives the repairman a more definite remedy than his old-established common-law remedy of being allowed to retain the article indefinitely.

The main purpose of these statutes, however, is to create a remedy for persons in the construction field, workers who have not been paid

---

1 Also attached to the deed and mortgage are an affidavit of due execution by the witness, an affidavit by the contracting party regarding his marital status for possible dower purposes, and an affidavit stating that the grantor is twenty-one years of age or over. The deed of conveyance will originally have been drafted by the vendor's lawyer, subject to the other lawyer's approval; and the mortgage by the buyer's lawyer, subject to the vendor's approval.

their wages, and suppliers of materials who have not received payment for them from the builder.

Their product has been affixed to the land, and is therefore no longer capable of being physically retained by the creditors. To protect their interests, the statutes have granted these people a lien on the land in connection with whose improvement their claims arose, even after ownership of it has passed from the building contractor to the buyer. These creditors have only a short time, however, (in Ontario, thirty-seven days after the last work was done) to register their *mechanics' lien* on the title. (The early use of the word "mechanic" encompassed artisans in all trades.)

While affording this protection to workers, suppliers, and sub-contractors, it would be unfair to penalize an owner who had made full payment to the contractor. Therefore, the Mechanics' Lien Acts require the owners of newly constructed buildings to withhold from the contractors a percentage of the contract price (in Ontario, 20% if the price is under $25,000, 15% if the price is higher). For the length of the protective period, this fund will be used to satisfy the mechanics' lien claims, as approved by the court, and only the balance (if any) need be paid to the contractor. Any purchaser of a new building should delay paying the contractor the full purchase price until he has waited thirty-seven days (in Ontario) and then searched for the registration of any mechanics' lien against the property.

Mechanics' liens enjoy priority over the claims of almost all other creditors; the two exceptions are an earlier mortgagee who has a first claim on the unimproved value of the land (i.e., the value of the land alone), and the person making a building mortgage loan for the value of any construction that has taken place up to the time of the claim under the lien.

If the lien is not sufficient to cover all the claims, the first claims to be met are those of workers for thirty days' wages; next in line are the unpaid suppliers of construction materials. Any claimants who have not been fully satisfied by the lien still have the right to sue for the balance as unsecured creditors.

Suppliers of materials can, by contract, waive their lien rights. But waivers by workers of their lien rights are valid only in some provinces; such waivers are void in others (e.g., Ontario).

307

QUESTIONS

1. Before signing the offer to buy a house, what points should the buyer have clarified and put in the contract regarding:
   (a) Fixtures.
   (b) The mortgage.
2. (a) What does a house buyer's lawyer investigate when he "searches"?
   (b) What are "requisitions"?
3. What takes place at the "completion" of a house sale?
4. Why do lawyers in Canada charge a relatively high rate for their legal work in conducting the purchase of land for a client?
5. Why is it important for a person to register his purchase of land?
6. Why should the buyer of a newly-built house not be prompt in making full payment of the purchase price to the builders?

CHAPTER TWENTY-EIGHT

Mortgages

TYPES OF MORTGAGES

We have already mentioned how a mortgage can come into existence on the purchase of a house or other property. If an existing mortgage is not taken over from the seller by the buyer, the buyer can borrow money by way of a mortgage either from the seller or from some outside party, such as a mortgage or trust company.

Mortgages can also be arranged at any later time; on giving the property as security, its owner (the mortgagor) can get substantial loans from a mortgagee. If the amount of the loan is conservative (e.g., not exceeding 50 to 66% of the appraised value of the property), the rate of interest to be paid on it will be more reasonable (6 to 7% at time of writing) than if the loan is for a higher percentage. If after borrowing money by way of mortgage on his house, its owner needs to raise more ready cash, he can do so by granting a "second mortgage." The rate of interest to be paid on the second (and any subsequent) mortgage naturally is much higher, since in the case of a forced sale the holder of the first mortgage is entitled to have his claim met in full before any balance becomes available to later mortgagees. Incidentally, as mentioned earlier, the order of precedence among mortgagees is established by registration; regardless of the dates at which loans were advanced or mortgages were executed, the person *registering* his mortgage first becomes the first mortgagee (unless it can be proved that this person had been given actual notice of the existence of an earlier mortgage).

A mortgage that is registered under the previously referred to Torrens land titles system is called a *charge*.

REPAYMENT AND DISCHARGE OF MORTGAGE

The mortgage can be made repayable in one lump sum after the expiry of a specified time limit, with only the interest on it to be paid meanwhile at stated intervals. It is more customary, however, to *amortize* the mortgage by repaying it in small monthly, quarterly, or half-yearly instalments, contemporaneously with making the interest payments on the remaining balance.

A mortgage is the conditional transfer to the mortgagee of the legal title to the land; he normally does not get possession of it. When the mortgage has been paid off in full:

1. The mortgage is either made to become void; or
2. Title to the property is retransferred to the mortgagor, and he is given a *discharge of mortgage* (which should be registered in the same manner as the original mortgage was).

Where the purchaser of property makes only a very small down payment, its vendor will be able to realize his security more readily if he does the following: instead of granting title to the purchaser and then taking back a substantial mortgage from him, the vendor will execute an *agreement of sale*. This operates in the same manner as a conditional sale of goods: the vendor agrees to transfer the title to the purchaser after the last instalment has been paid in full; until then, however, the vendor remains its legal owner with its attendant advantages. This method is common in the western provinces.

A mortgagor may do as he pleases with his property, provided that what he does is not to the mortgagee's detriment: he must not let it fall in ruins; he must not remove fixtures or commit waste (see Life Estates, Chapter 26); and he must carry full insurance on the property, with the mortgagee being named as the beneficiary in the policy.

ASSIGNMENT

The mortgagor may at any time "dispose of his equity of redemption"; that is, he may sell the property, subject to the mortgage. To do this, the mortgagor is not required to obtain the consent of the mortgagee, who need only be notified of the sale. If the purchaser continues to fulfil the obligations imposed by the mortgage he took over, the original mortgagor will be free of any further obligation to the mortgagee. However, if the mortgage obligations are not met, the original mortgagor will become liable under his *personal covenant* to the mortgagee to remain personally responsible until the mortgage (and interest) has been fully repaid.

The mortgagee may sell the mortgage without the mortgagor's consent. The assignee should, of course, notify the mortgagor to protect his rights, and he should register the transfer. Mortgages (particularly second mortgages) commonly are sold at a discount from their face value, by granting a "bonus" to the buyer (whether such a bonus represents income or capital gain is presently the subject of discussion for tax purposes). A mortgagee can also raise money on the mortgage he holds by sub-mortgaging it.

MORTGAGEE'S REMEDIES

A mortgagee's remedies on default of payment of interest or principal are as follows:

1. He may sue the original mortgagor under his personal covenant, even if the property has been sold to someone else, as explained above. He may only sue for the instalment actually due, unless the mortgage contained an acceleration clause, which appears in nearly all mortgages, entitling him to sue for the entire balance of the debt if default is made in just one payment.

The purchaser of the mortgaged land cannot be sued by the mortgagee under this personal covenant unless:

(a) He gave his own personal covenant to the mortgagee; this usually happens when he is granted a renewal of the mortgage by the mortgagee (this is a good example of novation—see Chapter 12); or

(b) In some provinces (e.g., Ontario), if the purchaser agreed with the vendor of the mortgaged lands to assume liability under the personal covenant—even though, in this case, there is no privity of contract between the purchaser and the mortgagee.

2. A standard form of mortgage usually gives the mortgagee the right to collect rents from any tenants the mortgagor has on his land or his building. Alternatively, he may sue for possession and install tenants who will pay him rent until the debt is paid.

3. He may exercise a landlord's right to distrain on the mortgagor's

chattels as if he were a tenant (see Distress in Chapter 29, Leases) if the terms of the mortgage reserved this right to him.

4. If the mortgage is four months overdue in being repaid, or if interest on it is six months in arrears, the mortgagee can apply to the court to have the mortgaged property sold so that he may realize his security. If the mortgage expressly reserved a *power of sale* to the mortgagee, the assistance of the court need not be invoked. Making use of all technicalities available to him, the mortgagor may be able to delay the sale for seven months, so that he may raise the necessary money in the meantime. The sale must be made under the most favourable terms available, and the mortgagee (or any undisclosed representative of his) must not buy the property for himself. Any excess realized by the sale must be accounted for to the mortgagor; while any shortage remains the responsibility of the mortgagor, for which he can be sued by the mortgagee.

5. By the remedy of foreclosure, the mortgagor is foreclosed from (he loses) his right to redeem his property, and the mortgagee becomes its full owner. The mortgagee will select this remedy if a sale of the property would be harmful to him; for example, if the market happens to be bad because prices are low or because there are no purchasers for this particular property. The mortgagor may oppose this application and ask the court to order a court sale instead; and upon request, a six-month extension is granted to him automatically.

Even if the court has ordered a foreclosure, and the mortgagee still has the property, it may reopen (cancel) a foreclosure in unusual cases of hardship or sharp practice. If a mortgagee forecloses on property and sells it, and the proceeds of the sale are less than the amount of the mortgage, he will have no further claim against the mortgagor; conversely, the mortgagee is entitled to keep any excess.

A second mortgagee who is not receiving proper payment of principal and interest has two alternatives: (1) To protect his interests, he may pay off the first mortgage and step into the shoes of the first mortgagee; i.e., he will then have all the above rights. (2) He may apply for a foreclosure order; if granted, he will become the equitable owner of the property, subject to the mortgage held by the first mortgagee.

QUESTIONS

1. You have just bought a house and paid the full price to the seller. Soon thereafter a claim is made upon you to pay off a mortgage you had not known of before. Set out the circumstances under which you would have to pay it.

2. (a) What is a mortgage?
   (b) What is an agreement of sale?
   (c) What is a charge?

3. (a) What are the remedies of a first mortgagee if the mortgagor of real property does not meet his obligations?
   (b) What are the remedies of the holder of a second mortgage under similar circumstances?

4. What are the advantages to a mortgagor of having an open mortgage? (See Chapter 27.)

Leases

DEFINITION AND FORMALITIES

A lease is a contract whereby the landlord (lessor) conveys to the tenant (lessee) the *use* of premises (land, house, apartment, rooms) for a term, at a rent.

Written form. Since a lease is an interest in land, the Statute of Frauds will generally require it to be in writing. For an executory lease to be enforceable, it must be in writing. However, leases up to three years require no writing, if there has been part performance consisting of the physical taking of possession and the payment of rent. The leaving of a piece of luggage or clothing on the premises is sufficient taking of possession, as is the leaving of a book; however, leaving a magazine on the premises as a symbolical taking of possession was held to be insufficient for the purpose.

Use of seal. Leases over three years must bear a seal. The presence of the seal is excused, however, if such a lease is in writing and possession has been taken of the premises. (A verbal lease for more than three years would not be enforceable.)

Registration. If a purchaser of premises discovers, after having made the purchase, that the premises are occupied by a tenant who has a long-term lease (over seven years in length), such a lease is not binding on the innocent purchaser unless it was registered. Consequently, a tenant who obtains a lease for a term of over seven years should register it. Although shorter leases may be registered, this is unnecessary since they are binding on the purchasers. The rights of lessees must also be respected by mortgagees when enforcing their claims against landlords, if they took a mortgage on premises that were already leased. However, if the mortgage was given before the lease, the mortgagee's rights come before those of the tenant. Therefore, a prospective tenant who wants to be assured of undisturbed tenure of the premises in this regard, should first search the landlord's title in the registry office.

IMPLIED COVENANTS

Leases are usually lengthy documents which try to foresee all possible future contingencies and make provision for them. These express conditions, or covenants, contained in the lease govern in case of a dispute between landlord and tenant. But if no lease is drawn up, or if the terms of a lease fail to cover certain points, the following *implied covenants* come into play:

Quiet enjoyment, The landlord covenants (gives an undertaking) that he will not disturb the tenant in his quiet possession of the premises; that is, the landlord will not go on the premises himself or authorize anyone else to do so; and he will not create conditions (unusual noise, smells, etc.) that will substantially lessen the tenant's enjoyment of the premises—or instruct others to do so. However, the landlord cannot be expected to guarantee that the tenant will remain unmolested by third parties trespassing or disturbing the peace. The landlord further covenants that no one else has a prior claim on the leased premises. Should the landlord be in breach of his covenant (e.g., where a prior mortgagee, in exercise of his rights, dispossesses the tenant), the landlord can be sued by the tenant for damages.[1]

Rent. The tenant is to pay the landlord whatever has been agreed upon in the way of rental. This is usually in the form of money, but it can also be in the form of goods; for example, farm produce or crops, or minerals from a leased mine. If no other arrangements have been made, it is the tenant's responsibility to "seek out the landlord"; that is, to take the rent to his office or abode on the required rent payment days. While rent can be paid at the end of a term, it is equally common for payment of rent to be required in advance. A landlord is not entitled to arbitrarily increase the amount of rent before the expiry of the agreed upon rental period.

Municipal taxes. In the case of rented apartments or rooms, property

---

1 A "superior landlord" (the landlord of a landlord) cannot be held responsible by an aggrieved tenant, however.

taxes are always paid by the landlord. In the case of rented houses, it is generally the local custom for the landlord to pay these taxes also; a lease may, of course, reverse this obligation (leases commonly contain a provision that the tenant is to pay any increase in taxes by reason of being a separate school supporter).

Assignment and subletting. Subject to his remaining personally liable to the landlord for the payment of the rent and for the observance of other conditions imposed on him in the lease, a tenant has the implied right to assign his lease; that is, to let someone else occupy the rented premises for the balance of the leased term. A tenant may similarly sublet the premises; that is, he may rent part of the premises to a sub-tenant, or he may sublet all of the premises for a period of time that is shorter than the term of the lease (e.g., a school teacher subletting his rented house during the summer months). A standard contract contains a clause stating that the tenant may not assign or sublet without the landlord's consent, but most of the provinces' Landlord and Tenant Acts state that "such consent may not be unreasonably withheld"; on the other hand, a stiff lease may even override this provision of the Act by expressly excluding its application.

Fixtures. When discussing the sale of a house, it was stated that anything affixed to the premises permanently, had to go to the purchaser. However, a tenant has the right, at the end of the rental term, to remove household fixtures (e.g., a water heater or TV antenna—but not its base plate) that he had affixed to the premises, provided he can do so without damage. His rights with regard to "trade fixtures" extend even further; for example, shelving and refrigeration equipment installed by a tenant in rented business premises may be removed by him provided he repairs the damage caused thereby. While the tenant of a private residence may not, on leaving, uproot and take with him shrubs and plants he has planted, a nurseryman may do so, since for him these plants represent trade fixtures. Any building erected by a tenant on rented land must be left behind for the benefit of the landlord, however. Such anticipated "improvements" are usually taken into account when coming to an agreement on the amount of rent to be paid.

Repairs. The question of who is to be responsible for repairs to the rented premises should be covered very carefully in the lease.

   1. In the case of a leased house, the landlord is often made responsible

for major repairs (roof, chimney, furnace, etc.), while the tenant must effect minor repairs (plumbing, wiring) and decorating (e.g., "the house to be painted every three years on the inside and every seven years on the outside").

2. If the lease contains a covenant by which the tenant is made responsible for the repairs, he becomes responsible for everything except the normal aging process. As double protection against this liability, the standard lease contains a clause stating: "reasonable wear and tear excepted." Also generally excepted by contract are "loss by fire, lightning, and tempest". If the lease contained no such exception clause, the tenant's covenant to repair would make him responsible for making good losses from even these causes. Such a "repairing lease" generally grants the landlord reasonable rights to enter the premises periodically to view the state of repair. If the premises need repairs, the landlord may not himself undertake them; he may sue the tenant for damages or for repossession. If anybody (whether the tenant or anybody else) is injured on the premises due to their non-repair, the landlord has no liability to him; only the tenant is liable, whose duty it was to effect the repairs.

3. If it was the landlord who covenanted to repair, he must effect all necessary repairs after he has been notified of their need by the tenant. If the landlord neglects to effect them, the tenant may sue him for damages. Alternatively, the tenant may have the necessary repairs effected himself (after having first given his landlord notice of his intention to do so), and then either sue the landlord for their cost or deduct their cost from his next rent payment(s).

Under a lease of this nature, the primary responsibility for injuries to third parties lies on the landlord. He is also liable for injuries to the goods of his tenant that were caused by his failure to effect repairs after having been properly notified of the need for them. He is not, however, liable for personal injury from such causes to the tenant, or to members of his household; the reason being that the tenant could, had he wanted to, have effected repairs himself in the first place.

4. If the lease contains no mention at all of repairs, we have the curious situation arising of *neither party* being legally responsible for effecting any repairs; with the following exceptions:
- The landlord must point out to the tenant any hidden dangers that

317

he knows of; otherwise he can be held liable for any injuries or damage resulting from his failure to do so.

- If the premises are furnished, they must be fit for habitation, but only at the start of the tenancy; otherwise the lease is voidable by the tenant.

- The tenant must repair his own breakages, and he must treat the premises in a "tenant-like" manner; that is, he must keep them weather proof. If the premises are destroyed by fire, neither party need rebuild them, but the lease comes to an end.

Thus, while theoretically neither party is obliged to repair a caved-in roof or a broken pipe that spews water all over the house, in practice the repair will be effected either by the tenant because he does not want to get wet, or by the landlord because he does not want his property to deteriorate.

LENGTH OF TENANCY

Fixed term tenancy. The length of tenancy may be a clearly expressed *fixed term* at the end of which the tenant may vacate, and the landlord may demand possession of the premises, without any previous notice having to be given by either party to the other.

If the tenant should move out before the expiry of this fixed term, he remains liable for the rent for the balance of the full term and can be sued for it on each rent day. However, the landlord must try to minimize the loss by seeking a suitable new tenant at the first opportunity. If the prematurely departing tenant surrenders the keys to the premises on leaving, the landlord, by accepting them, does not necessarily imply his concurrence to the termination of the lease.

Periodic tenancy is the name given to the leases of indefinite length (e.g., for rooms, flats, or apartments) that continue from year to year, from month to month, or from week to week, until proper notice is given. Such tenancies arise either by express agreement (verbal or written) or by implication. For example, when a fixed term expires and both parties continue as before, without bothering to make a new agreement, a periodic tenancy develops, along the same terms as the original fixed term. If the original term was for one year or longer, the new term is from year to year.

NOTICE.   Lacking specific agreement, the amount of notice to be given corresponds to the rent payment dates. Thus, where rent is paid by the week, notice must reach the other party at least one *clear* week before the planned day of vacating, even if rent is paid in advance. On a monthly tenancy, one clear month's notice is required; three months notice is required on a quarterly or half-yearly tenancy; and six months notice on a year-to-year tenancy. To remove any dispute regarding the giving of notice, it is wise to give it in writing and preferably by registered mail.

Tenancy at will—at the pleasure of the landlord, that is—is said to exist in arrangements such as the following: a prospective purchaser is given permission to occupy the house he is buying, before completion of all legal formalities in connection with its purchase; or where an employee is provided with rent-free living quarters by his employer at his place of work (e.g., a housekeeper or a janitor). Such a tenancy may be terminated by either party at any time; of course, it may not be assigned to anyone else. If the landlord accepts rent, a periodic tenancy may arise, unless a tenancy at will is expressly specified in the agreement.

Tenancy at (or "by") sufferance exists when premises are occupied by a "tenant" without the knowledge or against the will of the property owner; in other words, where the owner endures, or "suffers" the occupant's presence. Such an occupant can be an out-and-out trespasser or a tenant who will not vacate the premises at the proper time; he becomes liable for a reasonable amount of "use and occupation rent." In fact, if an "overholding tenant" was on a year-to-year basis, he becomes liable for double rent. Such a tenancy may, of course, be terminated by either party at any time.

TERMINATION OF LEASE

Leases may be terminated as follows:
- At the expiry of a fixed term.
- At the expiry of a proper notice period.
- On the accidental destruction of the premises (unless the contract imposed an obligation to rebuild them on the one party or the other).
- On a breach of covenant by one party or the other and—
  (a) the giving up of possession by the tenant; or
  (b) the taking of, or suing for, possession by the landlord.

319

LANDLORD'S REMEDIES

Where the tenant does not vacate the premises at the proper time (at the end of the term or for the breach of a covenant) the landlord must demand possession in writing, and he may then take court action for possession.

If the tenant does not pay his rent, he may be sued for it; or the landlord may repossess the premises; or the landlord may exercise his right of distress—that is, he may distrain upon (seize) certain goods of the tenant and sell them five days later at an auction sale. The regulations with regard to distress are very technical and must be observed meticulously; otherwise the landlord can find himself (and the bailiff he employed for that purpose) liable in damages for "wrongful distress." For example, distress may only be exercised for rent that is overdue and for which a demand had been previously made (not for taxes or other debts); in daylight hours on weekdays without force; and on goods belonging to the tenant or his family that are not "exempt from distress"—that is, goods that are not necessaries of life such as food for a month, clothing, bedding, tools of the trade, pets, utensils, sewing machine, furniture (e.g., if a tenant needs six chairs and he has more, he may keep his six best chairs).[2]

TO RENT OR TO BUY?

People who are about to establish a home of their own are faced with the decision whether to rent or to buy their living quarters. To help clarify their thinking about these two choices, the advantages and disadvantages of home ownership, as contrasted to renting, are summarized below.

Advantages of home ownership:

• Through having to make regular repayments of the mortgage principal, it represents forced savings.

• An investment in bricks and mortar will not suffer during a runaway inflation.

• Rent is "lost" money; only a handful of receipts can be shown for it.

---

2 Often a landlord will make an excessive or wrongful distress, and the impecunious tenant is unable to afford legal action to enforce his remedies.

- Credit is more readily obtainable (money can be raised by mortgage).
- Landlord can never increase rent.
- Prestige; social standing.
- Some voting privileges.
- Greater living space.
- No restrictions regarding children; pets; parties.
- Opportunity for gardening, hobbies.
- Permanence for widow and children (Lease may not be renewed).
- Joy in own furniture.
- Develops responsibility.
- All improvements made are not expenses but are additional investments.

Disadvantages of home ownership:

- Needs a substantial down payment.
- Property suffers from depreciation (but gains from an accretion of values generally).
- Ties up capital, which perhaps could be better employed in business.
- Many expenses (taxes, insurance, heating, mortgage interest, repairs); these may come to more than the rent for a small apartment.
- Extreme care needed in selection.
- Great caution needed when entering a building contract for a brand-new house.
- Cumbersome to move if house or neighbourhood prove unsatisfactory.
- Lessens mobility (e.g., when changing jobs).
- No janitor service for lawn, snow, furnace, garbage.
- Apartments provide central heating, hot water, and elevators.
- Stairs to climb in a house.
- Must buy furniture, etc.
- Burden of responsibility.
- Needed improvements and repairs *must* be made.

QUESTIONS

1. (a) You own a house which you plan to rent to a tenant. Draw

up a lease agreement that is favourable to you.

(b) You plan to rent a house from its owner. Draw up a lease agreement that is favourable to you.

2. You are the tenant of an apartment under a standard tenancy agreement. You are leaving town for a while and you wish to sublet your apartment to a respectable friend. Your landlord, who is a rabid Maple Leaf fan, gets to learn that your friend is a Montreal supporter and will therefore not permit the arrangement.

(a) What are your rights under the agreement?

(b) What would your rights have been if no formal agreement had existed?

3. Howey rented a furnished apartment on a monthly basis and paid one month's rent in advance on June 1, 1965. On June 30 he is about to give up the apartment when his landlord asks for another month's rent. Must Howey pay it? Explain.

4. What remedies does a landlord have against a tenant who has not paid his rent?

5. Do you prefer to own or to rent your residence? Give full reasons for your preference.

Special Transactions

CHAPTER THIRTY

Succession to Property

INTESTACY

When a person departs this earth, he may, by will, determine what is to happen to what he has to leave behind. If, however, he leaves no will; or if the will he made is declared by the courts to be invalid; or if his will does not fully dispose of all his property, the rules of *intestacy* (i.e., dying without having left a last will or testament) will determine how his estate is to be administered. In Ontario, the Devolution of Estates Act is the governing statute, and any legal decisions in connection with the administration of the estate will be made by the Surrogate Court.

APPOINTMENT AND DUTIES OF AN ADMINISTRATOR

Letters of administration issued by the court vest ownership of the estate in an *administrator* (*-trix*, if female), as trustee. If no near relative (next of kin) applies for letters of administration, they will be issued to any other applicant, such as a creditor of the estate (who must be bonded), or to the Public Trustee.

The administrator's duties are the following:

- He collects all claims that were due to the deceased and are now due to his estate.
- He advertises for creditors of the estate.
- He pays debts in the following order:
  1. Funeral expenses.
  2. Administration expenses.
  3. All other debts, following the order of the bankruptcy laws. If the funds of the estate are not sufficient to meet the claims of all the creditors, nobody else—not even the deceased's child-

ren—is legally responsible for their payment out of his own funds; unless, of course, a person has expressly guaranteed payment, or was a partner of the deceased, or had given his written promise to the creditors to pay them.

4. Federal and provincial estate taxes and succession duties.

• He obtains a *release* from the taxation authorities, allowing him free access to the deceased's bank accounts and safety deposit boxes.

• He distributes the estate among the beneficiaries as they decide, if they are all in agreement. If not, he realizes all the property and distributes the proceeds (in Ontario) as described below:

ORDER OF DESCENT OF PROPERTY

A surviving widow receives as her portion the first $20,000 of the estate (or all of it, if it amounts to less) and:

1. If there are no children or other lineal descendants, she gets two thirds of the balance of the estate; the remainder goes to the deceased's collateral relatives (see below); if he has none, it goes to the Crown.

2. If there is one child, the balance of the estate is divided equally between the child and the widow.

3. If there are several children, the widow gets one third of the balance of the estate, with the remaining two thirds being divided equally among the children.

If the widow chooses to exercise her right of *dower* (a life estate in one third of her dead husband's wholly owned improved real property), she thereby forfeits all the above rights.

A surviving widower also receives the first $20,000 as above and:

1. If there are no children, he receives one half of the balance; the remainder going to the deceased woman's collateral relatives; or, if she has none, to the Crown.

2. If there is one child or more, the widower receives one third of the balance, the other two thirds going to the child, or to the children equally.

Again, if he exercises his right of *curtesy*, he forfeits all the above rights.

Where the deceased left no surviving spouse all of his estate goes to his *next of kin* (i.e., blood relatives; thus all "in-laws" are eliminated) in the following order:

1. LINEAL DESCENDANTS. The lineal descendants of a deceased are:

(a) His child, or children equally. This includes posthumous and adopted children,[1] children born before their parents' marriage, and a woman's illegitimate children (but not a man's); not included are step-children, unless adopted.

(b) If any of these children died before the intestate did, the dead child's children (i.e., the intestate's grandchildren) will "represent" the dead child; that is, they will divide equally the share that the dead child would have received had he been alive at the intestate's death.

(c) Similarly, if any of the intestate's grandchildren mentioned in (b) above are dead, their children (i.e., the intestate's great-grandchildren) will represent their parent by sharing his share equally—and so on down the line indefinitely. In other words, representation is *per stirpes*, or "according to tribes."

If the deceased had no lineal descendants, the next of kin after that are as outlined below.

2. COLLATERAL RELATIVES. These can extend from the deceased's closest relatives to distant cousins. Whoever stands closest to the deceased in relationship gets all his estate, to the exclusion of all other relatives. If there are several relatives removed the same distance from the deceased, they share equally *per capita* (i.e., according to the number of heads, or by "counting noses").

(a) First place is occupied by the relatives just one step removed from the deceased, namely his two parents. In five of the provinces, the deceased's father and mother share his estate equally (if one is dead, the other gets it all). In Ontario:

(b) The deceased's siblings (brothers and sisters—whether of the whole blood or of the half-blood) share equally with the deceased's parents, although they are two steps removed (one step up from the deceased to the parents; another step down from the parents to the siblings).

(c) A sibling, who died before the intestate, is represented by his child or children *per stirpes*—but this right of representation does not extend beyond this one generation: a deceased nephew or niece cannot

---

1 If a child is adopted after it is twelve years old, the child will not get the succession duty preference accorded to a deceased's children.

be represented by his or her children; the share of the deceased nephew or niece is shared by the other nephews and nieces if any are alive.

(d) If the deceased is survived by no parent, sibling (or representing niece or nephew), the next in line are those of his four grandparents who survive him (standing two steps away), sharing equally.

(e) If none of the above are living, the next in line are kin three steps distant: nephews and nieces (if all the deceased's siblings predeceased him); uncles and aunts; great-grandparents. All of these share equally *per capita*.

(f) Four steps away are: first cousins, grand-nephews, great-uncles, etc. This counting of steps can go on as far as it is possible to establish a family relationship; and the Surrogate Court will often admit as evidence of relationship not only marriage and birth certificates, but also authentic entries in old family Bibles, etc.[2]

3. THE CROWN.   If the deceased had no kin at all, his property goes to the Crown; that is, the province. His land is escheated, and his personal goods are declared *bona vacantia* (vacated goods). In Alberta, the University of Alberta is the beneficiary instead.

Simultaneous death. According to the doctrine of *commorientes*,[3] if the order of death of two or more people in a common disaster cannot be established by evidence or logic, the younger will be deemed to have survived the older. Thus, if an intestate couple is killed in an auto wreck and the order of death is indeterminable, and the husband is older, the bulk of his estate will be distributed among his wife's relatives. (However, in a curious case where a couple died of exhaust fumes, it was held that there was definite evidence that the older husband survived the younger woman; namely, that a respiratory defect caused him to inhale the poisonous fumes more slowly than his healthy wife.) But, if one of the parties carries life insurance, the beneficiary is deemed to predecease the insured; and the proceeds of the policy will be distributed in accordance with the Insurance Act. Similarly, a beneficiary of a will is also presumed to predecease the testator, unless there is evidence to the contrary.

---

2 The rules of succession to the Crown and to titles of nobility are slightly different. There the right of representation extends also to collateral relatives and thus takes pre-eminence over the mechanical counting of steps of relationship; and since a crown or a title cannot be shared, two other important factors are the principles of primogeniture and of male supremacy.

3 From the Latin *commori*: to die together or simultaneously.

WILLS

An intestacy can be very cumbersome. It can tie up property for a very long time until all possible claimants have been located and disputes between them settled. Also, one's property may go to persons one least wants to benefit, just because they happen to be, technically, most closely related to one (e.g., an estranged wife from whom no formal separation has been obtained, or a renegade son). Therefore, it is far wiser for people to make wills. It is surprising how often this is neglected; either from superstition (some people dislike to contemplate their inevitable death—they probably carry no life insurance either); or because "he hasn't anything to leave anyway."

When a person decides to make a will, he should get a lawyer to draw it up (fees for drawing a simple will are modest). Failure to do so might result in more trouble than an intestacy; the do-it-yourself will forms, obtainable in stationeries, are said to have the blessing of unethical lawyers who hope to profit from the legal disputes to which the forms give rise. The experienced lawyer will remember to make provision for children as yet unborn; to avoid two or more sets of succession duties (e.g., by saying: "To *A*; however if *A* predeceases me or survives me by no more than thirty days, to *B*; and if *B* also predeceases me, to *C*."); and to take care of other circumstances of which the layman may not be aware. The chief danger of an "amateur" making a will lies in his use of words which bear a technical meaning, perhaps diametrically opposed to his intentions.

REQUIREMENTS FOR VALIDITY

Legal capacity of testator. Although a will is not a contract, the *testator* (*-trix*, if female; the person making the will or testament) must have legal capacity. The testator must be sane and of an understanding mind when the terms of the will are composed; and, at the time of the signing of the will, he must realize what he is doing. He must not be a minor; but a member of the armed forces on active duty or a mariner on a voyage may dispose of his personal property by an unwitnessed will even if he is under twenty-one.

Intent. The testator must have genuinely intended the terms of the will; if a person can prove that the will was made under duress, undue influence, or fraud, the Surrogate Court will not probate it; that

329

is, it will be declared void, and the estate will descend as on an intestacy. If a condition in a will is illegal, the condition is regarded as void, and the beneficiary on whom it was imposed may disregard it. A will that has been declared invalid on a breach of technicality can still effectively declare a beneficiary of the deceased's life insurance policy.

Technicalities of execution. Wills must be made strictly according to the law; a person now domiciled (permanently resident) in Ontario must draw up his will according to the Wills Act of Ontario *or* according to the laws of the province or country where he was originally domiciled. However, if he owns land outside Ontario, his will must also conform with the requirements of the territory where the land is.

Written form. A will must be in writing (see Writing Requirements in Chapter 22), and it must be signed at its end virtually simultaneously by the testator and two witnesses, all three being in the physical presence of each other. A testator may affix his mark (e.g., an X) instead of his signature; or, if incapable of signing, he may have someone else sign for him—in which case he must affirm the proxy's signature in the two witnesses' presence, as above. However, in six provinces, *holograph wills*—that is, wills entirely in the handwriting of the testator—require no witnesses.

A person who expects to benefit from someone's will should not sign it as a witness or let his spouse do so; the reason being that no witness (or his spouse) may benefit from the will he witnesses. A will bearing a beneficiary's signature will still be regarded as having been properly witnessed, but the lapsed gift will "fall into residue" (see below). This holds true in Ontario even for a person who signed a will as an unrequired third or fourth witness. This restriction can be waived, however, by the unanimous consent of the other beneficiaries. An *executor* (*-trix*, if female: the person named in the will to carry out the terms of the will) signing as a witness, however, does not forfeit his appointment and remains entitled to any fees he was authorized to charge; similarly, a creditor of the deceased forfeits none of his claims by signing the will as a witness.

PROVISIONS OF THE WILL

The opening words of the will usually declare it to be the testator's last one, and they expressly revoke all earlier testamentary dispositions (e.g., wills, codicils, and gifts to come into effect on death).

Appointment of an executor to administer the estate. The executor can be either a relative, a lawyer, a friend, or a trust company, or a combination of these. A person named as executor is, of course, entitled to refuse the appointment, and it is therefore wise to obtain such a person's approval beforehand. An executor is entitled to charge the estate for his services, to a maximum of 5% of the value of the estate. At this point, appointments will also be made of a *trustee*, if any (often a trust company) and of a *guardian* (usually the mother) for underage children.

Bequests. Various specific bequests are made (if of realty, they are technically called *devises*; if of personalty, they are called *legacies*). If any of these bequests lapse (e.g., due to a previous death of the legatee; or because the legatee will not or cannot fulfil a condition attached to the bequest), they go to the residuary legatee—or, they "fall into residue." But if the predeceased legatee was a lineal descendant or a sibling (e.g., a child or a brother) of the testator, the gift does not lapse, but goes to that person's heirs. Any bequest must be taken by the beneficiary subject to any mortgages or unpaid instalments attaching to it, unless the will expressly specified for the clearing of such charges by the estate. Similarly, succession duty must be paid unless the will expressed the gift to be tax-free; in which case, the estate must bear that expense.

Disposition of the residue. This important section of the will disposes of that portion of the deceased's estate which has not been specifically bequeathed. The residue will be relatively small if the specific bequests were substantial. As often as not, however, the specific bequests are trivial; in that case the residue should be carefully apportioned among all those whom the testator intends to benefit. If it is omitted to make a disposition of the residue, it will go as on an intestacy.

Date and signatures. At the end of the will are placed the date, the signature of the testator and of the two witnesses, and the carefully worded *attestation clause* which recites in detail how every requirement for signing by the testator and the witnesses has been exactly complied with.

REVOCATION AND CHANGE OF WILL

Since a will, as was said before, is not a contract, it can be revoked or changed at any time before death. An exception exists where the consideration by the testator, in a contract entered into by him in his lifetime, consisted of his promise to leave the other party a bequest. Another exception exists in the case of *mutual wills* (among married couples, partners, etc.) wherein the will drawn in favour of the one is valuable consideration for the will drawn in favour of the other.

Wills can be revoked or changed as follows:

By making a later will which bears terms contradicting the earlier will. If the later will does not expressly revoke earlier wills, any non-contradictory terms in it will supplement the provisions of the earlier will. However, if the later will expressly revokes all earlier wills (as a standard will usually does), even the non-contradictory provisions of earlier wills are cancelled.

By changing an existing will. Small changes in the will can be made by crossing out or erasing undesired words and substituting others. Each such change must be signed or initialled in the facing margin both by the testator and by the two witnesses under the rigorous conditions described above. If these are lacking, the court will ignore the changes.

By codicil. A codicil is virtually a footnote to an already existing will. However, it is a separate document, executed and attested in the same manner as a will, supplementing and/or changing the terms of an existing, valid will.

By destroying the will. A will is also revoked if it is deliberately destroyed by the testator, or by some authorized person in his presence, with the express intention of revoking it. If a will cannot be found, the presumption is that it has been so destroyed; such a presumption is, of course, open to disproof.

By a document of revocation. A will can also be revoked by a document, executed like a will, expressly revoking it. If a person made and revoked several wills (this is quite a hobby with some people), the revocation or destruction of one will does not bring back to life an earlier will. Thus, if a person made a will A; then made a new will B which expressly revoked will A: and then made a will C which contained nothing but a revocation of will B; then he will die intestate unless he expressly re-executed will A or declared in will C that the terms of will A are to come back into force.

332

By marriage. Marriage (or remarriage) by the testator also serves to revoke a will; unless the will states that it is drawn up in contemplation of an impending marriage to a specifically named person.

By being declared void by the court. A will is naturally also rendered invalid if it is declared void by the court.

DUTIES OF AN EXECUTOR

The executor (if none has been appointed, the court will appoint "an administrator with the will annexed") may apply to the Surrogate Court for *letters probate* (certificate of correctness), which will be granted if the will has not been successfully contested by some aggrieved party. The letters probate are needed if the testator owned company shares or real estate which require transfer to the heirs; otherwise not.

Then the executor proceeds as the administrator of an intestate estate (see above). After performing his duties, he will be wise to get a written release from every one of the beneficiaries and creditors and a *certificate of discharge* from the court.

MANDATORY PROVISION FOR DEPENDANTS

In some jurisdictions, certain minimum amounts *must* be left to a deceased's widow and children. In England no such requirement exists: a man's son may be "cut off with a shilling." Most of the provinces have an act like the Ontario Dependants' Relief Act; according to this the surviving dependants of the deceased are entitled to adequate amounts from his estate for their maintenance if they are inadequately provided for. Not included in this category is the separated wife of a deceased to whom a court had refused to grant alimony.

A widow is also entitled to her dower rights in addition to what has been left to her by will; unless the bequests were given to and accepted by her "in lieu of dower."

DEATH DUTIES

Ontario and Quebec require *succession duties* to be paid by persons receiving financial benefit from someone else's death, and the Canadian Estate Tax Act also entitles the federal government to a share of large estates before they are distributed among the beneficiaries.

The Ontario Succession Duty Act can be briefly summarized as follows:

• If the estate is valued at no more than $50,000 and it all goes to preferred beneficiaries (spouse, parents, grandparents; children, grandchildren and their spouses), no duty is payable.

• If the estate goes to collateral relatives, there is a similar "exemption" if the estate does not exceed $20,000. For strangers the exemption is $5,000.

• If the estate exceeds these exemptions, the beneficiary must pay duty on a sliding scale, depending on the amount, and on the degree of relationship.

The Canadian Estate Tax is paid as follows:

• No tax need be paid by estates under $40,000.

• If the beneficiary is the widow, the exemption is increased to $60,000; and it is increased by a further $10,000 for each dependent child of the deceased.

• If the deceased died from war wounds, these exemptions are increased by 50%.

• If succession duty has been paid in Ontario or Quebec, 50% only of the federal estate tax need be paid by the estate.

Gifts. The above duties and taxes must also be paid on gifts which the deceased made within three to five years before his death. And it should not be forgotten that even gifts of over $1,000 that are given during one's lifetime are generally taxable under the Income Tax Act in order to prevent a large-scale evasion of death duties.

On the next page is a very rough outline of federal and Ontario death duties payable by an Ontario resident's estate which is inherited, for simplicity's sake, by just one person.

QUESTIONS

1. Describe the circumstances under which a will must be signed and witnessed.
2. Describe the ways in which a will may be revoked.
3. What is the order of inheritance under an intestacy?
4. A man died, leaving no relatives except a son and a daughter. By

his will, he divided his estate equally between them, and he appointed his son executor. The son's wife was a witness to the will.
(a) Explain how the estate will be divided.
(b) Who will be executor?
5. (a) What is "representation"?
(b) Who enjoys this right?
6. (a) What is the doctrine of *commorientes*?
(b) What awkward problem is it designed to avoid?

Value of Estate	Widow	BENEFICIARIES Other Preferred Beneficiaries	Collateral Relatives	Strangers
$ 5,000	—	—	—	—
10,000	—	—	—	$ 1,563
20,000	—	—	$ 624	3,353
40,000	—	—	5,184	7,200
50,000	—	$ 550	8,690	9,925
60,000	$ 3,174	4,474	10,760	13,025
100,000	11,675	13,675	23,340	26,975

Patents, Trade Marks, and Copyrights

MONOPOLIES

The government is very reluctant to grant monopolies; it will do so only where it is in the public's interest (e.g., to utilities and transport companies), and then, hedged in with innumerable protective provisions; and as a reward to people who have enriched the nation's store of wealth and wisdom by creating something new. These inventors, authors, and artists are granted the exclusive right to reap a profit from their brain-children for limited periods of time and subject to certain restrictions, which shall now be examined.

PATENTS

Inventors of any machine, manufacture, or composition of matter that is *new* and *useful*, can, on application, be granted the right by *letters patent* to make, sell, and use the article or process in question exclusively for the next seventeen years.

WHAT IS PATENTABLE

A patent will not be granted for a particularly dexterous or ingenious manner of manufacturing an article; but the invention must consist of "that impalpable something which distinguishes things invented from things otherwise produced." Nor is the discovery of a hitherto unknown scientific principle patentable—for that is knowledge that should be made available to the world at large. Nor will a patent be granted for an invention that has an illicit object in view (e.g., burglary tools).

However, improvements to products, processes, etc., may be patented

336

even though the latter have been patented by someone else. The term "usefulness" is also interpreted quite generously, admitting new toys and games, such as "Monopoly"; but not articles that are just "cute."

HOW PROTECTION IS OBTAINED

In exchange for being granted the patent, its inventor must make full particulars of it available to the public, disclosing every ingredient of the material used and each step in the manufacturing process. Anyone may buy a copy of any patent for $1. If an inventor is (for technical reasons) unable to get a patent; or if he wants protection for more than seventeen years; or if he fears entanglement in law suits against possible patent violators, he may decide not to apply for a patent and thus publicize his invention, but to manufacture it by *secret process*. The danger in this proceeding is, of course, that the secret may leak out, leaving its inventor with no legal protection.

The inventor himself (or his heirs, if he has died) may apply for a patent within two years of having introduced his invention to the public; if he leaves it beyond that, it is too late; he is deemed to have made a gift of his invention to the public. He may, however, lodge a *caveat* with the federal patent office in Ottawa. A caveat is advance notice of an incomplete invention and will serve to protect the inventor's interests where a longer time than two years is unavoidable.

The patent application. The fee for a patent application is about $35, and its grant will cost a similar amount. An application is a most complicated and technical matter, consisting of a *petition*, an accurate *specification*, and an exhaustive list of *claims* which are made for the invention. These must all be lodged in scrupulous compliance with the wealth of mechanical detail that is demanded by the regulations. Therefore, to obtain the greatest degree of protection, the inventor should engage the services of a specialized patent attorney. It will be his responsibility to procure protection for the invention in foreign countries; with some (U.S.A. and U.K.) Canada has an international agreement, but individual steps will have to be taken in other countries where protection is sought.

The patent stamp or label. Patented articles must be stamped "Patented, 19......." If this is not possible, they must have attached to them a label so inscribed; and if this is not physically possible, then a similar leaflet must be enclosed. The words "Patent pending" have no legal significance; they only serve as a warning to someone who is contemplating manufacture of such goods not to invest too heavily in a plant he will have to abandon once the patent is granted. The words, "Made in Japan," "Made in U.S.A.," etc., are stamped on goods in their country of manufacture to comply with the regulations of countries which import them.

ASSIGNMENT OF PATENT RIGHTS

A patentee may sell his patent rights outright, or he may grant a licence to someone else to use his invention against the payment of *royalties*. Such an assignee or licencee should register his rights at the Patent Office within three months. If a patentee fails to use his patent for three years, he may be compelled to grant a licence for its use to someone else. The Crown has the privilege of using anybody's invention against proper payment. In fact, a government employee can be compelled to sell his inventions or patents to the Crown outright.

REMEDIES FOR PATENT INFRINGEMENT

A person, profiting from a patented invention by manufacturing, selling, or using it without permission, can be sued by the patentee or licencee for an accounting of the profits that the violator has made, and for damages. The patentee can also obtain an injunction against such further violation and an order for the destruction of goods produced in violation of the patentee's rights. A person is also subject to penalties under the Criminal Code for deliberately violating some of its provisions in connection with patents.

A patent violator's defense to such an action will be either:

1. That his process is different from that covered by the plaintiff's patent and thus does not constitute a violation: or

2. That the Patent Office was wrong in granting the patent to the plaintiff in the first place.

In these two cases the patent dispute will be heard in Exchequer Court.

If a prospective manufacturer disputes the validity of someone else's patent, he may, to avoid legal entanglements after beginning manufacturing, *impeach* the patentee's claim in Exchequer Court; that is, he may apply for a declaration that the patentee's claims are ineffective.

TRADE MARKS

It is a common law tort to "pass off" one's goods as those of another person by a *deliberate* use of the same or of a *similar* trade name, mark, or design as used by the competitor.

The federal Trade Marks Act of 1954 now affords statutory protection to the *first* actual *user* of such a device provided he registers it within six months at the Trade Marks Office in Ottawa. For a $25 fee, registration will stop others for fifteen years (this period is renewable for further fifteen-year periods) from using a mark in a manner that is liable to lead to confusion in the public's mind.

KINDS OF TRADE MARKS

Designs. Trade marks may consist of designs: for example, the CBS "eye" and the NBC peacock (or the NBC radio chimes); or Players' bearded sailor; or the "His Master's Voice" dog; or the Smith Brothers "Trade" and "Mark" of cough drop fame; or the Pontiac Indian head; etc.

Words. A trade mark may also consist of words: for example, "Vaseline," "Coca-cola," "Kodak," etc. To obtain 100% protection, such a word or words (containing not more than thirty letters in four groups) should generally not be a word of the common English or French language, even if misspelled or corrupted; nor a name; nor descriptive of the article's quality or ingredients; and a design should not pertain to national symbols. Eastman's spent a fortune in developing the word "Kodak" which does not violate any of the above requirements in any known language. That is why numbers are popular: for example, *4711* eau-de-cologne and *222* headache tablets.

The reason for these prohibitions is that one man should not be allowed to appropriate for himself alone, what is common property. An exception is made for certain marks (that are normally unregistrable) once they acquire distinctiveness (e.g., Hoover vacuum cleaners; Singer sewing machines). These are given more than six months in which to register. On the other hand, certain marks can lose their distinctiveness: for example, Linoleum; and, in the U.S.A., Aspirin (in Canada, Bayer's still have the exclusive use of this name).

339

Distinguishing guise. Also registrable is the "distinguishing guise" of a product or its container: Examples are the hole in Lifesaver candy, the corrugated Coke bottle, and the "flip-top pack" of a brand of cigarettes. For $5, industrial designs (e.g., patterns on carpets, china, textiles, etc.; or store front displays) can be registered for a five-year-period (renewable once) at the Patent Office. Trade marks may now be assigned separately from the product with which they were associated; this represents a recent change in the law.

INFRINGEMENT OF TRADE MARKS

Infringement of a trade mark consists of using or selling a mark which is the same or similar to all or part of a used and registered mark, on similar wares (although a Vogue hat was held to impinge upon Vogue magazine), without the owner's consent. The mark is held to infringe even if it is not an exact copy of the original. It is sufficient for it to create an impression of being the same in the mind of a general member of the buying public, who is not expected to memorize all the details of the original mark. But (as was stated when discussing partnership names) a person may use his own name for a product if he does not do this in a manner deliberately calculated to defraud; even if his use of his own name causes some loss. Similarly, he may use the name of the region where the goods are actually produced: for example, 1,000 Island salad dressing, Okanagan apples, St. Lawrence Corn Oil, etc.

Remedies. As in patents, the injured party can claim an accounting of profits and damages. An injunction against further use of the offending mark and an order for its removal from the product may be demanded. If this is not possible, the destruction of the product may be ordered. In cases of brazen fraud and forgery of trade marks, criminal action may also be taken.

COPYRIGHTS

The federal Copyright Act confirms the right of an author, composer, or artist not to have his original creations copied by others substantially without his permission, usually for the life of the author and fifty years thereafter. This right does not give to the owner of the copyright the same exclusive rights that a patent gives to an inventor: there is nothing to prevent a second painter from painting a picture of the same subject, or a second author from writing an account of the same happenings—as long, of course, as the second person goes directly to the source and does not copy from the first person's work.

WHAT CAN BE COPYRIGHTED

There is no copyright in ideas (e.g., weight reducing schemes) or in general information (e.g., a list of city residents or a logarithm table or a map) as such. However, the manner in which the idea or information is compiled, and the language with which it is presented, do enjoy protection. Nor need the original material possess artistic merit. No copyright exists in items that are blasphemous, pornographic, or otherwise illegal. There can be no copyright in names or in not-particularly-famous titles of books, paintings, etc.

For a composer to enjoy copyright in his music, he must have set it down in writing; merely performing it in public is insufficient. Also unprotected are *ad lib* lectures or poetry; unrecorded story plots or advertising campaigns; in other words, anything that is not set down in permanent form on paper, canvas, clay, film, tape, etc.

OWNERSHIP OF COPYRIGHT

An employer owns the copyright in material produced by his employees in the course of employment. An artist, having sold a picture or a sculpture, still retains the sole right of selling reproductions of it, unless he transferred this right to the buyer of the picture or sculpture by contract. However, if someone orders a picture or some other work of art from a commercial painter, photographer, etc., the buyer normally also acquires copyright in it. An author has a copyright in his work until he transfers this to the publisher by express contract.

Only the owner of the copyright (or a licencee—see below) has the right to publish or produce his work, with the following exceptions:

• Short passages may be quoted for the purposes of criticism or review; and for study or research purposes. Very short passages (e.g., famous quotations and snatches of music) may even be used for wider purposes; but playing a musical excerpt for a half minute without licence constitutes a violation of copyright.

341

• Schools, churches and charities may perform the work provided no private person profits from the performance and provided credit is publicly acknowledged to the copyright owner.

• Political speeches can be quoted; but a summary of such, or a comment on one, enjoys copyright.

• Works of art permanently situate in a public place may be copied freely.[1]

Duration of copyright. Copyright usually extends for the life of the author and fifty years thereafter; if there were two or more authors, then for fifty years after the last to die. Copyright in photographs, records, etc., lasts for fifty years from the making of the plate. If a work was not published during an author's lifetime, his heirs enjoy copyright in it for fifty years from the date of its posthumous publication. After these periods all works fall into the public domain.[2]

Assignment of copyright. The owner of a copyright may sell it; but such an assignment must be in writing. He may also grant a licence to others to use the copyright against the payment of royalties (e.g., two cents for each side of a phonograph record). Twenty-five years after the author's death, anyone may use his work on paying 10% royalties. If a foreign author's work has not been published in Canada, then anyone, after the author's death, may demand a licence to publish it in Canada.

REGISTRATION

If it is desired, a copyright may be registered at the Copyright Office in Ottawa for $2. The advantage of registration is that it constitutes constructive notice to the world at large of the existence of the copyright; thus, no violator can claim ignorance of it. Registration is a definite advantage to the assignee or the licencee of a copyright; it serves to establish his priority in case of a duplicate assignment by the copyright

---

1 A Canadian author has the "moral right" (only theoretical, since there have been no cases involving it since he was granted this *droit moral* in 1931) not to have his work distorted or mutilated so as to result in an imputation on his integrity. It also leaves him with the right to claim authorship even after having parted with the copyright in his work.

2 That is why, when ASCAP virtually went on strike a number of years ago, American radio stations could only play old tunes such as Stephen Foster's "Jeannie with the Light Brown Hair." ASCAP is the powerful American Society of Composers, Authors and Publishers which safeguards the interests of all its members against "pirates"; its Canadian counterpart is CAPAC, or Composers, Authors and Publishers Association of Canada.

owner. Until 1962 it was important for a Canadian author to be familiar with registration procedure in the U.S.A.; until then he enjoyed protection only in the countries of the Berne Convention: the British Commonwealth, Western Europe, Japan, Liberia, and Tunis. In 1962 all members, including the U.S.A., ratified the terms of the Universal Copyright Convention; since then all the formality required of a Canadian is to print "Copyright" or "© Canada 19............" in his book, etc.

REMEDIES FOR PLAGIARISM

Plagiarism, from the Latin word for "kidnapping," means infringement of copyright. The remedies for plagiarism are:
* Injunction against further infringement.
* Damages, and accounting of profits, *if* the infringement was committed knowingly. It is for this reason that registration is useful and why the existence of a copyright is prominently printed in books, articles, and the like.
* If committed deliberately, a destruction of the infringing material may also be ordered (but not of a building whose plans violated a copyright).
* Alternatively, a criminal prosecution may be lodged. The time limit for this is three years and the possible punishment is a $500 fine and/or four months imprisonment.
* A Canadian copyright owner has the right to request that the import into Canada of violating material be prohibited. (As was the import into Britain of the paperback TAUCHNITZ edition, printed in Europe in English.)

A person enjoys the protection of Canadian copyright laws if he is a citizen of a member nation of the Berne Convention, or if he is a resident of the British Commonwealth; or if his work was published in a member nation of the Berne Convention.

Two copies of any new book (and of new editions of it) must be supplied to the National Library.

QUESTIONS

1. What requirements must an invention fulfil before a valid patent is granted?
2. List the remedies for patent infringement.

3. (a) What forms can trade marks take?
   (b) Give an example of each form.
4. (a) What is a copyright?
   (b) For how long does it last?
5. Under what circumstances may someone else's artistic creation be reproduced without his consent?
6. Under what circumstances may a person demand to be granted a licence to use:
   (a) A patent.
   (b) A copyright.

Personal Law

IMMIGRATION, NATURALIZATION AND CITIZENSHIP

People who live legally in Canada may be either alien visitors, or residents; the latter may be either alien immigrants or Canadian citizens.

ALIENS

Aliens need a *passport* to enter Canada; as does a Canadian travelling to a foreign country. (This requirement is considerably relaxed by special agreements with countries such as the U.S.A., Bermuda, etc., where substitute evidence of nationality is generally sufficient.) Visitors from many countries and all immigrants must also bear a *visa* that is stamped in their passports by a Canadian consul abroad. They must additionally pass inspection by the Canadian immigration authorities when arriving at a Canadian "port of entry," which can be by sea (e.g., Halifax or Quebec City), or by land (e.g., Niagara Falls, Ontario), or an international airport. Known criminals, sufferers from infectious diseases, etc., will generally be refused admission.

A *visitor's visa* is valid only for a limited period of time and will not allow a person to take employment without a work permit. *Immigrant's visas* are granted to people who, in the opinion of the federal Department of Citizenship and Immigration, will become welcome additions to Canada's population. The Department's policy on immigration fluctuates considerably, depending on the country's need for immigrants and on the attitude of the administration in power at the time.

When the immigrants are also approved by the officials at the border point, they have the magic letters *L.I.* (Landed Immigrant) stamped into their passport. This entitles them to permanent residence in Canada with the opportunity of subsequently acquiring Canadian citizenship.

CANADIAN CITIZENSHIP

Canadian citizenship can be acquired by birth, by marriage, or by naturalization.

By birth. There are two ways of acquiring Canadian citizenship by birth:

1. By being born on Canadian soil (including a Canadian ship or aircraft), regardless of the parents' nationality.

2. By being born anywhere, but of a Canadian father (or of a Canadian mother, if the child is illegitimate). In this case, the birth should be registered at the local Canadian consulate within two years, if possible.

Since nationality can thus be derived from more than one source, a person may have dual (or even multiple) nationality; in which case he must make an *election* before becoming twenty-one years of age. If he fails to do so, he might find himself compelled to adopt a particular nationality and/or find himself deprived of another.

By marriage. Before 1947, most countries (but not the U.S.A.) gave a woman her husband's nationality on marriage. Since 1947, a Canadian woman does not lose her nationality on marrying an alien; and an alien woman, on marrying a Canadian, remains an alien.[1] If she wants Canadian citizenship, she must acquire it by naturalization as described below; however, in her case it will only take one year instead of the usual five years.

By naturalization. To qualify for naturalization, the applicant—

• Must have been lawfully admitted to Canada.

• Must be of good character.

• Must know English or French (unless he has been in Canada for twenty years).

• Must be twenty-one years of age; unless he is married to a Canadian, or is included in the application of a parent, or has a petition made out for him subsequently by a naturalized parent.

---

1 A non-Indian woman marrying an Indian becomes an Indian; and an Indian woman who marries a non-Indian ceases to be Indian.

- Must intend to live in Canada permanently (such an intention may, of course, be changed afterwards) and to become a loyal citizen.
- Must have resided in Canada for five years out of the last six—the last twelve months uninterruptedly. Physical presence in a Canadian prison or mental institution during this time does not count; nor do absences abroad if they were spent on Canadian government service or while working at a foreign branch of a Canadian business firm or organization, provided contact is regularly maintained with the Canadian consulate abroad.
- Must file a *declaration of intention* within one to five years before making application for citizenship.

After complying with the above requirements, the applicant may be examined by a judge in a special Immigration Court; if found acceptable, he is granted Canadian citizenship. He also becomes a *British subject* when he takes the *oath of allegiance to Her Majesty* (this is not required of British subjects from other parts of the Commonwealth).

The naturalized Canadian has the same rights as one natural-born: he may vote; he may stand for office; he is entitled to welfare benefits; he can call on the assistance of Canadian consuls abroad. He is also under the same obligations: he is subject to military service in time of war; he is subject to jury duty (unless exempted as a doctor, lawyer, etc.); and, even as a resident, he must come to the aid of police or fire rangers when called upon.

LOSS OF NATIONALITY

Any Canadian may deliberately relinquish his nationality by voluntarily acquiring another one; for example, by naturalization, or by serving in the armed forces of a country that is at war with Canada.

A *naturalized* Canadian may have his nationality revoked if he is found guilty of treason or disloyalty to Her Majesty; if he obtained citizenship by fraud; if he leaves Canada for six years without good reason and showing no intention to return (registering with a Canadian consul abroad is evidence of the intention to return); or by similarly spending two years in his country of origin. Staying away thus for ten years results in an automatic loss of citizenship.

CHANGE OF NAME

Quite frequently people wish to change their name for any number of reasons: for example, because their foreign name is long or difficult for a Canadian to understand; to anglicize their name out of affection for their new country; in compliance with the conditions attached to a gift or inheritance; or a woman wishing her maiden name back after a divorce or a marriage annulment.

Anyone may call himself by whatever name he pleases, provided he does not do so with the intention of defrauding someone (note stage and pen names; and career women retaining their maiden names, after marriage). But if he does not desire constant misunderstandings when registering in hotels (where one's true name must be given) or when applying for car licences, etc., it may be preferable to change his name officially. In Canada a person may change his first names and his surname, while in England only one's surname may be changed.

A woman, of course, acquires her husband's name on marriage in most countries; if, however, some feminist does not like this custom, she can get married in some territory (e.g., Gibraltar) where this is not the case.

An adopted child also acquires his new parents' name. (Subject to exceptions, a person to be adopted must be under twenty-one, and his new parents must be at least twenty-five years older than the child).

Under the Ontario Change of Name Act, a British subject who is at least eighteen years old may apply to the County Court judge of the county in which the applicant has lived for at least one year to have his name, and that of his family, changed. (The consent thereto must first be obtained from his wife and any children over fourteen years of age.) The fee is $15 for the applicant, plus $1 for each family member included in the application.

The judge will grant the application if he is satisfied that it is *bona fide* (i.e., not intended to cover up a criminal record or to cover the tracks of a debtor), and that it will not lead to confusion with someone else bearing a similar name. Once granted, the change of name must be advertised in the provincial Gazette, and for three consecutive weeks in the local newspapers. This is not required for minor spelling changes or if the new name has already become generally known by lengthy, unofficial use.

A change of name must then be registered for vital statistics purposes; as must also all births, still births, adoptions, foundlings, marriages, divorces, and deaths.

Any fraud committed in connection with a change of name is punishable by up to six months imprisonment and/or a $500 fine.

MARRIAGE

The requirements for marriage are as follows in Ontario:

- The parties to the marriage must not be mentally defective or suffering from the effects of alcohol or drugs.
- Neither one may already be married to someone else at the time.
- The parties must not be closely related to each other. While a person may marry his first cousin, he must not marry his step-child.
- If a party to the marriage is under eighteen years of age, his father's written consent must first be obtained. If there is no father, the mother's or a guardian's consent are acceptable. If a father unreasonably withholds his consent, a judge may dispense with it. If the party is under fourteen, such consent must be accompanied by a certificate (issued by a doctor with legal training) that, without a marriage, an illegitimacy would result.
- Both parties to the marriage must have been resident in Ontario for at least fifteen days. This requirement, and most others, can be waived by the Provincial Secretary who has the power to issue *special permits*. Otherwise, the parties must first either:

(a) OBTAIN A LICENCE.   In Toronto, marriage licences are issued at the City Hall for $5 (not payable by unenfranchised Indians). Thereupon the parties may get married three days later.

Before being granted a licence, a person who has been divorced in Canada must produce proof of the divorce. If he was divorced outside Canada, he must first obtain the Provincial Secretary's authorization to remarry. If this is not granted, the parties wanting to marry will have to do so in a country or state that recognizes the foreign divorce. Or:

(b) PUBLISH BANNS.   If the parties to the marriage do not obtain a licence, they must have their regular church publish the *banns* according to its usage. The parties may then get married within five days

349

at the earliest and three months at the latest. The publishing of banns is not available to divorcees.

If a person's spouse has been missing and untraceable for seven years, a judge, upon application, may declare such a person dead—but for the purposes of a remarriage only.

The marriage ceremony can be performed by someone ordained in a religious body (including Quakers); or in a civil ceremony (between 9 a.m. and 5 p.m.) by a judge, magistrate, or other authorized person (e.g., the captain of a ship on the high seas). The couple and two witnesses must, in all the above cases, sign a register kept for that purpose; and a marriage certificate will be issued to the parties on request.

Common law marriage is said to exist between couples living together permanently as man and wife, who have not gone through a recognized marriage ceremony—often because one of them has not been able to secure a divorce from his previous marriage partner. Such a common law partner has legal status in certain situations; for example, as a dependant under the Workmen's Compensation Act. Common law marriages between competent parties used to have full legal status in remote regions, such as the Scottish Highlands, where going through a formal marriage ceremony was coupled with considerable transportation difficulties.

ANNULMENT

A marriage will be *annulled,* or declared void, if it was performed between people ineligible to marry (e.g., relatives within the prohibited degrees of marriage); or if one of the parties was already married at the time.

A person can also *apply* to have a marriage annulled (even if he is a Roman Catholic) if he can show that he did not genuinely consent to it; for example, by being drugged or insane at the time, or by being tricked into it (perhaps by being told that it was part of a play he was acting in). It will also be annulled if the other party was never able to consummate the marriage.

DIVORCE

Each Canadian province has the right to have its own divorce courts. Quebec and Newfoundland have none; therefore, residents in these provinces who wish a divorce can only obtain one by having the Canadian Parliament declare the marriage terminated by a private Act of Parliament. The other provinces recognize adultery as the only grounds of divorce; except Nova Scotia which grants it on slightly wider grounds.

Even so, no divorce will be granted if it is shown that any of the following *bars* to divorce are present:

- If the adultery was committed only for the purpose of providing evidence for a divorce (*collusion*).
- If one party, by his conduct, virtually persuaded or forced the other to commit adultery (*connivance*).
- If the betrayed party resumed cohabitation with the other, after discovering the adultery (*condonation*, or forgiveness).

A divorce action (which takes place in the Supreme Court of the province in which the husband is domiciled) can be contested or not. If the application is successful, the court will issue a *decree nisi* (an interim order) which will be made *absolute* (in three months in Ontario), unless an official called the Queen's Proctor meanwhile finds evidence of the previously mentioned bars to divorce or evidence that the divorce evidence was fabricated.

Alimony. The judge will order the divorced husband to pay maintenance to his wife and children (but not vice versa) if he was the guilty party. In a contested divorce action, damages may also be sought and assessed against the *co-respondent*; that is, the third party in the triangle. The judge will also decide on the education of the children, and who is to be granted custody of them; the other parent will usually be granted limited access to them.

SEPARATIONS

A legal separation agreement grants both parties their complete personal and financial independence; except, of course, that they may not remarry. The court will force the husband to keep up payment of any sums he promised to pay his wife. The court will also issue an order for the wife's maintenance and the children's welfare on the grounds of her husband's adultery; two years' desertion; cruelty; insanity; criminality; etc.

SOCIAL SERVICES

Throughout this book reference has been made to various forms of taxation: income and corporation tax, sales taxes, property tax, customs and excise taxes, death duties etc. The bulk of the income derived from taxation is spent by the federal, provincial, and municipal governments on national defense, public debt charges, education, highways, the rendering of municipal services generally, and on health and welfare services. These last are summarized below.

Services rendered by the federal government:
- War veterans' pensions, allowances, and other benefits.
- Old age payments of $75 per month to everyone at age seventy if he has been in Canada for ten years. The provinces will start paying this amount at age sixty-five to people established as needy by a "means test."
- Blind and disabled persons receive similar payments at age eighteen.
- The operation of unemployment insurance; and of the national employment services.
- Family allowances to parents of $6 per month for every child under ten; and of $8 for every child between ten and fifteen years of age. Allowances of $10 per month are also paid for youths to age seventeen, if still in school.
- The operation of national hospital and health services.
- The care for about 175,000 unenfranchised Indians throughout Canada.
- The low interest charges offered by the Central Mortgage and Housing Corporation.
- The good interest rates and security afforded by Canadian savings bonds and government annuities.
- Interest-free loans to students up to $5,000 ($1,000 per year of study).

Services rendered by the Ontario government (with similar ones being offered by all the other provinces):
- Allowances to unsupported mothers, ranging from $195 to $255 per month.
- Homes for the aged and for children; day nurseries.

- Hospital and health services.
- Hospital insurance.
- Reform schools and institutions.
- Grants to universities.
- Technical education and adult retraining.
- Museums.
- English and citizenship classes for immigrants.
- Workmen's compensation.

Services rendered by the municipalities:
- General welfare for the needy and sick.
- Inexpensive housing for low-income groups.
- Medical services.
- Education: elementary and secondary, including books and supplies.
- Libraries.

QUESTIONS

1. What different kinds of visa are there?
2. Explain how a person may have multiple nationality.
3. How does an alien become a naturalized Canadian?
4. What restrictions are there in connection with a change of name?
5. Couples about to get married must comply with certain legal formalities. List the alternative forms.
6. What are the differences between divorce, annulment, and separation?
7. What are the "bars" to divorce?
8. Prepare a list of the medical services furnished by your community.

Major Variations
From Ontario Law
In the Other Provinces

BRITISH COLUMBIA

COURTS:

Small Debts Court: Jurisdiction to $200.

County Court: Jurisdiction to $3,000.

Supreme Court (Trial court, including Probate)

Court of Appeal

Civil jury of 5.

PERIODS OF LIMITATION:

Simple contracts: 6 years.

All other claims: 20 years.

A "habitual drunkard" loses the right to manage his property.

EMPLOYMENT: In contracts of employment any term in excess of 9 years is void.

WRITING: Writing is required not only for contracts of guarantee but also for contracts of indemnity.

Sales of goods of $50 or over should be in writing.

A *conveyance of land* need not be under seal.

CONDITIONAL SALES: A copy of the contract is to be registered within 30 days.

BILLS OF SALE AND CHATTEL MORTGAGES: A copy of the contract is to be registered within 21 days.

INNKEEPERS can limit their liability for guests' losses to $50 by posting a copy of the Innkeepers' Act.

DOWER AND CURTESY are replaced by *homestead* rights.

A WIDOW may attack a will in which her husband failed to provide for her adequately.

354

INTESTACY: The surviving spouse gets one half of the estate if there is one child; if there is more than one child, the spouse gets one third of the estate. If there is no child, the spouse gets $20,000 and one half of the balance of the estate; the remainder going to the deceased's next-of-kin.

PARTNERSHIPS, if composed of 21 to 35 persons, require special authorization. If composed of more than 35 persons, they must incorporate.

ALBERTA

COURTS:

Magistrate's Civil Court: Jurisdiction to $200.

District Court: Jurisdiction to $1,000.

Supreme Court (Trial and Appellate Divisions—including Probate)

Juvenile Courts

Civil jury of 6.

PERIODS OF LIMITATION:

Court judgments: 10 years.

All other claims: 6 years.

A written *acknowledgment* of a debt extends or revives it, without any implied promise being necessary.

Easements cannot be acquired by prescription.

FRUSTRATED CONTRACTS ACT—as in Ontario.

WRITING: Sales of goods of $50 or over should be in writing.

CONDITIONAL SALES ORDINANCE governs sales over $15. A copy of the contract is to be registered within 30 days, with the same exceptions as in Ontario.

Repossessions can be effected only by the sheriff.

After resale, the seller cannot sue the buyer for any deficiency.

BILLS OF SALE AND CHATTEL MORTGAGES: A copy of the contract is to be registered within 30 days.

DOWER AND CURTESY are replaced by *homestead* rights.

A WIDOW may attack a will in which her husband failed to provide for her adequately.

A HOLOGRAPH WILL needs no witness.

355

INTESTACY: The property of a person dying intestate without next-of-kin goes to the University of Alberta.

On an intestacy, the surviving spouse gets one half of the estate if there is one child; if there is more than one child, the spouse gets one third of the estate. If there is no child, the surviving spouse gets the entire estate.

PARTNERSHIPS, if composed of more than 20 persons, must register as a company.

SASKATCHEWAN

COURTS:

Justice's Civil Court: Jurisdiction to $200.
District Court: Jurisdiction to $1,200.
Court of Queen's Bench
Court of Appeal
Surrogate Court
Civil jury of 12.

PERIODS OF LIMITATION:

Simple and specialty contracts: 6 years.
Court judgments and claims to land: 10 years.
A written *acknowledgment* of a debt extends or revives it, without any implied promise being necessary.
Easements cannot be acquired by prescription.

EMPLOYMENT: Anyone who has been employed for more than 3 months with one employer is entitled to one week's notice.

WRITING: Sales of goods of $50 or over should be in writing.

CONDITIONAL SALES ACT governs sales of $15 or over. A copy of the contract is to be registered within 30 days, with the same exceptions as in Ontario.

BILLS OF SALE AND CHATTEL MORTGAGES: A copy of the contract is to be registered within 30 days.

DOWER AND CURTESY are replaced by *homestead* rights.

A WIDOW may attack a will in which her husband failed to leave to her at least one third of his estate.

A HOLOGRAPH WILL needs no witness.

INTESTACY: The surviving spouse gets $10,000 and one half of the balance of the estate if there is one child; if there is more than one child, the spouse gets one third of the balance. If there is no child, the surviving spouse gets the entire estate.

PARTNERSHIPS, if composed of more than 20 persons, must register as a company.

MANITOBA

COURTS:

Magistrate's Civil Court: Jurisdiction to $100.
County Court: Jurisdiction to $2,000.
Court of Queen's Bench
Court of Appeal
Surrogate Court, Juvenile Courts, Family Court
Civil jury of 6.

PERIODS OF LIMITATION:

Simple and specialty contracts: 6 years.
Court judgments and claims to land: 10 years.
A written *acknowledgment* of a debt extends or revives it, without any implied promise being necessary.

EMPLOYMENT: In contracts of employment any term in excess of 9 years is void.

FRUSTRATED CONTRACTS ACT—as in Ontario.

WRITING: Sales of goods of $50 or over should be in writing.

CONDITIONAL SALES are governed by the Lien Notes Act.

BILLS OF SALE AND CHATTEL MORTGAGES: A copy of the contract is to be registered within 30 days.

DOWER AND CURTESY are replaced by *homestead* rights.

A WIDOW may attack a will in which her husband failed to provide for her adequately.

A HOLOGRAPH WILL needs no witness.

INTESTACY: The surviving spouse gets one half of the estate if there is one child; if there is more than one child, the spouse gets one third of the estate. If there is no child, the surviving spouse gets the entire estate.

QUEBEC

COURTS:

Magistrate's Court: Jurisdiction to $200.

District Court: Jurisdiction to $1,000.

Court of Queen's Bench

Superior Court

PERIODS OF LIMITATION:

Simple contracts: 5 years.

All other claims: 30 years.

Easements cannot be acquired by prescription.

EMPLOYMENT contracts can be entered only for a limited term or project.

Notice:

If employment is by the week, 1 week's notice is required.

If employment is by the month, 2 weeks' notice is required.

If employment is by the year, 1 month's notice is required.

WRITING: All sales of goods of $50 or over (even if there is part perform-ance) should be in writing.

By forfeiting any *earnest* he has given, a buyer is released from his contract. A seller who has accepted something in earnest, is released from his contract if he repays a double amount to the buyer.

SALES OF GOODS: The seller is deemed to give an implied warranty against latent defects in the sold goods, even if he was unaware of them. (This can be excluded by contract.)

A true owner of stolen goods may reclaim them from an inno-cent third party, but he must pay him (unless the third party acquired prescriptive ownership after three years' possession).

BILLS OF SALE AND CHATTEL MORTGAGES: Quebec has no Bills of Sale and Chattel Mortgages Act. Therefore, a non-owning possessor may transfer title to an innocent third party.

Hypothecation (mortgage) is possible only of land; but there is no foreclosure.

TENANCIES:

On a yearly tenancy 3 months' notice must be given.

Three days of grace may be added to a notice to quit.

A tenant, with the consent of the landlord, staying in possession for 8 days after expiry of a lease, acquires a fresh term.

Duty to repair rests on the landlord.

Leases over 1 year are not binding on a purchaser unless sealed and registered.

358

INCAPACITY: Prodigals, habitual drunkards, and narcotic addicts can be interdicted from contracting.

Infants:

An infant trader can be sued.

An infant over 14, when suing for earned wages, can do so without a tutor or next friend.

An infant is emancipated on marriage; but for certain transactions (e.g., making or witnessing a will) he needs the co-operation of a curator.

Married Women:

There is community property (administered by the husband) between husband and wife, unless this was excluded in the pre-nuptial contract. But a wife keeps land she owned before marriage, or land which she gets after marriage by gift or inheritance. A wife cannot contract regarding her estate or become a trader without her husband's consent.

Spouses (consorts) cannot contract with each other.

A wife has dower rights to one half of her husband's real estate.

WILLS:

A *holograph* will needs no witness.

Notarial (or, authentic) wills are for persons unable to read. They need not be probated.

"English wills" must be probated.

There is no *commorientes* rule.

INTESTACY: A widow gets one half of the estate if there is one child. She gets one third if there is more than one child, or no children.

A widower gets one third of the estate if there is a child or children. He gets one half if there is no child.

If the intestate died without spouse or child, one half of his estate goes to his parents and the other half to his brothers and sisters.

PARTNERSHIPS: Commercial partners have unlimited liability. But civil partners (e.g., professional men) are liable to creditors equally.

MANDATE is the name given to agency, and to bailments of repair, service, etc.

NEW BRUNSWICK

COURTS:

> Magistrate's Civil Court: Jurisdiction to $200.
> County Court: Jurisdiction to $1,000.
> Supreme Court—Queen's Bench, Chancery and Appeal Divisions
> Probate, Juvenile and Divorce Courts
> *Civil jury* of 5 or 7.

PERIODS OF LIMITATION:

> Simple contracts: 6 years.
> All other claims: 20 years.

FRUSTRATED CONTRACTS ACT—as in Ontario.

WRITING:

> Ratification of ex-minors' contracts must be in writing.
> Sales of goods of $40 or over should be in writing .

CONDITIONAL SALES, BILLS OF SALE, CHATTEL MORTGAGES: A copy of the contract is to be registered within 30 days, with the same exceptions as in Ontario.

INNKEEPERS can limit their liability for guests' losses to $100 by posting a copy of the Innkeepers' Act.

YEARLY TENANCIES: Three months' notice is required.

WILLS:

> A married minor may dispose of his property by will.
> A widow may attack a will in which her husband failed to provide for her adequately.
> A *holograph* will needs no witness.

INTESTACY: The surviving spouse gets one half of the estate if there is one child; if there is more than one child, the spouse gets one third of the estate. If there is no child, the surviving spouse gets $20,000 and one half of the balance of the estate; the remainder going to the deceased's next-of-kin.

PARTNERSHIPS: A partnership must publish its registration in the Royal Gazette; after which, "Registered" (or "Reg'd.") is appended to the firm name.

NOVA SCOTIA

COURTS:

> Municipal Court: Jurisdiction to $500.

County Court: Jurisdiction to $1,000.

Supreme Court

Probate Court, Juvenile Court, Divorce Court

Civil jury of 5; *grand jury* of 8.

PERIODS OF LIMITATION:

Simple contracts: 6 years.

All other claims: 20 years.

WRITING:

Ratification of ex-minors' contracts must be in writing.

Sales of goods of $40 or over should be in writing.

CONDITIONAL SALES: A copy of the contract is to be registered within 20 days.

BILLS OF SALE AND CHATTEL MORTGAGES: A copy of the contract is to be registered within 30 days.

INNKEEPERS can limit their liability for guests' losses to $40 by posting a copy of the Innkeepers' Act.

TENANCIES: Three months' notice is required for yearly tenancies. One month's notice is required for 3 or 6 month tenancies.

A WIDOW may attack a will in which her husband failed to provide for her adequately.

INTESTACY: The deceased's real estate goes to his or her child(ren), subject to the surviving spouse's right of dower or curtesy, respectively. If there is one child, the spouse gets one half of the personal property; if there is more than one child, the spouse gets one third of the personal property. If there is no child, the estate is divided equally between the surviving spouse and the deceased's next-of-kin. If there are no next-of-kin, the spouse inherits the entire estate.

PRINCE EDWARD ISLAND

COURTS:

County Court: Jurisdiction to $500.

Court of Chancery

Supreme Court

Probate Court; Juvenile Courts

Civil jury of 7; *Grand jury* of 12.

PERIODS OF LIMITATION:

Simple contracts: 6 years.

All other claims: 20 years.

The right to "ancient lights" (or windows) can be acquired after 20 years' prescription.

FRUSTRATED CONTRACTS ACT—as in Ontario.

WRITING:

Ratification of ex-minors' contracts must be in writing.

Sales of goods of $30 or over should be in writing.

CONDITIONAL SALES: A copy of the contract is to be registered within 20 days.

BILLS OF SALE AND CHATTEL MORTGAGES: A copy of the contract is to be registered within 30 days.

TENANCIES: Three months' notice is required for yearly tenancies.

WILLS must be probated (within 30 days).

INTESTACY: The surviving spouse gets one half of the estate if there is one child; if there is more than one child, the spouse gets one third of the estate. If there is no child, the surviving spouse gets $8,000 and one half of the balance; the remainder going to the deceased's next-of-kin.

PARTNERSHIPS: There are no limited partnerships in P.E.I.

NEWFOUNDLAND

COURTS:

Magistrate's Court: Jurisdiction to $200.

District Court: Jurisdiction to $1,000.

Supreme Court (including Probate)

Family Court

Civil jury of 9; *grand jury* of 23.

PERIODS OF LIMITATION:

Simple contracts: 6 years.

All other claims: 20 years.

The right to "ancient lights" (or windows) can be acquired after 20 years' prescription.

WRITING:

Ratification of ex-minors' contracts must be in writing.

Sales of goods of $50 or over should be in writing.

CONDITIONAL SALES: A copy of the contract is to be registered within 30 days, with the same exceptions as in Ontario.

BILLS OF SALE AND CHATTEL MORTGAGES: There is no Bills of Sale and Chattel Mortgages Act, but a copy of the contract may be registered within 5 or 30 days.

INNKEEPERS can limit their liability for guests' losses to $150 by posting a copy of the Innkeepers' Act.

CHATTELS REAL is the name for real estate.

DOWER: A wife has no right of dower.

WILLS:

The minimum age for making a will is 17.

A *holograph* will needs no witness.

INTESTACY: The surviving spouse gets one half of the estate if there is one child; if there is more than one child, the spouse gets one third of the estate. If there is no child, the surviving spouse gets $20,000 and one half of the balance of the estate; the remainder going to the deceased's next-of-kin.

PARTNERSHIPS: A partnership may not consist of more than 10 persons.

INDEX